Globalization and Islamic Finance

Convergence, Prospects, and Challenges

Globalization and Islamic Finance

Convergence, Prospects, and Challenges

HOSSEIN ASKARI, ZAMIR IQBAL, AND ABBAS MIRAKHOR

WILEY

John Wiley & Sons (Asia) Pte. Ltd.

Other Wiley Editorial Offices

John Wiley & Sons, 111 River Street, Hoboken, NJ 07030, USA

John Wiley & Sons, The Atrium, Southern Gate, Chichester, West Sussex, P019 8SQ, United Kingdom

John Wiley & Sons (Canada) Ltd., 5353 Dundas Street West, Suite 400, Toronto, Ontario, M9B 6HB, Canada

John Wiley & Sons Australia Ltd, 42 McDougall Street, Milton, Queensland 4064, Australia

Wiley-VCH, Boschstrasse 12, D-69469 Weinheim, Germany

Library of Congress Cataloging-in-Publication Data

ISBN 978-0-470-82349-1

Typeset in 10.5/13pt Sabon Roman by Macmillan Publishing Solutions

Printed in Singapore by Toppan Security Printing Pte. Ltd.

10 9 8 7 6 5 4 3 2 1

Contents

Preface

The global financial turmoil that started in 2007 and picked up steam in 2008 has again emphasized the fragility of a debt-based financial system. Debt financing during times of turbulence is akin to relying on "hot money." Equity financing, by comparison, is more permanent and assumes risk. Moreover, with the rapid innovation in debt instruments, transparency has been replaced by opacity. As a result of unknown and opaque risks and failed financial regulation of debt instruments and debt financing, debt may be losing much of its attraction to investors, at least for the foreseeable future.

The last two decades of the 20th century witnessed a number of global bouts with financial instability and debt crises with devastating consequences for a large segment of humanity, thus raising consciousness regarding the vulnerability and fragility of financial systems that are based, at their core, on fixed-price debt contracts. While numerous international banks have seen their reputation tarnished by the sub-prime crisis, Islamic banks have been largely unscathed. They did not, and given their premise indeed *could not*, park their assets in mortgage-backed assets. This success has spiked interest in Islamic, equity-based finance, not only in Islamic countries but also in countries that support the conventional system, by both Muslims and non-Muslims. Given the state of the global financial markets in 2009, the growing interest in Islamic finance outside of Islamic countries, especially in large Western financial markets such as London, could provide the all-important boost to the internationalization of Islamic finance and promote its growth. In turn, the growing internationalization of Islamic finance will afford equity-based finance added impetus in the West. In other words, conventional finance and Islamic finance could begin to reinforce one another.

In this book, we address an overarching question regarding the future of financial globalization, and of Islamic finance: Will conventional finance, at the heart of the current financial globalization, and Islamic finance converge? There is evidence that financial globalization has not been as helpful as expected, given the potential of its benefits for growth of investment, employment, and income, as well for reducing income inequality and poverty. In our view, the success of financial globalization will depend on the spread and degree of risk sharing around the world. The greater the momentum, the deeper the markets, and the wider the spectrum of risk-sharing instruments, the greater will be the shared ownership and participation in finance. Faster, deeper, wider financial development has a symbiotic relationship with globalization, as the feedback process between the two strengthens both. Evidence suggests that, thus far, the degree of risk sharing achieved by globalization is insignificant.

While Islamic finance has experienced phenomenal success in the last two to three decades, it still has a long way to go to achieve its objective of maximizing risk sharing. In the following chapters, we argue that the institutional structures within which Islamic finance is required to operate to promote good state and corporate governance, trust, protection of rights, and contract enforcement. In the case of Islamic finance, the progress achieved to date is a negligible fraction of the potential. The reasons are identical to those offered in financial globalization. Financial, legal, and institutional developments, and the greater pace of instrumentalization of basic modes of transactions permitted, would accelerate the progress of Islamic finance. As it would appear that Islamic finance and financial globalization share a *common objective* of achieving maximum risk sharing, it is not too unrealistic to expect convergence as we continue down this path.

We also believe that legal and institutional developments, as well as further advances in information technology, will reduce informational problems and lead to growing trust, which is essential for risk sharing. The result will be the dominance of equity in financial structures and relationships. The breakdown of trust as a result of repeated wars and catastrophes as well as financial innovations, particularly the securitization of government debt in the late Middle Ages, created the right milieu for the dominance of debt and debt finance which has lasted to the present day. We believe that conflicts and wars are the factors that most seriously threaten the future of globalization and financial globalization. How the world handles these threats may be the single most important factor determining the course of financial globalization and the possible convergence of Islamic and conventional finance.

For Islamic finance to sustain long-term growth, Muslim countries must liberalize their economies, embrace efficient institutions, and adopt consistent macroeconomic policies. They need to grow on a sustained basis and more rapidly, while also addressing the all-important issues of social and economic justice. Their sustained economic growth would be the most important impetus for a thriving Islamic financial sector; in turn, a thriving Islamic financial sector may be the best inducement for non-Islamic countries to embrace Islamic finance and equity-based assets more generally. In a globalizing world, the development of both Islamic finance and conventional finance can be expected to reinforce one another. We believe that Islamic countries are beginning to show signs that they are on the path to faster economic growth and financial market development, and they are turning increasingly to Islamic finance and risk-sharing instruments. Affluent Muslim communities in the West are doing the same.

This book addresses the overarching question: How likely is it that conventional and Islamic finance will converge as they both go through the globalization process? The answer would be "quite likely," if global finance relied more extensively on equity or equity-like flows, on the one hand, and invented/innovated a wider spectrum of risk-sharing instruments, on the other. A similar process of innovations in Islamic finance, coupled with financial and institutional reforms, would invigorate the growth and development of Islamic finance and enable an asymptotic convergence of the two.

CHAPTER 1

A Brief History of Globalization and Islamic Finance

Globalization is a process that enhances the flow of goods, services, capital, people, technology, and ideas across national borders. It is a phenomenon whereby numerous countries combine and increasingly appear as one country; complete globalization is akin to the unification of states that today make up the United States of America. The process of globalization proceeds more rapidly when barriers between countries that affect the movement of goods, services, capital, technology, and labor are reduced, and is enhanced by reduced information and transportation costs. It is a multifaceted and multidimensional process of growing interconnectedness among the nations and peoples of the world. Its main dimensions are: (i) economic and financial, (ii) cultural, and (iii) socio-political. Its economic and financial dimensions include growing trade flows across countries, flows of capital and investment, flows of technology, and labor flows (both skilled and unskilled), accompanied by standardization of processes, regulations, and institutions, all facilitated by the free flow of information and ideas. Its cultural implications are the amalgamation of cultures, adverse impact on languages (diminution of their use) that are used by a few and are not important to business and commerce, and diminution of distinct cultural identity. Its socio-political tendencies are convergence of ideas, political and economic institutions, and norms. It is a process that affects every dimension of life and existence. The reverse of globalization may be termed de-globalization. Globalization and de-globalization are ongoing processes, and at any point in time one dominates the other; as such, the process is continuous, whether the world is becoming more, or less, global.

While the impact of globalization on conventional finance has been studied and recognized, its impact on Islamic finance, a relative newcomer, has not been addressed. Islamic finance is a system of finance that prohibits debt-based financing; thus, it prohibits interest, and the financing of activities that are not permitted in Islam, such as gambling and the manufacturing

1

and distribution of spirits and wines. Islamic finance is based on risk sharing, trust, transparency, and the upholding of Islamic values. It has developed and grown side by side with conventional finance over the last 40 or so years.

How will globalization affect both conventional and Islamic finance? Will they continue to flourish as two distinct financial systems, or converge over time, or will one absorb the other? How will conventional and Islamic finance affect globalization? What does their history and the history of globalization reveal about their future?

1.1   A Brief History of Globalization

Globalization is not a recent phenomenon but has a long history, as indicated by its definition as a continuous process. When the process began, nobody knows. As Findlay and Lundahl (2002, pp. 1–2) note:

> *Even the most cursory inspection of the rapidly accumulating literature on the subject indicates that there appears to be about as many answers to the question as there are authors who have posed it.*

Findlay and Lundahl (2002, p. 2), however, do assert that:

> *It is more than sufficient to note that if we go back eight centuries what was up to that point the strongest wave of or effort at globalization hitherto in history emanated from the Mongols. They were the main agents of the process, that is, they "pushed" globalization as it were.*

The Mongolian event of the 13th century was in some sense the earliest truly global event and, as Findlay and Lundahl note, the Mongolian Empire still has the distinction of being the largest continuous empire in recorded history. As a result of the Mongolian push, trade routes were opened from England to China. Muslims, in turn, created sea trade along the ports of the Indian Ocean and the Persian Gulf. Trade, perforce, resulted in the movement of people, and even of diseases (such as the Black Death). The rapid expansion of the Chinese economy and the power of the Mongols in China were the forces that integrated the world economy.

Beginning in the 18th century, trade started to be dominated by British, French, and Dutch overseas companies, all chartered by the state. These conditions continued until structural changes occurred in the world economy in the late 18th and early 19th centuries—railroads and steamships, and the advent of the Industrial Revolution. At the same time, the American

Revolution and independence movements elsewhere meant that nation states wrested control of their resources from foreign domination, while simultaneously European countries used their military power to expand the commercial interests of their nationally chartered companies. The British, the French, and the Dutch extended their economic imperialism into Asia and Africa, while the United States started to reach into Latin America, with military might and economic expansion going hand-in-hand. At times, global integration has been fueled by economic forces, sometimes by military conquest, and sometimes by both economic and military forces. Yet, the process of globalization has not always been unidirectional; that is, toward ever-higher levels of global integration. It has proceeded in fits and starts, with globalization and de-globalization going hand-in-hand.

The most recent periods of this continuing process of globalization, whether boom or bust, are:

1. The globalization boom of 1820–1914
2. The globalization bust, or de-globalization, of 1914–45
3. The globalization boom of 1945–?

Again, as may be inferred from the titles of the above three periods, globalization is not unidirectional as witnessed over the last two centuries. Before the onset of the hostilities that led to World War I, trade, capital, and labor flows across national borders had been increasing steadily. World War I, nationalism, and the Great Depression (accompanied by protectionism as countries attempted to protect their domestic markets) reversed the process. It was not until after World War II that there was the will to reverse the process and reduce barriers. Even then, only trade barriers were reduced, followed much later by a reduction in barriers limiting financial flows, with labor flows across most borders still highly restricted even today.

The first of these globalization phases, as in earlier periods, was imposed by military power, underpinned and supported by industrial might. England forced its way into China and conquered all of India. France colonized North Africa. A number of European powers carved up Africa. The United States enhanced its domination over South America. During the first globalization boom, the lowering of barriers and the dramatic reduction in transportation costs (steamship, rail, canals) enhanced trade and mass migration of labor, with significant convergence in commodity prices and real incomes (Lindert and Williamson, 2001). This process was widespread—across Asia, Europe, and the Americas.

In the case of labor flows, labor migration was prevalent in the 19th century, as the motivation (real wage differential and social networks) was significant with little government impediment. For example, the labor force in Argentina and in the United States increased by 86 percent and 24 percent, respectively; while Ireland's labor force was diminished by 45 percent, and, as to be expected, with varied impacts on wage rates and economic growth (Lindert and Williamson, 2001, p. 14). International monetary reform, as embodied in the convertible currencies of the gold standard (and the silver standard), was adopted by the vast majority of countries in 1870. At the same time, given the high rates of return on foreign investment, cross-border capital flows increased significantly to levels not seen again until the last decade of the 20th century (Lindert and Williamson, 2001, p. 13). The lowering of barriers and the convertible currencies helped increase international trade/gross domestic product (GDP) from 10 percent to over 20 percent between 1870 and 1914, and cross-border capital flows/GDP from 7 percent to nearly 20 percent (Mishkin, 2005, p. 1). But capital did not flow from capital-abundant to capital-scarce countries, as would be predicted by theory (Lindert and Williamson, 2001, p. 17). Instead, capital inflows and GDP per capita were positively correlated. Thus, capital flows were not a force for convergence, indicating that the so-called Lucas paradox was a fact of life even in the 19th century. (Economic theory predicts that capital should flow from where it is plentiful to where it is scarce—that is, from developed to developing countries—but in fact the most significant flows are between developed countries; thus the paradox.) Lindert and Williamson (2001, pp. 17–18) have summarized the effect on income inequality during this period:

> *Within rich, land-abundant New World countries, more trade and more immigration augmented inequality. Within poor, primary-product-exporting Third World countries, they did the same. Within poor, land-scarce, participating Old World countries, more trade and more emigration reduced inequality. As for income gaps between countries, migration had an equalizing effect, one that was only partly offset by the fact that capital flowed to rich New World countries ... Overall, prewar [World War I] globalization looked like a force equalizing average incomes between participating countries, but with mixed effects on inequality within participating countries.*

The second era, the period of de-globalization of the inter-war years, was marked by political upheavals (such as the Bolshevik Revolution in Russia and the rise of fascism in Western Europe), rising nationalism, and policies erecting barriers and disincentives to the flow of goods, labor, and capital across countries. In North America in the face of growing domestic income inequality prior to World War I, and later during the Great Depression (high unemployment and negative economic growth), the government adopted policies to reduce imports and to stop the inflow of emigrants. These policies were counterproductive and, in turn, affirmatively anti-global, as they slowed the flow of goods, labor, and capital across national borders. Other countries followed suit to protect their own markets in a futile bid to preserve employment and economic prosperity. Trade, labor migration, and capital flows across countries slowed dramatically. This slowdown was accompanied by acceleration in the rising inequality between countries (Lindert and Williamson, 2001, p. 19). By the end of World War II, the world economy was at a standstill, with almost no trade or capital flows across borders and little emigration. The paramount lesson from this de-globalization period is clear: if globalization marginalizes a big segment of the population of a country, especially one that is organized and influential, then the globalization process will be threatened. This simple lesson is even more valid today, when instantaneous communications around the globe are possible. The forces of anti-globalization and nationalism rise when interests are threatened. While, on the one hand, labor, and trade and capital flows affect wage rates and rates of return to capital, on the other hand, those that are affected do not directly see the impact of trade and capital flows on real wages. While the effect of trade and capital flows on wage rates is somewhat invisible, affected workers can see plainly the emigrants who have taken their jobs or reduced their real wages. As a result, in times of falling wages or rising unemployment, labor flows may be more sensitive to populist attacks than trade.

The ongoing third period, the post-World War II globalization boom, was motivated and has been driven by the shortsighted policies and the economic trauma that marked the inter-war years. The world attempted to undo the damage of those years by adopting institutions and policies that would promote cross-border flows. At the international level, the United Nations (UN), the International Monetary Fund (IMF), the World Bank, the General Agreement on Tariffs and Trade (the GATT), and more were established to promote economic reform and lower barriers to trade and capital flows. The Bretton Woods Agreement was adopted to avoid disruptive exchange rate changes and to provide short-term financing for countries facing balance of payments difficulties in order to avoid the damaging global economic contractions that had occurred in the 1930s, especially in the aftermath of Austria's inability to secure short-term financing. However, this post-World War II reversal in policies was adopted only slowly. Countries were still reluctant to dismantle trade barriers quickly, as attested to by the fact that they could not agree on setting up a World Trade Organization (WTO). A number of countries, most prominently the United States, were reluctant to compromise on important issues, especially when they felt that their national sovereignty was threatened. The best they could do was to set up a system with little enforcement, or teeth, that was subject to periodic painful negotiations to reduce tariffs on goods alone—the GATT. Numerous trade rounds under the GATT reduced barriers to the movement of goods across national borders. The process, though not always smooth, is continuing under the more recently established WTO, with coverage extending to services and including capital flows, and with enforcement powers.

This latest period of globalization differs in many important ways from the earlier one that ended prior to World War I (Lindert and Williamson, 2001, p. 20). Labor migration has been less significant than in the earlier period. The impressive gain in the cross-border movement of goods, services, and capital has not been matched by cross-border labor flows. Even capital exports have been less significant than in the earlier period of globalization; for example, the capital exports to GDP ratio in the United States during 1989–96 was 1.2, while it was 4.6 in Britain during 1890–1913 (Lindert and Williamson, 2001, p. 20). While various measures of capital flows, especially foreign direct investment (FDI), may still be below their pre-World War I levels, the trade to GDP ratio is higher today, supported by lower trade barriers and lower transportation and communication costs. The reason for these differences between the two periods has been largely attributed to changes in US policy (Lindert and Williamson, 2001, p. 20):

> These differences are tied to policy changes in one dominant country, the United States, which has switched from [being] a protectionist welcoming immigrants to a free trader restricting immigration. Another difference . . . the postwar world started out much more unequal than the world of 1820 or 1870, and international income gaps, not income gaps within countries, now dominate the global inequality of living standards.

During this recent phase, the process of globalization has been especially rapid since 1973: the ratio of world trade to GDP increased from 22 percent to 42 percent in 2000 (Estevadeordal and Taylor, 2002) and the share of capital inflows to GDP increased from about 3 percent in 1990 to about 14 percent in 2005 (IMF, 2007a).

But, as in an earlier period, globalization is being blamed for a number of emerging economic, social, and environmental ills: disparity in income across countries, income inequality within countries, labor standards (with countries maintaining low standards to attract foreign investors), labor conditions (with multinational firms attracted to low labor cost countries no matter what the conditions), poverty, climate degradation, and the global financial meltdown of 2007–09. While the effects of globalization on income inequality across countries and within countries are being hotly debated (see Chapter 2), the rising inequality within the United States and the United Kingdom in the last two decades is readily confirmed by adverse changes in Gini coefficients and shares of income accruing to differing percentiles. The result is more nuanced for other OECD countries (Lindert and Williamson, 2001, p. 31). But to what degree are these effects due to globalization? While labor and environmental conditions may have suffered, to what extent are these a failure of government policy or directly attributable to globalization? It is evident that globalization, as with most other things in life, may have both positive and negative effects. The issue may be whether governments can ameliorate the negative effects through policies to enhance the benefits and become net beneficiaries of the process of globalization. In assessing the impact of globalization and devising policies to maximize its net benefits, it must be remembered that globalization is not the most direct instrument for affecting incomes, growth, income distribution, poverty, or more. Governments have an arsenal of policy instruments at their disposal for addressing such issues much more directly.

1.2 How Complete Is Globalization?

Today, the broad global economic picture is one of diversity, or more accurately, one of gross inequality (see Table 1.1). While the US per capita income was around US$38,000 in 2007, the world average was in the neighborhood of US$6,000 and that of low-income countries was a mere US$334. For the countries that comprise the Islamic Conference (OIC), representing nearly 25 percent of the global population, per capita income was only US$1,501, a figure that was a fraction of the Organization for Economic Co-operation and Development (OECD) average, only a quarter of the global average, and would fit neatly in the "lower middle income" category as defined by the World Bank.

Globalization is today far from "complete." For instance, consider a country whose share of global GDP is 25 percent and whose trade/GDP is 15 percent. Is globalization "complete" for such a country? The answer is an emphatic "no." If a country's share of global GDP is 25 percent (roughly similar to the United States today), for "complete" trade globalization, its trade/GDP should be 75 percent, not 15 percent (again, the rough US share today). By this measure, globalization in the area of trade has a long way to go (compare Tables 1.1 and 1.2). The United States represented 29.3 percent of global GDP but had an export/GDP of only 10.5 percent (which should be in the order of 70 percent for complete globalization) and the OIC represented 5.5 percent of global GDP but had an export/GDP of 30.6 percent (which should have been in the order of 95 percent for complete globalization).

In the case of financial globalization, such a ready measure is not available, as a country's share of global finance is difficult to define. One could

TABLE 1.1   Economic Indicators

	GDP (US$ billion)		Per Capita (US$)		Population (million)	
	2000	2007	2000	2007	2000	2007
OIC[1]	1,567	2,194	1,228	1,501	1,276	1,461
United States	9,765	11,564	34,600	38,338	282	302
Euro area	6,245	7,069	20,400	22,182	306	319
High income	25,934	30,398	25,793	28,777	1,005	1,056
High income: OECD	24,730	28,781	26,767	29,805	924	966
High income: non-OECD	1,207	1,656	14,793	18,257	82	91
Middle income	5,647	8,506	1,425	1,997	3,962	4,260
Upper middle income	2,903	3,833	3,715	4,659	781	823
Lower middle income	2,745	4,671	863	1,359	3,181	3,437
Middle East & North Africa	431	585	1,561	1,868	276	313
Low income	370	538	334	415	1,108	1,296
World	31,949	39,436	5,258	5,964	6,076	6,612

Source: World Development Indicators, The World Bank.

[1]Limited or no data for some countries, including Afghanistan, Iraq, Qatar, and Somalia.

TABLE 1.2   Trade and Capital Flows

	Exports (% of GDP)		Imports (% of GDP)		FDI Inflows (%)		FDI Outflows (%)	
	2000	2007	2000	2007	2000	2007	2000	2007
OIC[1]	38.53	30.63	31.44	36.74	0.56	2.94	0.18	0.60
United States	11.2	10.5	15.1	16.3	3.3	1.4	1.6	1.8
Euro area	36.6	39.8	35.9	38.5	10.2	3.8	3.5	5.5
High income	23.9	25.7	24.4	26.4	5.3	2.7	3.5	3.5
High income: OECD	22.1	22.5	22.8	23.9	5.2	2.6	3.4	3.4
High income: non-OECD	69.8	112.4	62.2	99.5	0.0	8.7	0.0	0.0
Middle income	27.4	31.0	25.9	31.2	2.8	3.1	0.4	1.2
Upper middle income	27.8	30.5	26.2	29.5	3.4	3.3	0.6	1.7
Lower middle income	27.1	36.8	25.6	33.9	2.1	2.9	0.1	0.7
Middle East & North Africa	26.8	33.9	25.6	39.1	1.3	4.2	0.1	0.0
Low income	28.0	30.5	30.0	36.1	1.7	3.1	0.0	0.0
World	24.6	27.0	24.7	27.2	4.9	2.8	3.0	3.0

Source: World Development Indicators, The World Bank.

[1]Limited or no data for some countries, including Afghanistan, Iraq, Qatar, and Somalia.

venture a proposition that, with globalization, the domestic investment to GDP ratio should be comparable to foreign investment to GDP ratios. Taking FDI as a surrogate for foreign investment, the reported FDI ratios are not comparable to what we assume to be domestic investment to GDP ratios. At the same time, the FDI ratios are diverse across country groups and are quite low for most country groups. Globalization is clearly limited in the area of finance; flows between the rich countries dominate these flows (the Lucas paradox), indicating that flows to developing countries have a very long way to go. Moreover, if Shiller (2003) is even partially correct in foreseeing the future of financial markets and the new financial order, then the management of risk, especially cross-border diversification of risk, has barely begun.

While trade and capital flows may have a considerable way to go before being truly globalized, the "tap" on labor flows has not even been opened in the current globalization phase. The severe restriction on labor flows is dramatized by the number of would-be illegal immigrants who die on the high seas or in railroad cars, and stand in long lines at the embassies of advanced countries and wait, sometimes for years, to secure legal immigrant status. Today, the legal flow of labor is largely limited to those with higher levels of education. The cross-border flow of educated labor increased in the latter half of last century, and especially following the change in immigration laws in the United States in 1990. But quotas and other restrictions still severely limit the flow of even educated and skilled labor. The flow of labor has a long way to go before "complete" labor globalization can be claimed, with similar wage rates paid for comparable labor skills all over the world.

The unimpeded flow of technology across borders also has far to go. Many countries, but especially the United States, have imposed ongoing sanctions on dozens of countries, especially in the area of advanced technology. Companies are afraid to license their most sensitive technologies until they are afforded better protection against piracy.

No country in the world comes close to meeting these targets indicated for complete globalization in terms of the flow of goods, capital, labor, and technology. If countries today feel the pressures of globalization, they have seen nothing yet compared to what lies in store should the globalization process ever be permitted to continue unabated.

Globalization has both its fans and detractors. Some argue that globalization increases economic growth and prosperity, no matter what; others believe that faster growth can come about only *if* countries are properly positioned to take advantage of it, requiring sound institutions and policies; and yet others argue that globalization is bad for everyone, no matter what policies and institutions are embraced. Some assert that globalization increases income inequality between countries, others that it has an adverse effect on income equality *within* countries. Still others argue that globalization increases global poverty. Because globalization can be so all-encompassing, there have been some attempts to examine the effects of individual components of globalization (largely, trade and financial flows) on these variables. The danger for the future of globalization is that if enough countries—or large constituencies within countries—either do not gain from globalization or feel threatened by it, then the forces of protectionism will increase, as was experienced early last century and which reached a pinnacle during the Great Depression, a case of near autarchy where every country was a loser. Similarly, during periods of severe economic contraction, as is occurring currently with the onset of the sub-prime mortgage crisis in the United States, protectionism raises its ugly head and globalization is threatened at its very foundation. As of late summer of 2009, unemployment in the United States was 9.4 percent and was expected to peak at about 11 percent by the end of the year. Moreover, economic recovery was likely to be slow during 2010.

After this brief summary of globalization, a few observations should be evident. Globalization is an ongoing process; it has a long way to go to be "complete," but it is not monotonic and could be reversed. The impact of globalization is multidimensional. Some segments of society will gain while others will lose, or at least the gain or the loss will not be equally shared. This is the nature of the beast. If and when a large segment of society in a country loses out and becomes disadvantaged, then the voices of protectionism become loud, as was the case from around 1910 until the end of World War II. In fact, even today, by some measures (such as flow of FDI and labor mobility across national borders), globalization may be less advanced than at the beginning of last century.

The overall extent of potential benefits depends on how a country is organized, its competitiveness in global goods and services markets, the flexibility of its markets, and its policy and regulatory infrastructure. All countries have to develop the necessary economic and social policies, the appropriate regulatory and supervisory environment, flexible markets, financial stability, and the needed institutions to benefit from globalization, while guarding the economic welfare of *all* segments of society and preventing social and economic upheavals by means of increased access to education, healthcare, labor training, and the like. It is all too easy to blame all of a country's ills on globalization. Even if there were no such process as globalization, countries would still need to address the economic welfare of *all* segments of society and promote social and economic harmony and justice, with increased access to education, healthcare, labor training, and the like. The development of policies and institutions is the key, with or without the process of globalization. We believe that globalization may have an additional, all too hidden and never mentioned, benefit: the need and the push for governments to adopt better policies, institutions, and governance structure.

1.3   A Brief Introduction to Islamic Finance¹

Islam defines guiding principles and a set of rules for all aspects of human life, including economic aspects. These laws, most commonly known as *Shari'ah*, consist of constitutive and regulative rules according to which individual Muslims, and their collectivity, must conduct their affairs. The basic source of the law, in Islam, is the *Qur'an*, whose central reality in the life of Islam and its influence upon the life of Muslims cannot be overemphasized. It includes all the necessary constitutive rules of the law as "guidance for mankind." The principles enunciated in the *Qur'an* were explained, amplified, practiced, and exemplified by the Prophet (*pbuh*) whose personality, actions, and sayings, known as *Sunnah*, leave an indelible mark on the consciousness of the individual Muslim. Hence, after the *Qur'an*, the Prophet's sayings, and his actions, are the most important sources of the law and a fountainhead of Islamic life and thought.

Although the *Qur'an* and the *Sunnah* are the primary sources of *Shari'ah*, *ijtihad* (from the same root as *jihad*) plays a critical role. *Ijtihad*, through which efforts are expended by individual jurists to extract solutions to problems based on the primary sources, is the vehicle by which rules of behavior not explicitly addressed to problems that arise as human societies evolve are determined. *Ijtihad* is exercised through the earlier consensus of jurists (*ijma*), anology (*qiyas*), judicial preference (*istihsan*), public interest (*maslaha*), and customs (*urf*). Secondary sources of *Shari'ah* have to satisfy the condition that they do not introduce any rules that are in conflict with the main tenets of Islam. Compliance with the rules of the *Shari'ah* is essential to the preservation of the community and is assured by the fact that the individual's behavior is constrained by adherence to the binding norms of the socio-economic order and through coercion by the collectivity.

Throughout their history, Muslims have endeavored to develop their societies by following the principles of *Shari'ah*, and there were no exceptions for economic activities. An economic system according to Islam is based on preservation of property rights, emphasizing sanctity of contracts, ensuring justice in exchange and markets, expecting high ethical standards, sharing risks, and promoting social justice. The financial system is pivoted on the prohibition of *riba*, which includes payment and receipt of interest in all forms as understood in today's business world. The term "Islamic finance," which is a relatively new term and has emerged in only the last two to three decades, is often reduced to a system where "interest" is prohibited. However, this simple description is not only inaccurate, but is also a source of further confusion. The most significant implication of this prohibition is the removal of pure "debt-based" contracts from financial transactions. There is no doubt that the most critical and distinguishing feature of such a system is the prohibition of *riba*. The Islamic financial system also encourages risk sharing, innovation, and entrepreneurship, and emphasizes "materiality," by which we mean that it endorses a strong linkage between the real and the financial sector and promotes asset-based financing as opposed to pure lending-based financing. Islamic scholars have argued that when the notions of economic justice and risk sharing are combined with other fundamental principles of Islam, it can lead to a financial system that is inclusive, efficient, and stable, and which promotes economic development. The box below summarizes the basic principles of an Islamic financial system.

BASIC PRINCIPLES OF AN ISLAMIC FINANCIAL SYSTEM

Prohibition of interest. Prohibition of *riba*, a term literally meaning "an excess" and interpreted as "any unjustifiable increase of capital whether in loans or sales," is the central tenet of the system. More precisely, any positive, fixed, predetermined rate tied to the maturity and the amount of principal (that is, guaranteed regardless of the performance of the investment) is considered *riba* and is prohibited. The general consensus among Islamic scholars is that *riba* covers not only usury but also the charging of "interest" as widely practiced. A direct implication of prohibition of interest is prohibition of pure debt security with a predetermined interest rate.

This prohibition is based on arguments of social justice, equality, and property rights. Islam encourages the earning of profits but forbids the charging of interest because profits, determined *ex post*, symbolize successful entrepreneurship and creation of additional wealth, whereas interest, determined *ex ante*, is a cost that is accrued irrespective of the outcome of business operations and may not create wealth if there are business losses. Social justice demands that borrowers and lenders share rewards as well as losses in an equitable fashion, and that the process of wealth accumulation and distribution in the economy be fair and representative of true productivity.

Risk sharing. Because interest is prohibited, pure debt security is eliminated from the system and therefore suppliers of funds become investors instead of creditors. The provider of financial capital and the entrepreneur share business risks in return for shares of the profits and losses.

Asset-based. The prohibition of debt and encouragement of risk sharing suggests a financial system where there is a direct link between the real and the financial sector. As a result, the system promotes a "materiality" aspect requiring linking of financing directly with the underlying asset so that the financing activity is clearly and closely identified with the real sector activity. There are strong linkages between the performance of the asset and the return on capital used to finance it.

Money as "potential" capital. Money is treated as "potential" capital—that is, it becomes actual capital only when it joins hands with other resources to undertake a productive activity. Islam recognizes the time value of money, but only when it acts as capital and not "potential" capital.

Prohibition of speculative behavior. An Islamic financial system discourages hoarding and prohibits transactions featuring extreme uncertainties, gambling, and risks.

Sanctity of contracts and preservation of property rights. Islam upholds contractual obligations and the disclosure of information as a sacred duty. This feature is intended to reduce the risk of asymmetric information and moral hazard. Islam places great importance on preservation of property rights; defines a balance between the rights of individuals, society, and the state; and strongly prohibits encroachment of anyone's property rights.

Sources: Mirakhor (2003a); Iqbal and Mirakhor (2007).

In modern history, interest in conducting *Shari'ah*-compliant business rose with the first sign of expansion of conventional "interest-based" commercial banking in the Arab and Muslim world. In the late 19th century, a formal critique and opposition to the element of "interest" started in Egypt when Barclays Bank was established in Cairo to raise funds for the construction of the Suez Canal. Further, a formal opposition to the institution of "interest" could be found as early as 1903, when the payment of interest on post office saving funds was declared contrary to Islamic values and therefore illegal by *Shari'ah* scholars in Egypt.

During the first half of the 20th century, there were several attempts to highlight the differences between the emerging conventional financial system and the areas where it conflicted with Islamic values. By the 1950s and 1960s, several Muslim countries had begun to regain their freedom after years of colonial rule and, along with this new-found freedom, there were attempts to rediscover their Islamic values and heritage. By 1953, Islamic economists had offered the first description of an interest-free bank. By the start of the 1960s, there was a growing demand for *Shari'ah*-compliant banking, resulting in the establishment of the Mit Ghamr Local Savings Bank in Egypt in 1963 by the noted social activist Ahmad-al-Najjar. It is worth noting that Dr. Najjar chose not to label this institution as an "Islamic bank" but promoted it as a social welfare institution (Martin, 2007). Unfortunately, this experiment lasted for only four years. Around the same time, there were parallel efforts in Malaysia to develop a saving scheme for Muslims wishing to undertake the pilgrimage to Mecca.

The establishment of the Dubai Islamic Bank in the United Arab Emirates (UAE) by some traders in 1974 is considered to be one of the earliest private initiatives. The 1970s witnessed a rise in the price of oil, leading to rising oil revenues and financial assets in several oil-rich Islamic countries, especially in the Middle East. Oil revenues of the 1970s, sometimes referred to as "petro-dollars," offered strong incentives for creating suitable investment outlets for Muslims wanting to comply with the *Shari'ah*. Interest-free or Islamic banking, which was only a concept in the early 1970s, was subsequently given a strong business foundation. This business opportunity was exploited by both domestic and international bankers, including some of the leading conventional banks.

In 1975, the Islamic Development Bank (IsDB) was established along the lines of regional development institutions with the objective of promoting economic development in Muslim countries, as well as offering development finance according to the rules of the *Shari'ah*. Since its inception, IsDB has played a key role in expanding Islamic modes of financing and in undertaking valuable research in the area of Islamic economics, finance, and banking. The 1980s proved to be the beginning of a trend of rapid growth and expansion of an emerging Islamic financial services industry. The major developments of the 1980s included continuation of serious research work at the conceptual and theoretical level, constitutional protection in three Muslim countries, and the involvement of conventional bankers in offering *Shari'ah*-compliant services. The Islamic republics of Iran, Pakistan, and Sudan announced that they would transform their overall financial systems to make them compliant with the *Shari'ah*. Other countries such as Malaysia and Bahrain started Islamic banking within the framework of their existing system. The IMF initiated research into understanding the macroeconomic implications of an economic system that operates without debt financing and interest as the rationing price of money. Similar research was conducted to understand the issues of profit- and loss-sharing contracts and the financial stability of a system based on the sharing of profit and loss.

During the early stages of growth of the Islamic financial market in the 1980s, Islamic banks faced a dearth of quality investment opportunities. This created business opportunities for conventional Western banks to act as intermediaries to deploy Islamic banks' funds according to the guidelines given by the Islamic banks. Western banks realized the importance of the emerging Islamic financial markets and started to offer Islamic products through "Islamic windows" in an attempt to attract clients directly, without having an Islamic bank as intermediary. The number of conventional banks offering "Islamic windows" grew and several leading conventional banks, such as the Hongkong and Shanghai Banking Corporation (HSBC) and Citicorp, began to pursue this market aggressively.

By the early 1990s, the market had gained enough momentum to attract the attention of public policy makers and of institutions interested in introducing innovative products. In 1996, Citibank was one of the earliest Western banks to establish a separate Islamic bank—Citi Islamic Investment Bank (Bahrain). HSBC today has a well-established network of banks in the Islamic world. With the objective of promoting Islamic asset securitization and private equity and banking in OECD countries, HSBC Global Islamic Finance (GIF) was launched in 1998. With the growth of Islamic products and services, the need for regulation and standards increased, resulting in the establishment of a self-regulatory agency—the Accounting and Auditing Organization for Islamic Financial Institutions (AAOIFI) in Bahrain, which has played an important role in furthering growth.

By the late 1990s and early 2000s, Islamic finance began to attract international attention as more and more countries began to embrace the concept that a system without interest (debt) is workable. This recognition can be attributed to two major factors. First, during its history of more than 30 years, no major Islamic bank has failed; indeed, such banks have proved to be as efficient and profitable as their conventional counterparts. Although there were cases of bank failures, these failures were caused by and were attributed to bad governance and lack of risk management. In none of the failed banks was the issue of any Islamic product or the design of financial intermediation questioned. This success of over 30 years has engendered confidence and trust in customers and skeptics alike. Second, the advancement of financial theory in both conventional and Islamic literature, in the area of portfolio theory and understanding of financial intermediation, has been supportive. Such an advancement in theory has shown that a system without interest can be designed and that, under certain conditions, such a system may prove to be more stable than the conventional one (Khan, 1987).

More recently, during the period 2005–08, there had been another wave of interest in Islamic finance. Similar to the situation in the 1970s, the recent surge is stimulated by increased oil revenues in the Middle East. Whereas during the 1970s interest in Islamic finance was limited to the high net worth class, current growth is the result of demand by a much wider group, including small investors and retail consumers. Several countries where Islamic finance was dormant are experiencing a sudden surge in demand for *Shari'ah*-compliant products. One example is Saudi Arabia, where a long-entrenched skepticism about Islamic finance and lack of encouragement for its growth has suddenly given way to an increasing public pressure to embrace *Shari'ah*-compliant finance. For example, Saudi Arabia's largest bank, National Commercial Bank, has converted its entire branch network to *Shari'ah* principles (RedMoney, 2007). Both Bahrain and Malaysia have taken an active role in the development of Islamic finance and have made serious efforts to establish world-class financial centers to promote it.

There is no formal or systematic source of statistics on Islamic finance, but several estimates are often quoted by different commercial and non-commercial sources.[2] According to the 10-Year Master Plan for the Islamic Financial Industry prepared by IsDB and the Islamic Financial Services Board (IFSB), by the end of 2005, more than 300 institutions in over 65 jurisdictions were engaged in Islamic finance. In a broad sense, the Islamic financial industry consists of a number of components such as Islamic banks, Islamic windows, capital markets, Islamic insurance (*takaful*), and other non-bank financial institutions. "Islamic banking" usually refers to offshore and onshore deposit taking, and commercial and investment banking, and is the most dominant sector of the market. Islamic windows are specialized windows available through conventional banks catering to the demands of Islamic products. Historically, Islamic banking and windows have been the most active sector, but in the last decade, other forms of financial products and services have been gaining momentum. Activities in the capital markets in the form of Islamic funds or Islamic bonds (*sukuk*) are increasing and there are institutions specializing in asset management, mutual funds, and brokerage houses. Islamic non-bank financial institutions include specialized institutions offering financial services through leasing (*ijarah*) or partnership (*mudarabah*) similar to conventional fund management companies. There is also a limited but growing number of institutions engaged in micro-finance, venture capital, and private equity financing.

Table 1.3 shows the total size of different segments of the market, compiled from various sources. Due to a lack of transparency of financial disclosure by financial institutions in developing countries, these estimates are if anything on the conservative side, and the actual size of assets under management is considered to be significantly higher.

Financial intermediation performed by Islamic banks is based on the principle of profit and loss sharing. The depositors agree to share profits

TABLE 1.3   Total Assets under Management, 2007

Sector	Amount (US$ billion)
Islamic banks	300
Islamic windows	200
Sukuk	70
Islamic funds	20
Takaful	4
Total	594

Source: Askari, Iqbal, and Mirakhor (2008).

TABLE 1.4   Theoretical Balance Sheet of an Islamic Bank

Assets	Liabilities
Cash balances	Demand deposits (*amanah*)
Financing assets (*murabahah, salaam, ijarah, istisnah*)	Investment accounts (*mudarabah*)
Investment assets (*mudarabah, musharakah*)	Special investment accounts (*mudarabah, musharakah*)
Fee-based services (*joalah, kifalah,* and so forth)	Reserves
Non-banking assets (property)	Equity capital

Source: Van Greuning and Iqbal (2007).

and losses with a bank that uses its skills and market knowledge to invest depositors' funds in *Shari'ah*-compliant assets. Table 1.4 shows a stylized balance sheet of a typical Islamic bank. Depositors' funds are invested in either financing instruments used to finance trade activities or leasing or manufacturing/construction activities, or in investment instruments through partnership and equity-partnership arrangements.

Distinct intermediation raises two concerns. First, Islamic banks' assets are dominated by short-term trade and leasing-based financial instruments. These instruments tend to be of short-term maturity and are not highly liquid assets. This poses a serious problem for Islamic banks that are unable to transfer illiquid assets in the secondary markets, and because of this illiquidity, Islamic banks tend to shy away from medium- to long-term financial instruments. Second, Islamic banks are often characterized by their small size, in terms of assets and capitalization. Several studies have suggested that the industry should seriously consider consolidating smaller banks to reap the benefits of economies of scale and scope. However, the larger the institution, the greater the risk of financial contagion in the case of institutional failure.

As the science of financial engineering developed in conventional finance, its application in Islamic finance also led to innovation. The first wave of innovation came in the form of Islamic funds where portfolios of commodities, equities, Islamic leases, and other Islamic products were established. In the case of equities, special screening and filters were developed to comply with *Shari'ah* and to filter out stocks of companies whose businesses or practices involved dealing in debt, or in prohibited activities such as gambling, alcohol production, and socially irresponsible practices. Research has shown that the application of such screens or filters does not impact the benefit of diversification. Today, the FTSE, Dow Jones, and S&P maintain benchmark indices consisting of *Shari'ah*-compliant stocks, which are used as performance benchmarks by portfolio managers.

The other significant breakthrough came in the form of *sukuk* (Islamic bonds), where a pool of *Shari'ah*-compliant financial instruments is securitized in the form of a fixed-income security. The issuers of *sukuk* include both sovereign and corporate entities, and the success of *sukuk* is evident by the high growth this market has enjoyed. *Sukuk* have also proved to be a bridge between Islamic and conventional markets and have led to the gradual development of capital markets, as discussed in the following section. The *sukuk* market grew from approximately US$1 billion in 2002 to US$47 billion in 2007. For example, 207 *sukuk* were issued globally in 2007, compared to 199 in 2006 and 89 in 2005 (IFIS). Slow growth in the number of issues was attributed to the sub-prime crisis in the global financial markets but this did not have an adverse effect on the size of issuance, which doubled between 2006 and 2007. Dow Jones and Citicorp have introduced an index of *sukuk* to serve as a benchmark for portfolio managers.

With the growth of institutions providing Islamic financial services, considerable research and practical advancement has taken place in the area of regulatory framework, supervision, risk management, and corporate governance. In this arena, a close collaboration among the industry, public sector, multilaterals, and other stakeholders is evident. The results of these efforts are beginning to show, as many countries that were averse to the idea of non-conventional financial institutions are now more open to the idea; and the fear of the unknown has been reduced because of the dissemination of practical experience and knowledge. From a research standpoint, this area has attracted the most research, making a number of valuable contributions.

As the number of financial institutions and their geographical reach spread and expanded, there was a need to formalize the self-regulatory aspect of the Accounting and Auditing Organization for Islamic Financial Institutions and to establish the Islamic Financial Services Board with a wider scope. The IFSB was established in 2000 with the efforts of the IMF and more than 10 central banks of Muslim countries with a strong commitment to this industry. On the occasion of its 14th meeting—held in Riyadh, Saudi Arabia in 2009—the Council of the IFSB admitted two new regulatory and supervisory authorities as full members, and eight new financial institutions as observer members, which brought the IFSB membership to 185 members operating in 35 jurisdictions.

Since its inception, the IFSB has made significant contributions by issuing standards on capital adequacy, risk management, and corporate governance.[3] These standards are issued in consultation with all stakeholders and follow a thorough process of peer review. A working group of technical experts in the relevant area was formed to review and draft documents before they are approved by member countries. The IFSB's standard on capital adequacy was issued in December 2005, offering a comprehensive framework for the identification of risk weights for *Shari'ah*-compliant products and the methodology for computation and determination of capital requirements for Islamic financial institutions.

The IFSB issued guiding principles of risk management for institutions offering Islamic financial services in December 2005. These principles deal with risk profiles of different products and make suggestions on how to deal with credit, market, and operational risk of Islamic products. The principles also identify risks specific to Islamic instruments and the ways and means to control such risks. The IFSB strongly urges Islamic financial institutions to have in place a comprehensive risk management and reporting process, including appropriate board and senior management oversight, to identify, measure, monitor, report, and control relevant categories of risks and, where appropriate, to hold adequate capital against these risks. In December 2006, the IFSB issued guiding principles on corporate governance for institutions offering Islamic financial services. The IFSB defines seven guiding principles classified into four broad categories: general governance approach; rights of investment account holders (IAH); compliance with Islamic *Shari'ah* rules and principles; and transparency of financial reporting in respect of investment accounts. These principles—which exclude Islamic insurance (*takaful*) institutions and Islamic mutual funds—are considered merely for the purpose of guidance, as the IFSB recognizes that there is no "single model" of corporate governance that can work well in every country or every organization.

In December 2007, the IFSB issued guidance on key elements in the supervisory review process of institutions offering Islamic financial services. The objective was to offer guidance on the practices that supervisory authorities are expected to apply concerning capital adequacy, risk management, internal controls, and corporate governance. The guidelines take a risk-based approach to the process of supervisory review. The IFSB recommends that the supervisory authority should fulfill the adequacy of various compliance aspects, including the *Shari'ah* rules and principles, with reference to the IFSB's standards, including those on capital requirements, risk management, governance structure and processes, transparency, and market discipline. The latest achievement of the IFSB is the establishment of the Prudential Islamic Finance Database (PIFD), with the purpose of facilitating macro-prudential analysis and helping to assess the structure and state of development of the Islamic financial services industry. Some key standards and drafts are shown in Table 1.5.

Shari'ah scholars play an important role in the governance of Islamic financial institutions. *Shari'ah* scholars provide guidance to the institution on product development and work closely with the management to ensure that the institution is conforming to the principles of *Shari'ah*. Once a product or financial instrument is cleared or certified by the *Shari'ah* scholars, it gives comfort to other stakeholders that the financial institution is not engaged in any activity that is against the essence of their religious beliefs. During the early stages of Islamic finance, there were limited numbers of *Shari'ah* experts and most of them were not well versed in the English

TABLE 1.5   Key IFSB Standards and Exposure Drafts

	IFSB Issued Standards
2009	Capital Adequacy Requirements for *Sukuk*, Securitizations, and Real Estate Investment
2009	Guiding Principles on Governance for Islamic Collective Investment Schemes
2007	Guidance on Key Elements in the Supervisory Review Process of Institutions offering Islamic Financial Services (excluding Islamic Insurance (*Takaful*) Institutions and Islamic Mutual Funds)
2006	Guiding Principles on Corporate Governance for Institutions offering only Islamic Financial Services (excluding Islamic Insurance (*Takaful*) Institutions and Islamic Mutual Funds)
2005	Capital Adequacy Standard for Institutions (other than Insurance Institutions) offering only Islamic Financial Services (IIFS)
2005	Guiding Principles of Risk Management for Institutions (other than Insurance Institutions) offering only Islamic Financial Services (IIFS)
	Exposure Drafts (work-in-progress)
	Guiding Principles on Governance for Islamic Insurance (*Takaful*) Operations
	Conduct of Business for Institutions offering Islamic Financial Services (IIFS)
	Guiding Principles on *Shari'ah* Governance System

language and/or the principles of economics, finance, and banking. Each institution formed its own *Shari'ah* board and made every effort to attract prominent names to establish credibility for the institution. With the entry of Western institutions, demand for *Shari'ah* scholars who were reasonably conversant in the English language also increased, and with the increased demand, remunerations also increased.

With the continuing growth of Islamic finance and the scarcity of properly trained *Shari'ah* scholars, competition among *Shari'ah* scholars increased and many started to represent multiple *Shari'ah* boards. This sharing of resources raised concerns about the transparency and confidentiality of decision making by scholars representing multiple institutions. Siddiqi (2006) makes very pertinent observations that, in the beginning, during the 1970s, issuing a *fatwa* (religious proclamation) was considered a sacred duty and an action of public good, as compared to legal experts in conventional banking charging significant fees. However, this changed over time when competition and compensation created a lucrative market for experts who could bless a transaction and make it *Shari'ah*-compliant. With this commercialization, innovation went from the public domain to behind the closed doors of financial institutions that guarded the deals to maintain their competitive advantage.

Today, it is standard practice for financial institutions to maintain a *Shari'ah* Supervisory Board (SSB) that provides an oversight of the institution's dealings in *Shari'ah* matters. Each SSB is subject to an institution's internal procedures and processes to ensure compliance. From the governance point of view, the functioning of SSBs raises five main issues for corporate governance: independence in decision making; confidentiality of decision making; competence of members; consistency of decision making; and disclosure requirements (Grais and Pellegrini, 2006). In addition to internal corporate governance arrangements, national regulators and international standard setters in several countries have implemented guidelines for SSBs. These often refer to the general duty of SSBs to ensure *Shari'ah* compliance of transactions and, less frequently, indicate areas of competence, composition, and decision making. For example, regulators in Bahrain, Malaysia, Pakistan, Kuwait, Jordan, Lebanon, and Indonesia have defined terms of reference for SSBs, and Bahrain, Pakistan, Jordan, Lebanon, and Indonesia have developed guidelines for the appointment and dismissal of members of SSBs (Grais and Pellegrini, 2006).

There is more awareness today of the importance and the role of *Shari'ah* boards, and a realization that the industry should move toward defining *Shari'ah* standards. The need for standards stems from the existence of different schools of Islamic jurisprudence and different practices in different jurisdictions. The AAOIFI took early initiatives in defining *Shari'ah* standards, and as of 2008, it had drafted 23 accounting standards, five auditing standards, six governance standards, two codes of ethics, and 30 *Shari'ah* standards (see www.aaoifi.com). Similarly, the idea of a centralized *Shari'ah* Supervisory Board (also referred to as a High *Shari'ah* Authority, or Fatwa Board) has been implemented in some countries. For example, Malaysia, Sudan, Kuwait, Pakistan, United Arab Emirates, and Indonesia have established centralized boards to provide guidelines and to perform an oversight function over individual *Shari'ah* boards (Grais and Pellegrini, 2006).

Islamic finance has begun to go global; that is, it is gradually being introduced in countries other than Muslim countries. Although Western financial centers and financial intermediaries have always played an important part in executing and innovating Islamic transactions, such activities have been mostly carried out in the private sector and in a discrete fashion. By early 2000, this trend began to change and several non-Muslim countries began to take an interest in this emerging financial market. This interest can be attributed to several factors, such as booming oil revenues leading to the accumulation of investible funds looking for attractive investment opportunities, increased awareness of regulatory issues relating to Islamic financial intermediaries, and the desire by sovereign and corporate entities to tap into alternative funding resources.

Given the historical significance of London as a financial center, its reputation, sound regulatory framework, reputable financial houses, financial depth, and attractive time zone with respect to the Middle East have made it a popular choice for Islamic financial transactions. It is claimed that more money flows through the London financial center in terms of the most-widely used Islamic financial instrument, commodity *murabahah*, than through any other center (Oakley, 2007). With a Muslim population of almost two million, there was sufficient demand in the United Kingdom to establish the Islamic Bank of Britain in September 2004, which by the end of 2006 had attracted deposits worth £83 million from 30,000 customers and whose assets stood at £120 million (Martin, 2007). Similarly, the European Islamic Investment Bank (EIIB) began its operations in April 2006 with the objective of promoting *Shari'ah*-compliant investment banking. In 2008, European Finance House (EFH), a unit of Qatar Islamic Bank, was awarded a banking license in the United Kingdom to provide *Shari'ah*-compliant banking. EFH plans to target the European Union's 14 million Muslims who will have access to Islamic financial products (Spikes, 2008). Table 1.6 lists the top UK Islamic financial institutions and their ranking among top Islamic banks.

The UK has also attracted researchers on Islamic finance. A number of universities, including CASS Business School, Reading University, Durham

TABLE 1.6   Top UK Islamic Financial Institutions

Rank	Institution	As of Date	Asset Size (US$ million)	Top 500 Ranking
1	HSBC Amanah	June 2008	15,194	10
2	Bank of London and the Middle East (BLME)	June 2008	1,196	85
3	European Islamic Investment Bank (EIIB)	Dec. 2007	648	112
4	Islamic Bank of Britain (IBB)	Dec. 2007	337	146

Source: RedMoney (2009).

University, Loughborough University, and Surrey University, are engaged in research and offer courses in Islamic finance. The Chartered Institution of Management Accountants (CIMA) now also offers a certificate in Islamic finance, the first global qualification to be offered by a professional chartered accountancy body (RedMoney, 2009).

Realizing the significance and potential for Islamic finance domestically and internationally, the UK government has taken steps to make its markets "Islamic finance friendly." To tap into the increased liquidity looking for *Shari'ah*-compliant venues for investments, the UK government in 2007 started evaluating the possibility of launching a sovereign *sukuk* with the objective of encouraging the domestic Islamic financial market and developing a global benchmark. It was also declared in the 2007 budget that *sukuk* were to be accorded the same tax status as conventional debt instruments, and that the income to *sukuk* investors was to be treated as interest income. These measures were introduced to send positive signals to potential *sukuk* investors and to ensure a level playing field with conventional securities.

As more steps are taken to develop London as a hub for Islamic finance, the city poses serious threats for regional financial centers such as Bahrain and Malaysia that are trying to develop dedicated Islamic financial centers. Some argue that this may lead to capital flight, which can hamper the development of regional financial centers. However, others argue that London can play a complementary and enhancing role through financial innovations, cost-effective execution, and access to other markets.

Islamic finance has a long history of a silent presence in Europe. The major early development was the establishment in Geneva in 1981 of the Dar al Maal al Islami Trust, an investment company that holds stakes in several Islamic banks (Wilson, 2007). Many high net worth clients demanding *Shari'ah*-compliant investments deal directly with European banks—notably with UBS of Switzerland, the leading provider of *Shari'ah*-compliant wealth management services. The pioneering *sukuk* in Europe, was set up by the German Federal State of Saxony-Anhalt, which raised US$100 million through an issuance of five-year *sukuk* in July 2004 (Wilson, 2007). Although London has been active in the market, in the rest of Europe the idea of Islamic finance has yet to attract attention on a large scale. For example, in France, where the Muslim population of six million is three times that of the UK, the authorities and regulators have been slow to realize the potential of this market (Oakley, 2007).

In the rest of the world, Japan and Hong Kong are also engaging in Islamic finance. The Hong Kong Monetary Authority (HKMA) has given permission for the operation of the first Islamic banking window by Hong Leong Bank of Hong Kong (HLBHK), with limited operations to take Islamic deposits to be invested in commodity *murabahah* (RedMoney, 2009). Tokyo has taken concrete steps to capture a slice of the Islamic finance market. For example, Japan's trade promotion body, the Japan Bank for International Cooperation (JBIC), has announced plans to issue a *sukuk* to attract Middle East petro-dollars (Martin, 2007). Several Japanese banks and their securities divisions are keen to establish themselves as a gateway to Malaysia for Japanese investors to tap into this market. Japan based Toyota Motor Corporation issued two *sukuk* in Malaysian ringgit in 2008 and 2009 worth US $31M and US $11.4M respectively. (IFIS).

The presence of Islamic finance is beginning to be felt all over the world, and multilateral institutions are also engaging with the market. While the World Bank and the IMF have made contributions to this field through research, other institutions are also now getting involved. The International Finance Corporation (IFC)—the private sector arm of the World Bank—has executed several *Shari'ah*-compliant transactions. In 2007, Multilateral Investment Guarantee Agency (MIGA)—one of the agencies of the World Bank Group—provided its first-ever guarantee for *Shari'ah*-compliant project financing, worth US$427 million.[4]

Islamic financial institutions (IFIs) have also been impacted by the financial crisis, but for different reasons. Due to the prohibition of interest, IFIs do not have access to debt and therefore were unable, in the lead-up to the crisis, to create leverage as was done excessively by conventional banks. In addition, IFIs did not have any exposure to toxic assets, which are not considered as *Shari'ah* compliant. As a result, IFIs were not impacted during the early stages of the financial crisis. However, as the crisis developed into an economic slowdown and recession, IFIs started to feel the pinch. Exposure to IFIs appears in the form of a drop in real estate prices in the Gulf Cooperation Council (GCC) countries, a sharp correction in regional stock markets, and deteriorating asset prices in US and European financial and real estate markets (RatingsDirect, 2009). The real test of IFIs will be how to manage the expectations of the investors (depositors) who are expected to share the profits and losses of assets of the bank. Some financial institutions maintain reserves known as profit equalization reserves (PER), which they can tap into to give better returns to their investors during slow times. It is widely anticipated that IFIs will be making use of such reserves in the near future.

The financial crisis has highlighted a vulnerable area for Islamic financial institutions: liquidity management. IFIs do not have access to the liquidity management tools available to conventional banks, but in addition depressed asset prices made managing liquidity more difficult. Access to liquidity through *sukuk* issuance was also limited. Total *sukuk* issuance worldwide declined to US$14.9 billion in 2008, compared to more than US$34.3 billion a year earlier.[5] The liquidity issue can become a serious one if the economic recovery is delayed. Stakeholders have started to address this issue and efforts have begun to find solutions to the problem. The IFSB has formed a working group to understand the issues and to suggest solutions to the problem.

While the financial crisis poses challenges to Islamic financial institutions, it also offers opportunities to exploit. Depressed asset prices in the developed economies are attracting investors and Islamic financial institutions to make long-term investments. Such opportunities can become another venue for the introduction of Islamic finance in economies less familiar with this form of finance. Both developed and developing economies can tap into this market by understanding the requirements of Islamic finance and providing a level playing field at the legal and regulatory level.

The future of Islamic finance in Muslim countries will depend in large part on the pace of economic growth in OIC countries, the success of privatization programs, the extent and quality of economic and financial reforms, oil price developments and the size of available investment funds in oil-exporting countries, the quality of governance and supervision in Islamic countries, and the evolution of the global financial crisis that started in 2007 and continues unabated in 2009. As economic performance improves in OIC countries, as financial liberalization continues, as financial regulatory and supervisory administration of Islamic financial practices matures, as Muslims are afforded diverse and better opportunities to save and invest in accordance with their religion, and as the inherent stability of an Islamic financial system becomes acknowledged and accepted, the growth of Islamic finance should be more rapid than anything we have seen in the past.

1.4 Islamic Finance and Globalization: Convergence or Divergence?

After examining the various facets and manifestations of globalization and Islamic finance in Chapters 2–6, we will attempt in Chapter 7 to answer this central question: Is it likely that, with continuing globalization, conventional finance and Islamic finance will converge over time?

Our answer to this question will turn on the core elements of Islamic finance, conventional finance, and globalization. Islamic finance is based on risk sharing, trust and transparency. Islamic values, which are the foundation of an Islamic economic and financial system, preach the importance of economic and social justice, universal access to education, a level playing field, hard work, the rule of law, economic and material growth and progress, and state intervention to correct deviations from the accepted norm. These are the values that Muslim countries have to embrace and adopt in their quest to be more Islamic.

Recent progress in conventional finance has centered on unbundling risk and developing instruments to appropriate risk. While the net effect of financial globalization may be debated, the fact that it has a significant effect on risk sharing, financial stability, economic growth, incomes, cross-country income differentials, within-country income inequality, poverty alleviation, and more, cannot be denied. Whether Islam embraces financial globalization or not will depend on the extent that globalization supports Islamic values and goals and, even more importantly, on the ability of Islamic governments to develop policies and institutions to benefit from globalization, while minimizing the effects that are not compatible with Islam. At the same time, the global financial crisis of 2007–09 will undoubtedly affect the evolution of both conventional and Islamic finance. The role of debt financing and leveraging will have to be addressed. The impact of debt financing on financial stability will be important to both conventional as well as Islamic finance. The extent and role of cross-border transmission of financial shocks will have to be studied. The evolution of financial regulation and supervision will be key factors in the financial system that will evolve from what is likely to be the biggest financial meltdown since the Great Depression. The financial stability characteristics of conventional and Islamic finance will be important determinants of how Islamic finance may affect globalization and globalization affect Islamic finance. Will the world at large reduce its reliance on debt financing and leveraging and move more toward equity-based financing?

Ideally, Muslim countries should preserve, and hopefully even enhance, their Islamic character while reaping the benefits of globalization. If the required policies and institutions to benefit from globalization are universal access to high-quality education, a level playing field, the rule of law, efficient institutions, and state intervention to correct deviations from the accepted norms, it might appear that globalization may even afford Muslim countries additional policy support in their quest to be "more" Islamic.

Endnotes

1 For an introductory text on Islamic economics and finance, see Iqbal and Mirakhor (2007).
2 General Council of Islamic Banks and Financial Institutions (CIBAFI) is making efforts to maintain statistics on Islamic financial institutions.
3 For further details, see www.ifsb.org.
4 www.miga.org/news/index_sv.cfm?aid=1696.
5 Standard & Poor's, February 20, 2009.

CHAPTER 2

The Consequences of Globalization: Convergence or Divergence with Islam?

Globalization is the proverbial whipping boy used to justify or refute any development or position. Sometimes it seems that globalization is the most malleable of all doctrines, as it lends support to seemingly opposing views. In this chapter, we first ask what are the broad theoretical economic and financial effects of globalization. Second, we briefly review the empirical implications of globalization. Third, we examine the impact of financial globalization in more detail. Fourth, we present the core principles of Islam to assess where globalization supports, and where it conflicts with, fundamental Islamic teachings. Fifth, we outline the policies that may be helpful in making globalization compatible with, and even supportive of, Islam.

2.1 Theoretical Consequences of Globalization: Growth, Income Distribution, Poverty Alleviation, and Regulation

Globalization is essentially the process of eliminating all barriers so that countries "appear" as if they were one integrated country. Barriers that inhibit economic interactions, or flows, between countries include those on: goods and services, capital (portfolio, foreign direct investment, and debt), technology, and labor (both skilled and unskilled). The lifting of barriers, in turn, leads to an enhanced level of competition. The manifestation of this competition from abroad is multidimensional:

- Increased flow of goods into the country at a lower price
- Increased flow of services (including banking and other forms of financial services) at a lower price

- Increased flow of capital (FDI, portfolio, and debt) at a lower cost
- Increased flow of technology
- Increased flow of labor (professional, skilled, and unskilled)

These flows, in turn, affect a number of critical economic indicators, including: (i) real wage rates or the real rates of return to differing categories of labor (professional, skilled, and unskilled); (ii) real rates of return to capital; (iii) real incomes; (iv) income distribution (including poverty alleviation); (v) employment and unemployment; and (vi) economic growth. Before we look at the impact of globalization on these indicators, we must stress an important point. In all instances, there are numerous other forces, besides globalization, that affect these outcomes, and there are more direct policy options than globalization for governments to adopt to affect these variables. For example, governments can directly affect income distribution through taxation. In other words, globalization by itself does not determine any of these important economic developments. Globalization can, however, be a major determinant of developments.

Globalization is, in the first instance, advocated because of its presumed positive impact on overall economic growth. The classical argument in support of trade is quite appealing. Free trade and the unimpeded flows of labor, capital, and technology, by moving from where they are plentiful to where they are scarce, increase global output and enhance the welfare-promoting movement of factors and goods. The presumption is that these forces allow a country to expand its production possibility frontier by taking advantage of efficiency gains afforded by a larger market, specialization, and better technology through economies of scale, learning by doing, higher investment, and the like. A more recent argument (Balassa, 1978; Krueger, 1980) is that outward-oriented policies reflect a real exchange rate that promotes the development of exports, whereas inward policies are accompanied by an overvalued real exchange rate, retarding the growth of exports; the clear presumption here is that the benefit of outward-oriented policies is from better exchange rate management. Thus, it is presumed that economic growth can normally be expected to accelerate as a result of globalization. But this theoretical positive association of globalization with economic growth and the indicated policy of opening up all markets may be questioned, for a variety of reasons.

First, there is the standard infant industry argument against complete and indiscriminate liberalization: some industries, especially those where economies of scale and learning by doing are important, cannot develop, in the early stage of their evolution, in the face of price competition from already established and advanced industries from abroad. Infant industry protection has clearly been a positive factor for growth and development in a number of countries, including Japan and South Korea (Chang, 2007). A country that does not protect its infant industries may inhibit their eventual development. While many countries, including Japan and South Korea, disavow this pro-protection argument today, they are forgetting their own path to development (Chang, 2007).

Second, whether trade liberalization may be unequivocally beneficial or not depends on the exact form of existing barriers in all countries, as well as other factors that accelerate or decelerate growth. It is time (and environment or condition) specific.

Third, it must be remembered that not all trade flows occur under perfect competitive market conditions. Foreign firms may resort to "dumping" to get their goods into a country's market. There are three motivations behind dumping: sporadic dumping (excess inventory, and so on), persistent dumping (to maximize profits if price elasticities vary across markets), and predatory dumping (to drive domestic firms out of business). Dumping can clearly impair growth and be detrimental. As a result, countries may need to monitor dumping and impose barriers when it occurs.

Fourth, the inflow of services, especially financial services, can cause more widespread effects than the flow of goods. Financial deepening resulting from capital inflows and the appearance of foreign institutions can be expected to increase the liquidity of the local stock market and reduce the cost of capital. Foreign financial institutions will normally introduce new financial products. Capital flows will force recipient countries to adopt better macroeconomic policies or be subject to heightened economic and financial volatility. To fully benefit from these changes, countries need a well-developed financial oversight structure. If regulatory oversight is not well developed, then foreign participation could be harmful to the real as well as the financial sector of the economy. Foreign banks could drive out domestic banks, reducing competition; or they could drive out some domestic banks and render other domestic banks more efficient, increasing competition. Capital flows could cause financial and exchange rate volatility. Financial volatility and financial turmoil can be costly for economic growth and be especially harmful for the disadvantaged members of society. The net effect on economic growth and income distribution (poverty alleviation) cannot be a priori determined, but may largely depend on the quality of regulatory oversight.

In addition to affecting the rate of return to capital, the flow of capital also brings in foreign investors in the form of foreign direct investment. A multinational corporation (MNC) can invest in an existing firm or a new firm (greenfield). The appearance of MNCs could enhance or damage competition; it all depends on whether FDI increases or decreases the market power of individual firms. The MNC brings its own culture and management.

Its business approach may, in turn, affect employment and working conditions. At the same time, the presence of foreign management will impact the salaries of local managers. Again, regulation and oversight may be needed to address these and related issues in order to maximize benefits and minimize disruptions and costs.

What is the net effect of globalization on economic growth? An unequivocal answer cannot be given. The net result is that the impact of globalization on growth is country, case, and time specific. Thus, while we can say very little a priori about the net effect of globalization on economic growth for all countries, we *can* say more about individual countries if we are given their specific circumstances.

How does globalization affect real incomes and income distribution? The flow of goods and services directly affects the domestic price of goods and services, and as a result the real return to labor (different for each labor classification) and capital. The impact on the return to labor and capital is due to the fact that goods and services are essentially the embodiment of the inputs that are used to manufacture or deliver them. If a country—say, the capital-abundant country—imports labor-intensive goods and exports capital-intensive goods (as predicted in the Heckscher-Ohlin trade model— two countries, two goods, two factors of production which are mobile within countries but immobile across countries, diminishing marginal productivity of factors, constant returns to scale, zero transportation cost, and broadly similar consumption taste patterns), then real wage rates (assuming for the moment that all labor is the same) decline with more trade. This is because the import of labor-intensive goods is akin to importing more labor; in other words, similar to increasing the domestic labor supply and in turn reducing the return to labor.

The opposite of reducing barriers to trade—namely, the imposition of barriers to trade—is the famous Stolper-Samuelson Theorem. In the same country—that is, the capital-abundant country—the real rate of return to capital goes up at the same time as the demand for capital-intensive goods, and thus the demand for capital inputs, has effectively increased (from abroad). The decline in the real wage rate and the increase in the rate of return to capital will, in turn, affect the level of real income. Those who have only their labor to sell lose relative to those who own capital, resulting in a change in income distribution. The opposite is the case for the labor-abundant country. Globalization gives birth to both winners as well as losers, and inevitably to conflict! And conflict affects the ebb and flow of globalization.

In order to examine the return to different labor categories, we can simply replace capital and labor inputs by skilled and unskilled labor (as the two factors of production) and apply the Heckscher-Ohlin model as before.

Then, in the unskilled labor–abundant country (the developing country), trade would increase the real return of unskilled labor and reduce the real return of skilled labor, in turn, improving income distribution (reducing inequality between the two classes of labor). But in the skilled labor-abundant country (advanced country), the return to skilled labor would increase while return to unskilled labor would decrease, adversely affecting the income distribution (higher inequality). Thus the impact on income distribution is country dependent; in some countries income distribution will improve, and in others, it will deteriorate.

Income distribution is also affected by the flow of technology across borders. To the extent that the flow of technology increases or decreases the relative demand for skilled labor (unskilled labor saving or unskilled labor dissaving), returns to different labor categories—and thus income distribution—will be affected. The presumption is that most technological change increases the relative demand for skilled labor (increasing its return relative to that of unskilled labor) and thus tends to increase income inequality (IMF, 2007b, p. 59), but this is an empirical issue and need not always be the case.

A further effect on income distribution is attributable to trade in non-competing goods (goods that are not produced in the importing country), a possibility that is excluded in the standard Heckscher-Ohlin model of trade. If tariffs on these goods are reduced, their import prices decline and imports of them increase. If these non-competing goods are a significant part of the basket of goods consumed by unskilled workers, then income inequality will be reduced. It should be stressed that this reduction in income inequality can be expected to occur in both the advanced (skilled labor-abundant) and the developing country as long as the countries are importers of such goods and they are a significant component of consumption.

Finally, if a critical assumption of the Heckscher-Ohlin model—immobility of factors (capital and labor) across countries—is relaxed, then the sharpness of the Stolper-Samuelson result is blunted. The flow of labor across countries may reduce or increase inequality in both the advanced and developing country, depending on the category of labor flows and its destination. If unskilled labor (the abundant category of labor in a developing country) flows from the developing country to the advanced country, then inequality can be expected to decline in the developing country and increase in the advanced country; but if skilled labor flows from the developing country, the inequality can be expected to increase in the developing country and decrease in the advanced country. Capital flows can have an adverse or positive effect on income equality, depending on whether the capital flow, in turn, increases the relative demand for skilled or unskilled labor. Moreover, in the case of capital flows there are additional effects.

First, to what extent do capital flows enhance the financial access of the disadvantaged members of society? If the answer to this is that cross-border capital flows improve the relative access of the poor, then capital flows can be expected to improve income distribution. Second, capital flows may affect financial and exchange rate stability. This, in turn, may have a disproportionately adverse effect on the poor. If this is the case, then income inequality may increase.

Where does this all lead to concerning the impact on real incomes and income distribution? As can be seen, there are a number of opposing forces at work here. The net result clearly depends on the specifics of the country and the type of flows that are stimulated—in goods, labor, capital, and technology. Any conclusion has to be country and time—in other words, case—specific. Similar considerations affect the impact of globalization on poverty alleviation. Whether globalization reduces global poverty will depend on the particular circumstances of individual countries. Thus the overall impact of globalization (liberalization of trade, labor, capital, and technology flows) on income equality and income distribution cannot be a priori and unequivocally stated for all countries. It is not a theoretical issue but an empirical one that has to be assessed on a case-by-case basis. Again, it must be recalled that globalization is not the most direct policy instrument for addressing issues such as economic growth, income distribution, and poverty alleviation. Macroeconomic policies have a more direct and immediate impact.

Besides the effect of globalization on economic growth (and, in turn, on employment), income distribution, and poverty alleviation, there is a tendency for globalization to encourage competition in regulation, taxation, labor standards, and environmental protection. These are sometimes referred to as a "race to the bottom," or harmonization of regulations and standards. On the one hand, in their quest to be competitive, countries have an incentive to adopt legislation and regulations in the areas of labor, healthcare, environment, and taxation, among others, that will make it cheaper to manufacture goods and deliver services. Such legislation is often to the detriment of the citizenry and may be in conflict with fundamental social values. On the other hand, in a globalizing world, countries may be pressured by other countries to harmonize their regulatory regimes to attract foreign MNCs. Again, this may conflict with societal values.

In sum, we can say very little that is unequivocal about the theoretical impact of globalization on economic growth (and employment), real incomes, income distribution, and regulations in countries. Everything is country, case, and time specific. To benefit from globalization while minimizing the adverse effects, governments should develop policies and institutions to address adverse effects on income growth and income equality in order to preserve economic prosperity and social cohesion (employment and income equality). For instance, if a segment of the labor force becomes unemployed, then better access to education and labor retraining will be needed to absorb displaced labor into new sectors of comparative advantage. If the demand for highly skilled and educated labor is expected to increase, then education and its accessibility should be promoted. If income equality is adversely affected, better opportunities for advancement, such as enhanced access to higher-quality education, tax enforcement, or a revision of the tax code may be necessary. If competition is impaired, regulatory oversight is needed to ensure that markets are competitive and function smoothly and that harmful dumping is recognized and addressed. It would appear that, in the face of adverse developments accompanying globalization (such as those described above), countries should not resort to isolation but should instead adopt policies to mitigate any adverse developments while capturing the benefits.

To benefit, governments need targeted policies, thoughtful regulations, and efficient institutions. This simplistic conclusion was probably obvious and expected at the outset of this discussion. Many forces besides globalization, both positive and negative, affect growth. Globalization itself embraces many elements, some having positive and some negative effects on growth. It would therefore seem reasonable to assert that to benefit, countries need to adopt policies that minimize the negative and maximize the positive effects of globalization. While there are important theoretical indications that globalization would be growth promoting, the conclusion must be that the net benefits of globalization are likely to be country, case, and time specific. Much the same can be said for real incomes, income distribution, and poverty alleviation. In conclusion, economic benefits—in particular, welfare gains—from globalization are not guaranteed. Governments must adopt prudent policies to benefit.

2.2 Some Empirical Consequences of Globalization

At the outset we should again repeat the obvious. Globalization (trade, labor, financial, and technology flows across countries) may or may not improve economic growth and income equality, a prediction confirmed by the many forces both promoting and retarding economic growth and income equality at the theoretical level. We should expect mixed results, as the net impact of the many effects of globalization is case specific. Be that as it may, what do empirical results indicate about economic growth and income equality? We start out by presenting the broad results on growth, poverty reduction, and income equality; in the following section, we then provide a longer discussion of the impact of financial globalization.

We must first emphasize an oft-forgotten point. There is no obvious and accepted empirical definition of trade openness. The degree of openness of trade is not readily measurable, as tariffs, quotas, non-tariff barriers (NTBs), subsidies, procurement policies, and more all have an effect on "trade openness." In turn, the impact of "opening" trade on growth will depend on the conditions and circumstances prevailing in the country at that time. And explanations of differential growth between countries are attributable to many factors and have gone through a metamorphosis. For quite a while, Solow's classical theory of growth (capital, labor, and technical change) was the universal theory. More recently, "the new growth theories" (Roemer, 1986, 1987; Lucas, 1988) place extra emphasis on the important contribution of education or human capital and increasing returns to knowledge.

The economic growth experience of countries has differed when countries have been grouped on the basis of their policy orientation (that is, openness to trade). The experience of four country groups is indicative: over 1963–73, 1973–85, and 1980–92, countries with strongly open trade policies had average annual GDP per capita growth rates of 6.9 percent, 5.9 percent, and 6.4 percent; moderately open economies 4.9 percent, 1.6 percent, and 2.3 percent; moderately anti-trade 4.0 percent, 1.7 percent, and –0.2 percent; and strongly anti-trade 1.6 percent, –0.1 percent, and –0.4 percent (Lindert and Williamson, 2001, p. 50, reporting from various World Bank sources).

The impact of globalization on growth has been studied in cross-country cross-sectional regression studies and in detailed case studies of individual, or a small group of, countries. As an example of cross-country studies to assess the impact of globalization on growth, Dollar (1992) obtained the empirical result that countries that adopted outward-oriented policies had achieved higher growth than those that looked inward; he estimated that per capita GDP growth would be between 1.5 and 2.1 percentage points higher for Latin American and African countries if they adopted outward-oriented policies. Sachs and Warner (1995) concluded that open trade leads to higher growth, and to higher growth in developing countries than in developed countries (that is, also closing the income gap between the richer and poorer countries); the sub-par performance of some countries that had adopted open trade policies was attributed to financial crises and exchange rate mismanagement. Rodriguez and Rodrik (2000) concluded that the results of cross-sectional studies supporting the positive effect of trade openness on growth were not as strong as the authors claimed. Theory does not unequivocally support such a result (that is, the infant industry argument). There is no single correct way to measure trade restriction. The model specifications are not robust. Edwards (1993), in a review of the literature, concluded that the results of such cross-country regressions were flawed because of two-way causation: does growth promote exports, or do exports promote growth (as both trade policy and growth policy are endogenous variables)? Moreover, these results may be further questioned on grounds of data limitation or measurement errors. In short, and as to be expected from the theoretical discussion above, empirical results are not definitive.

Bekaert, Harvey, and Lundblad (2001) looked at the effect of financial market liberalization in emerging markets using both time series and cross-sectional data; they concluded that liberalization increased growth by 1–2 percent and that the growth effect is larger for countries with higher education levels. Bekaert, Harvey, and Lundblad (2005) examined the impact of financial globalization on growth and obtained the result that equity market liberalization increased the annual real income growth rate by 1 percent in countries that had high-quality institutions. Capital account liberalization was also found to be growth promoting and did not subsume the positive effect of equity market liberalization. The impact of financial globalization is discussed in more detail in the next section.

What about the empirical impact of globalization and trade openness on poverty reduction and income equality? Again, as with the definition of trade openness, we note that there is no acceptable aggregate definition of poverty and that aggregate data may hide real poverty through the aggregation process. Lindert and Williamson (2001, p. 38) provide a summary of the long-term (1500–2000) global change in income inequality:

> *World income inequality has risen since 1820, and probably since the sixteenth century. Most of that increased world inequality took the form of a rise in income gaps between nations, not a rise in within-nation Country inequality. However, the gaps between nations were not widened by participating in globalization. As for the visible inequalities within countries, the effects differed by region and by historical era. Before World War I, globalization raised inequality within the United States and other New World countries, but it had the opposite effect in those European countries that were committed to trade and sent out emigrants. After World War I, globalization once again widened inequality within the United States and perhaps other OECD countries. Globalization may also have raised inequality in the newly trading and industrializing countries, such as the Asian tigers, China, Mexico, and Brazil. Yet, the rising inequality in these countries was not evident among persons and households in the newly-trading regions and sectors. Rather it took the form of widening gaps between them and the less prosperous, non-participating regions. The poorest regions and the poorest countries were probably not hurt by globalization, they just failed*

to be part of it. Where the non-participants were actively excluded,
the policies yielding that inegalitarian result can hardly be called
liberal, but globalization cannot be made to take the blame.

For more recent developments, Dollar and Kraay (2002) examined
cross-country data over four decades for 92 countries. They asserted that
the average income of the bottom fifth in a country rose in proportion to the
overall average income; the factors that explain differences in cross-country
growth—such as the rule of law, openness in trade, and developed financial
markets—have no systematic effect on the share of the bottom fifth in society; and there was no evidence to support the systematically and relatively
favorable effect on the poor of four government actions: primary education
attainment, public spending on health and education, labor productivity
in agriculture relative to the rest of the economy, and formal democratic
institutions. Ravallion (2004a) used both macro (cross-country, time series,
and aggregate data) and micro (household data and modeling specific trade
reforms) to assess the impact of reducing barriers on poverty. His conclusion was that increased openness to trade is not the key to poverty reduction and it is doubtful that it hurts more people than it helps, while there
are both winners and losers among the poor. If an important goal is poverty alleviation, then his results indicate the importance of combining trade
reform with social protection policies.

Harrison (2006) reviewed the result of cross-country studies (using
aggregate data) on the number of poor, income growth rates and inequality, and country case studies (using micro data) on the incomes of the poor.
While focusing on globalization as reflected only in international trade in
goods and in capital flows (ignoring flows of services, technology, and labor),
she concluded that: (i) the poor in unskilled labor-abundant countries do
not always gain from trade reform; (ii) the poor gain more if complementary policies are in place; (iii) export growth and foreign investment reduce
poverty; (iv) financial crises adversely affect the poor; and (v) there are both
winners and losers among the poor. In short, it would appear that there is
a great deal of doubt concerning the oft-quoted adage that "a rising tide
lifts all boats."

What about the impact of globalization on labor flows and, in turn, the
effect of labor flows on real incomes and income differentials? And are labor
flows sufficiently significant to make a difference?

Migration can be expected to increase with the real wage differential
between the receiving and sending country and the availability of social
networks to assist migration in the receiving country, and to decline with
migration costs, including government restrictions in both the receiving
and sending countries. In the 19th and early 20th centuries, many receiving and

sending countries encouraged migration. In the 20th century, encouragement turned largely to discouragement, especially with the onset of the Great Depression. More recently, beginning in the latter part of the 20th century, the flow of educated labor has been encouraged in some receiving countries. As a result, labor flows have become increasingly important. The United Nations estimated the total number of skilled migrants for the period 1961–72 at about 300,000 (Docquier and Rapoport, 2004). However, the 1990 US Census estimated the number of highly educated immigrants living in the United States alone to be 2.5 million (Docquier and Rapoport, 2004). The flow of skilled labor has further accelerated since 1990 due to changes made in US immigration laws to attract skilled foreign labor, later followed by similar changes in other OECD countries. The flow of labor across borders has become for some countries, both as recipients (for example—and especially—the US, which is the destination for about 40 percent of immigrants to the OECD (Docquier and Rapoport, 2004) and as originators (for example, Iran and El Salvador), an important globalization mechanism today. Overall figures (all labor categories) indicate that (Hanson, 2007):

> *Between 1990 and 2005, the number of individuals living outside of their country of birth increased from 154 million to 190 million, reaching a level equivalent to 3 percent of the world population.*

Given that labor flows are again becoming more important, it is timely to consider what characterizes labor flows. Carrington and Detragiache (1998), among others, find that the level of education is a key factor in today's *legal* labor migration. Labor with little education has more limited migration possibilities, and migrants tend to have a much higher level of education than the average education of their country of origin. In their study, Carrington and Detragiache discovered that for almost all countries, labor with tertiary education (highly skilled labor) had the highest migration rate. Their broad conclusion is that (p. 6):

> *In absolute terms, the largest flows of highly educated migrants are from Asia, but relative to the number of highly educated individuals the "brain drain" is small for most Asian countries (although Iran and Taiwan are notable exceptions). In contrast, the outflow of highly educated individuals reaches above 30 percent in a number of countries in the Caribbean, Central America, and Africa. These countries have very high overall migration rates, but the outflow of educated people is exceptionally strong. The exodus of workers with secondary education is also substantial in most Central American countries, reaching more than 60 percent in El Salvador.*

Thus, from this pattern of labor flows it would appear that labor migration tends to increase inequality (widening the wage gap between skilled and unskilled labor) in developing countries and decrease it in advanced countries. Aydemir and Borjas (2007) examined the impact of migration on wages and inequality in Canada (inflows), the United States (inflows), and Mexico (outflows). Their result confirms the expectation that change in labor supply inversely affects wages, with an elasticity of roughly 0.3–0.4 in the three countries. However, the impact on wage structure was very different in the three countries: in Canada, wage inequality was narrowed; in the US it was increased; and in Mexico it increased the wages of those with average skills and reduced the wages of those at the bottom of the skill distribution.

The flow of labor, besides affecting wages, has other effects on the country of labor origination through: remittances, diaspora investment in the country of origin, return migration, resulting development in trade and business networks, and incentives for future human capital formation. (For a discussion of these and the net effect on developing countries, see Docquier and Rapoport, 2004; and Ozden and Schiff, 2006.) Remittances were estimated to be US$216 billion for 2004, with US$150 billion destined for developing countries alone (Ozden and Schiff, 2006, p. 1). Thus the broader impact on developing countries has to take account of these factors and will differ from country to country. While the net effect of immigration on developing countries could still be negative (the historical presumption), these compensating factors could play an important positive role in economic development in developing countries, if they are effectively employed (see Ozden and Schiff, 2006).

One already mentioned factor connected to labor flows should be emphasized. While labor, and trade and capital flows, affect wage rates and rates of return to capital, those that are affected do not see directly the mechanism through which it occurs; it is more akin to an invisible effect. But affected workers can see with their own eyes the emigrants who take their jobs or reduce their real wages. As a result, in times of falling wages or rising unemployment, labor flows are more sensitive than even trade and capital flows, although the effect may be similar.

What of the *overall* (from trade, financial, technology, and labor flows) impact of globalization on income equality? It would seem that the answer depends on the country and its circumstances. In a recent survey, the IMF (2007b) summarized the relationship between rapid trade and financial globalization and the rise in income inequality in many countries as follows:

The analysis finds that technological progress has had a greater impact than globalization on inequality within countries. The limited overall impact of globalization reflects two offsetting tendencies: while trade globalization is associated with a reduction of inequality, financial globalization—and foreign direct investment in particular—is associated with an increase in inequality. It should be emphasized that these findings are subject to a number of caveats related to data limitations, and it is particularly difficult to disentangle the effects of technology and financial globalization since they both work through processes that raise the demand for skilled workers. The chapter concludes that policies aimed at reducing barriers to trade and broadening access to education and credit can allow the benefits of globalization to be shared more equally.

One further point must be emphasized. It should be remembered that no matter how globalization affects income equality and poverty, countries can always address both of these developments through taxation, well-designed economic and social policies (education, social safety net, and the like), and appropriate and targeted expenditures.

In sum, the overall impact of globalization—trade, labor, technology, and financial—on growth, poverty reduction, and income inequality cannot be generalized. While there is a strong presumption to support a positive impact on growth and, to a lesser extent, on the other indicators, the impact is country, case, and time dependent. Although globalization is unlikely to be the most important or most direct policy for reaching these important goals, its positive contribution can be significantly enhanced by other supportive policies, such as universal access to high-quality education, better institutions and regulations, consistent macroeconomic policies, and the like.

2.3   Financial Globalization

There is an organic, interactive relationship between financial globalization and financial integration. On the one hand, the degree of progress of the latter depends on how well developed a country's financial sector is. On the other hand, financial globalization plays an important catalytic role in the liberalization and development of domestic financial markets (Häusler, 2007). An important dimension of the process of financial sector development is the expansion and quality improvement in credit and share markets (Levine, 1997; Levine and Zervos, 1998). The process of financial development deepens markets and services that channel savings to productive investment and strengthens risk sharing. Liberalization of the stock market reduces the cost of equity capital (Stulz, 1999a, 1999b), leading to a surge in the growth rate of investment and expansion of employment and output. The effect would be stronger when stock market development is accompanied by privatization, as the latter would be a signal of the country's commitment to liberalization (Perotti and van Oijen, 1995, 2001).

Financial sector development constitutes the most important channel of economic growth, particularly in countries that are finance constrained (Ayyagari et. al., 2006; Acemoglu and Guerrieri, 2006). Empirical research over the last two decades, which has established the strong link between financial development and economic growth, has also identified the conduits between the two. These channels include: (i) greater involvement of the private sector and better risk sharing; (ii) reduced risks that lower expected returns, leading to lower cost of capital and resulting in investment in higher-risk, higher-return projects; (iii) enhancement of competition and innovation; (iv) improved productivity; (v) lower output and income volatility; (vi) cost-efficiency gains in mobilizing resources for public investment; (vii) financial deepening as financial development leads to greater financial intermediation by banks, capital markets, and non-bank financial institutions; and (viii) reduced income inequality and poverty (Honohan, 2006; Demirgüç-Kunt et. al., 2006; Beck et. al., 2007; Beck and Levine, 2004; Batra et. al., 2003; Watkins, 2007; Ravallion, 2004a, 2004b, 2005; Ravallion and Chen, 2001; Aizenman and Jinjarak, 2006; Claessens and Perotti, 2006; Clarke, 2004; Goodhart, 2004).

The benefits listed above would accrue if legal and institutional developments accompany financial development. The most important dimensions of the former are legal protection of creditor, investor, and property rights, as well as contract enforcement (Clementi and MacDonald, 2004). Good governance, transparency, and accountability are the important institutional aspects that support financial development (Johnson et. al., 2002). It is considered that, once a threshold level of availability of these legal and institutional developments is surpassed, the beneficial effects will accrue (Prasad et. al., 2004). Empirical evidence suggests that countries with weak governance and low transparency receive less FDI and equity flows and have to resort to debt financing through bank loans that, as mentioned earlier, expose them to vulnerabilities and volatilities, leading to financial crises (Wei, 2001; Gelos and Wei, 2002; Wei and Wu, 2002; Smarzynska and Wei, 2000; Wei, 1997, 2000a, 2000b, 2000c, 2001; Kaufman et. al., 2005; Abed and Gupta, 2002). Another factor that could exacerbate these problems is economic instability, with research suggesting macroeconomic policies as an important determinant of the composition of capital flows (IMF, 2007a, 2007b).

On the other hand, better legal institutions and improved governance and transparency reduce informational problems (adverse selection and moral hazard) and market frictions (Acemoglu et. al., 2004; Acemoglu and Johnson, 2003; Balgati et. al., 2007). This will assist in the process of integration and deepening in the financial sector, which, in turn, will allow the emergence of active and liquid equity markets, reduced cost of capital, and improved credit rating (Yartey, 2006). As a result, more investment projects become viable, leading to greater risk sharing. More active equity markets are also associated with reduced volatility, again suggesting improved risk sharing. On the other hand, equity market opening against a backdrop of a weak financial sector, inadequate institutional and legal development, and an unstable macroeconomy could even increase variability (Bekaert and Lundblad, 2006).

Research suggests that an interactive relationship exists between financial sector liberalization and the development of an active equity market when a country achieves a threshold level of higher bureaucratic quality, a lower level of corruption, and strengthened legal institutions (Prasad et. al., 2004). It would appear that in countries where the financial system is characterized by a more advanced legal and institutional infrastructure, stock market transactions are increased and the effects of financial market openness are enhanced (Stulz, 2006). In short, financial sector development—which is accompanied by legal and institutional developments that protect investor, creditor, and property rights, enforce contracts, improve transparency, and lower corruption—promotes equity markets, which in turn increase risk sharing (Wei, 2005; Faria and Mauro, 2004; see also Black, 2000, for a helpful list of the core institutions needed to support the emergence, development, and operations of a strong securities market).

Domestic financial sector development allows integration with the global market, as it increases diversification opportunities and expands the set of financial instruments available for risk sharing. Economies that are open to two-way investments—domestic investors can invest in foreign assets and foreign investors in domestic assets—are said to be globally integrated. Financial integration, in turn, becomes an important channel of global risk sharing. There appears to be a symbiotic and interactive relationship between domestic financial development, financial integration, and financial globalization. Importantly, there is empirical evidence that financial development and integration reduce poverty through increased investment, employment, and income, and reduced income inequality. Recent research has found that: (i) the impact of financial development on poverty exerts two independent influences, with half of the impact on economic growth and the other through a reduction in income inequality; (ii) financial development leads to considerable deceleration in the rate of growth of income inequality; and (iii) as the process of financial development gathers momentum, the rate of reduction in the proportion of the population living in poverty accelerates (Atje and Jovanovic, 1993; Beck et. al., 2007; Claessens and

Feijen, 2006; Ravallion and Chen, 2001; Ravallion, 2005; Claessens and Perotti, 2006; Harrison, 2006). In sum, there appears to be considerable benefit to financial sector development and financial integration; such development and integration are increased and accelerated, as globalization of finance positively impacts and interacts with these two processes.

On the assumption that significant informational problems and transactions costs are absent, the theory suggests that integration and globalization of finance allow portfolios to be well diversified internationally and that capital flows into markets with the most favorable risk–return profiles. Thus, as risk sharing expands globally, capital is allocated more efficiently and welfare increases. There are important paradoxes contradicting this theory: (i) the Lucas paradox; (ii) the home equity bias puzzle; and (iii) the equity premium puzzle. First, Lucas (1990) argued that this theory suggests that capital-scarce countries have high rates of return to capital and should be able to attract investment from rich countries. The then data, however, did not show a large flow of capital from the latter to the former. Indeed, most of the international capital flows, especially FDI and portfolio equity flows, took place among rich countries (Obstfeld and Taylor, 2003). Also, even then, equity flows were much more biased in favor of domestic (rather than international) markets than the theory suggests (Coval, 1999; Tesar, 1995b; French and Poterba, 1991). Research indicates that a very high percentage of aggregate stock market wealth is composed of domestic equity (Aurelio, 2006). Furthermore, even in the domestic markets of rich countries, investment in stock markets is a fraction of what the theory suggests, given that the returns to equity are much larger than justified on the basis of aversion to risk (Halaissos and Bertaut, 1995). Mehra and Prescott (1985) demonstrated that, over many decades, a larger differential existed between the real rates of return to equity than to safe assets—that is, US Treasury bills. They also demonstrated that this differential was too large to be explained by existing theories of rational investor behavior. The implication presents a puzzle as to why rational investors, noting the differential, would not invest in equities up to the point where the remaining differential could be explained as the risk premium on equities. While Mehra and Prescott focused on the US data in their 1985 paper, subsequent research emphasized that it existed in a number of countries, including India (Mehra, 2006). Recent research has shown the global character of this puzzle and has attributed a significant part of it to institutional factors (Erbas and Mirakhor, 2007). Interestingly, in one of his recent papers, Mehra (2003) reports that the real worth of one dollar invested in equity in 1802 would have been nearly US$560,000 in 1997, whereas the real worth of the same US$1 invested in Treasury bills in 1802 would have been only US$276 over the same period.

Empirical evidence, however, suggests that risk sharing within countries and across borders is as yet an insignificant fraction of its potential (Shiller, 2003). Shiller presents six ideas for a new risk management infrastructure: (i) insurance (long-term livelihood and home equity insurance), (ii) financial markets (macro markets), (iii) banking (income-linked loans), (iv) taxation (inequality insurance), (v) social welfare (intergenerational social security), and (vi) agreements with other countries (international agreements). While Shiller's insight is bold, still other areas of risk management could be added to his list.

There is validity in the critics' arguments on globalization that, despite the fact that globalization was expected to help the poor, poverty has not been reduced and inequality has not decreased (Stiglitz, 2003, 2006; Lindert and Williamson, 2001; Mody and Murshid, 2005; Ranciere et. al., 2006; Tornell et. al., 2004; Tesar, 1995a; Goldberg and Pavcnik, 2007; Kaminsky and Schmuckler, 2002; Van Wincoop, 1994, 1999; Wei and Wu, 2002). Moreover, there is empirical evidence of increased risks of volatility and financial crises (Aizenman, 2002; Kose et. al., 2007). In response, researchers argue that the process of globalization is far from complete and that, at present, the global economy and finance are undergoing major structural changes, creating a situation of "fluidity" as a result of changes to the usual "determinants of market valuation, volatility, leverage, velocity, and liquidation." Each of these structural changes is significant both on its own and in the way it interacts with others (El-Erian, 2007). These changes are: (i) positive productivity shocks associated with the growing integration of large segments of the labor force in developing economies, rendering them a significant portion of global expansion; (ii) a significant increase in commodity prices, which has turned their producers, as a whole, into net global creditors; and (iii) considerable retrenchment in the barriers to entry (El-Erian, 2007). Additionally, even rapid innovation in the design of instruments of risk sharing has focused on a fraction of the possibilities, and large potential markets that allow trade in broad claims on national income (called "macro markets") have yet to be developed and tapped. "Some of these markets could be far larger in terms of the value of the risks traded than anything the world has yet experienced, dwarfing today's stock markets" (Shiller, 2003). Shiller notes that "stock markets are claims on corporate dividends which are only a few percent of national income."

Finally, researchers suggest that, while the benefits of globalization have not been fully forthcoming with the scope and magnitude expected, the problem has not been the process of globalization, but rather the way in which it has proceeded, where the playing field has not been quite leveled and where many financial markets have a long way to develop to allow meaningful integration of wider and deeper risk sharing. Financial globalization does not automatically provide the expected benefits to many countries unless they have attained a threshold level of legal and institutional development, as mentioned earlier (Chinn and Ito, 2002; Kose et. al., 2007).

Evidence suggests that countries that attain an optimum threshold level of legal and institutional development are likely to attract more FDI and portfolio equity flows. In one such study, Faria and Mauro (2004) measured institutional quality as the average of six indicators—(i) voice and accountability, (ii) political stability and the absence of violence, (iii) government effectiveness, (iv) regulatory quality, (v) rule of law, and (vi) control of corruption—and found that countries that ranked higher on these indicators attracted more equity-like flows. Wei (2005) found evidence in a study on mutual funds that countries with a high degree of government and corporate transparency attract more equity investment because, as explained by Erbas and Mirakhor (2007), transparency reduces adverse incentive and ambiguity effects. There is also empirical evidence that poor public institutions bias the composition of inflow of capital against equity-like flows and toward debt, exposing these countries to currency and financial crises and adversely affecting their ability to use a given amount of capital inflow to stimulate economic growth.

Stulz (2005) indicates that in many developing countries there is a "twin agency" problem stemming from poor corporate and state governance, which feed on each other. In countries with a "twin agency" problem, the risk of expropriation by corporations and the state is high because "those who control a country's state can establish, enforce, and break rules that affect investors' payoffs within that country. When expropriation risks are significant, it is optimal for corporate ownership to be highly concentrated, which limits economic growth, risk sharing, financial development, and the impact of financial globalization" (Stulz, 2006). One study found that one dollar of cash is, on average, worth US$0.91 in countries with low corruption and only US$0.33 in countries with high corruption (Pinkowitz et. al., 2004). Where the "twin agency" problem exists, diffusion of ownership is weak, the financial sector is poorly developed, and investment and economic growth are low (Antunes and Tiago, 2003). Once a country begins to liberalize its financial market and to improve its legal institutions and governance, a virtuous circle becomes possible: globalization begins to play a positive role in encouraging further development of the legal and institutional infrastructure, which allows further development of the financial sector (Chinn and Ito, 2002).

The IMF (Mauro and Ostry, 2007) provides a list of the policies that enhance a country's benefits from financial globalization: developed domestic financial markets insulate a country from external shocks; strong institutions (rule of law, low corruption, and the like) enable better risk sharing; consistent macroeconomic policies encourage better private sector financial policies: trade integration facilitates economic recovery; and the opening of financial markets should be done deliberately and in a cautious manner to avoid costly disruptions. Akitoby and Stratmann (2009) use panel data to demonstrate that political institutions are important for financial markets and result in lower sovereign risk spreads. Obstfeld (2009) argues that there is no solid evidence to support the contention that financial opening enhances economic welfare and economic growth, but may increase the frequency and severity of economic crises.

Mishkin (2005, pp. 28–29) provides a summary that captures quite well the state of professional thinking on the effect of financial globalization on developing countries:

> *Financial globalization can play an important role in encouraging development of institutions so that financial markets can effectively perform the crucial function of getting capital to its most productive uses which is the key to generating growth and reducing poverty. However, as we have seen, although financial globalization can be a strong force for good, it can also go very wrong if a country doesn't manage the process properly. The increased likelihood that countries will experience financial crises when they open up their financial markets to foreign capital explains why there is no clear cut relationship between financial globalization and economic growth. Botched financial globalization also poses a danger because it may create a backlash against globalization.*
>
> *Bad policies are the reason that financial development does not occur and why financial globalization often leads to harmful financial crises. Instead of rejecting financial globalization, we can greatly improve the environment for economic growth if we develop policies that promote successful financial development and financial globalization.*

2.4 Basic Islamic Economic and Financial Doctrines and Globalization

Although Muslim scholars have addressed the issues pertaining to the economic and social life of Muslim communities throughout history, it was only in the 1970s that research efforts were made to explain how Islam proposes to organize the modern economy. The now classic works of As-Sadr (1987) provided groundbreaking ideas on the main features of an Islamic economy in comparison with those of socialism and capitalism. His work on an Islamic economy was followed by that of, among others, Chapra (1975, 1979), Siddiqi (1981), Khan and Mirakhor (1987), and Mirakhor (1989), who provided further groundbreaking research on why there is a need for an alternative system, what are the essential features of an Islamic economic system, and how a system will function in the absence of interest. Seminal works of Chapra (1996, 2000) and Siddiqi (1985, 2001) laid the foundation for and emphasis on the social justice aspect of Islamic economic system.

Let us now examine what is at the foundation of an Islamic economic system and how it might be affected—supported or undermined—by the process of globalization. Are Islamic doctrines and globalization compatible?

Islam is the only major religion that imparts detailed prescriptions for the economic life of its followers. Islam addresses the value of natural resources, sets standards for the exploitation of minerals, and stipulates guidelines on inheritance, finance, taxation, and banking. It emphasizes the importance of education, healthcare, hard work, investment, a social safety net, and especially social and economic justice, among other things. An economy may be classified as Islamic *only* if it chooses to base its economic and public policies on these essential doctrines. For our purpose, we extract these few fundamental economic principles as outlined by the *Qur'an* in order to capture the essence of an Islamic economy and how it might be supported or undermined by globalization.

The central goal of Islam is to develop an egalitarian social structure in which all men and women can maximize their intellectual capacity, preserve and promote their health, and actively contribute to the economic and social development of society. Economic development and growth, along with social justice, are the essential elements of an Islamic economic system. People of all genders, ethnicities, and religious creeds are considered equal in an Islamic society because *all humans* are required by God to partake in the formation of an educated, economically secure, and ethical society.[1] Natural resources were bequeathed to humanity by God with the sole purpose that they be utilized for the formation of a public order promoting social justice, economic equity and prosperity, and personal responsibility. Humans must use their reason to formulate strategies that will eliminate any factors hindering society's intellectual development, economic progress, and social freedom. Because it is humanity that must establish and develop a just and prosperous Islamic social order, the economic and social advancement of the Muslim community is ultimately determined by the extent to which individual Muslims participate in the administration of daily societal affairs. It is for this reason that the *Qur'an* made the pre-Islamic concept of *shura*, governing by mutual consultation and consensus, a central feature of an Islamic government.[2]

Islam espouses a capitalistic economic philosophy that encourages adherents to work hard for economic gain, compete in business, own private property, and take risks in investment. Individuals may earn a return on their investments, and are encouraged to work productively in their own self-interest. Islam recognizes, however, that the economic and emotional strains of poverty may compel an individual to resort to unhealthy or unethical means of earning an income. The essential components of the Islamic economic system were, therefore, formulated to ensure the availability and accessibility of education and employment, poverty reduction and prevention, and continuous social and intellectual development for all individuals. This viewpoint is affirmed by the *Sunnah*, which stress that economic prosperity and social stability are essential for continued adherence to moral–ethical behavior and the maintenance of faith.[3]

Islam holds that the community's physiological, safety, security, and social needs must first be satisfied for positive intellectual and economic growth to take place. Basic physiological needs for food, shelter, clothing, and rest must be assured; safety, security, and social cohesion should be maintained; and public freedom of speech and religion must be guaranteed. Islam has deemed the fulfillment of these essential needs, along with free and easy access to education, to be a prerequisite for the promotion of economic growth and social development (Ul Haq, 1995). Poverty is considered by Islam to be a threat to the very existence of the faith. Thus, specific capitalistic strategies looking to "maximize efficiency and productivity" must be qualified if they leave the basic physiological and educational needs of a significant part of the populace unfulfilled and hinder public access to equitable economic opportunities. Thus the Islamic system can be summarized as a capitalistic system with essential safeguards to ensure social and economic justice.

Progressive human development is considered by Islam to be the foremost guarantor of an economically just and socially stable society. The pursuit of knowledge and the practice of innovation are, thus, activities of supreme importance, and must be consistently encouraged by all members of the *ummah*.[4] Human beings, according to Islam, have the intellectual capacity and necessary resolve to develop intellectually, spiritually, and physically. Islam insists that its adherents cultivate their potential by ridding themselves of ignorance through study and spiritual growth. It not only views education as the requisite mode of attaining personal and earthly prosperity, but also considers it to be the primary means of resisting tyrannical manipulation (Sachedina, 1988). Muslims are, therefore, required to obtain an education, and must enhance and incorporate what they learn into their personal and public policy decisions.[5]

Islam's goal is to fashion an economic system in which each member of the *ummah* can produce enough income to satisfy his or her individual and familial consumption needs.[6] Islam pushes for the maximum exploitation of the earth's natural resources, and has made the utilization of these resources through hard work a religious obligation second only to prayer.[7] Work is considered by Islam to be the most crucial aspect of economic success, and hard work on the part of *any individual*—regardless of his or her religious convictions—is the best guarantee for economic and social progress. Islamic law permits all forms of labor, production, and economic commerce, except for routine beggary and freeloading, and any vocations that may promote social instability or political, economic, or social oppression.[8] Recognizing that an individual's capacity to produce may vary according to his or her talent and ability, Islam does not call for perfect income equality and does not stipulate a limit on the amount of income an individual may earn. It strives to reduce and prevent exceptionally large inequalities in wealth and income, and thus requires that employees receive no less than a living wage that can sufficiently cover basic expenses (Iqbal, 1986).[9] Islam has left it up to the *ummah* to determine what minimum or living wage value can adequately cover a worker's basic living expenses at a specific point in time (Ul Haq, 1995).

According to Islam, work and investment are the only legitimate means of acquiring property rights. Islamic law maintains that all individuals have the right to keep what they earn, and acquire a right of priority in the use of any goods they produce. Property may also be transferred by means of an exchange, contract, grant, or inheritance. Ownership rights are held inviolable, and private property cannot be forcefully appropriated or confiscated. The violation of legitimate property rights is considered by Islam to be oppressive and exploitative (Mirakhor, 2003a).

Thus, Islam recognizes the importance of institutions, the guarantee of property rights, and the enforcement of contracts to economic growth and development. However, in Islam, because natural resources (such as raw land, water, and mineral deposits) are considered to be a gift bestowed on humanity by God, *absolute* ownership can only be claimed by God (Cummings et. al., 1980). Because humans did not actually *create* any of the world's natural resources, they cannot exert unequivocal ownership over them. They may only privately own anything they produce with their work or gain through legitimate investment and inheritance.

An individual who earns more than what he or she consumes must pay a charity tax, called *zakah*, which is calculated according to his or her level of net worth. Business capital and housing are exempt from *zakah* taxation in order to promote investment in capital and construction and encourage home ownership (Ul Haq, 1995). It is important to note that *zakah* is not a substitute for taxation by the state, which may institute other forms of taxation to finance additional social, economic, infrastructural, and related programs (Askari et. al., 1982).

While Islam encourages people to save their earnings after consumption, it denounces the hoarding of wealth and views taxation as a mode of social investment.[10] It reasons that because God bestowed natural resources to the entire human population, all people are entitled to a share of world production. Thus those who are impoverished, unemployed, underemployed, or lack the ability to work are the primary beneficiaries of *zakah* payments.[11] Individuals who are employed but underpaid may receive *zakah* payments so that they can earn a living wage; those with refugee status may receive *zakah* as well. Surplus *zakah* funds may be saved, invested in infrastructure and development, or donated to impoverished countries (Ul Haq, 1995). Islam holds that the payment and distribution of *zakah* promotes a more equitable income distribution that ultimately enables those on a lower income scale to begin saving as their standard of living improves (Zaman, 1999). Evading this obligation, according to Islam, will promote an inequitable distribution of income and encourage an increase in poverty (Mirakhor, 2003a). Mirakhor (1989) summarizes these assertions succinctly:

> *Islam asserts unambiguously that poverty is neither caused by scarcity and paucity of natural resources, nor is due to the lack of proper synchronization between the mode of production and the relation of distribution, but as a result of waste, opulence, extravagance, and nonpayment of what rightfully belongs to the less able segments of the society. This position is illustrated by the Prophetic saying that: "Nothing makes a poor man starve except that with which a rich person avails in luxury."*

Compulsory *zakah* payments were instituted by Islam because every capable member of the *ummah* is required somehow to contribute to the development of a learned and economically prosperous social order. *Zakah* is a major component of *infaq* and *sadaqah*, compulsory and voluntary social expenditures made for the creation of non-profit and non-governmental institutions such as schools, health clinics, hospitals, and libraries (Ul Haq, 1995). Poverty exists, Islam reasons, not because natural resources are scarce, but because they are misallocated, inefficiently managed, unproductively hoarded, and unevenly distributed.[12] Independent social spending, according to Islam, is the best possible way for members of the Islamic social order to promote a more equitable distribution of wealth and resources.

Muslims with the financial capacity to donate beyond their *zakah* requirements are therefore strongly encouraged to invest further in *infaq* and *sadaqah*.[13] Islam does not require social institutions built through *infaq* and *sadaqah* to register with or be approved by a central political authority (Iqbal, 1986). Thus, by advocating extensive popular participation in the development of society, Islam reduces the need for an authority to intervene on behalf of the socio-economic interests of the community (Mirakhor, 2003a).

Islam holds that state authority is needed for the preservation, cohesion, and general welfare of society. It must be an elected body (although exact procedures for elections are not stipulated) that maintains fiscal stability and transparency, social cohesion, and an adequate national standard of living. *The state's most fundamental duties are the alleviation of poverty and the prevention of extreme income inequality (social and economic justice).* Although Islam ultimately holds the *ummah* responsible for the creation and administration of public development institutions, it authorizes the state to intervene on the community's behalf if an adequate living standard, referred to as *fard kifaya*, has not been established and if members of the *ummah* stop making their *zakah* payments.[14] The state authority, with the approval of the *shura*, may institute any new policies it considers necessary for the restoration or attainment of an equitable income distribution.[15] The state may therefore formulate its own additional tax policies, borrow money, and increase spending if doing so will result in economic growth (Mirakhor, 2003a). Islam encourages state authorities to avoid accumulating significant debt, however, and strongly discourages deficit spending (Ul Haq, 1995).

While the Islamic social order is not supposed to function as a welfare state, the primary national authority must ensure that all citizens have a reasonable standard of living. Thus if any members of the community cannot afford food, shelter, or healthcare and do not have easy access to education, the state is obligated to provide it for them. The state must ensure the proper collection and distribution of *zakah* funds, and may collect and administer *zakah* disbursements if the *ummah* lacks the capacity to do so. It is also allowed to provide non-profit and non-governmental organizations with *zakah* funds if they need them. Because Islam prohibits the excessive accumulation and hoarding of wealth, the state should not permit the presence of monopolies, and should formulate economic policies that encourage investment and competition.[16] In cases where the *ummah* is suffering from extreme income inequality and mass poverty, putting its survival at stake, the state is authorized to impose substantial taxes on the wealthy to collect money for basic living expenses, and may restrict and redistribute property rights.[17] Feudalism and absentee landlordism, for example, are considered to be socially detrimental and un-Islamic, and would thus warrant land confiscation and redistribution (Ul Haq, 1995).

The state must ensure organizational transparency and ethical business and social practices by instituting a *hisbah*, a judicial organization that monitors and ensures the fair treatment of laborers and consumers (Ul Haq, 1995). If the state fails to uphold basic human rights to sustenance, protection, education, healthcare, and social and religious freedom, the *ummah* is entitled either to take the state to court or, via *shura*, to choose a new authority (Ul Haq, 1995). Irfan Ul Haq (1995) provides a summary in this regard:

> *The limits of allegiance to a government have also been given by the Prophet. He [the Prophet] states: "No obedience is due in sinful matters; behold obedience is due only in the way of righteousness" and "No obedience is due to him who does not obey God." For such situations as outright immoral and illegal behavior or unjust policies on the part of government, the Prophet has made it virtually obligatory for Muslims to speak up and stand up for justice: "The highest kind of self-exertion (jihad) is to speak the truth in the face of a government that deviates from the right path."*

2.5   Convergence or Divergence?

2.5.1   Is Islam compatible with globalization?

Both the theoretical and empirical impacts of globalization on economic growth, income equality, poverty alleviation, and more are country and time specific. There is very little that can be determined a priori for all countries. But while the net effect of globalization—broadly defined to include financial globalization, and the flow of goods and services, labor, and technology across countries—may be theoretically and empirically questioned and debatable, the fact that globalization affects numerous critical economic and social variables is undeniable. From an Islamic perspective, the critical factors affected by globalization are: economic growth; relative incomes of different segments of society and, in particular, income inequality; poverty; employment; and, more generally, the accessibility of economic and social advancement. If all these goals are positively affected by globalization, then the state should embrace globalization. But if some are adversely affected by globalization, then the state must take steps to offset these adverse effects, while preserving the beneficial results; and if it cannot, then the state would have to reject globalization.

Given the mixed theoretical and empirical predictions of globalization, the direction and details of state intervention will by force differ from country to country. There can be no universal policy prescription for all Islamic countries. However, when Islamic goals are adversely affected by globalization, countries must adopt policies to reverse such developments. Still, some broad generalizations have emerged from the literature. To enhance growth prospects and protect the poorer segments of society, it is important that the state adopt a number of policies. In no particular order of importance, the required policies include those pertaining to: education, labor training, healthcare, social safety net, taxation, appropriate regulatory bodies and institutions in the areas of finance and banking, competition and the rule of law, and consistent and stable macroeconomic policies.

Education and the acquisition of skills must be promoted at all levels and to every segment of society. This will increase a country's potential benefits from globalization—economic growth, poverty reduction, income equality, and employment. At the same time it will support the most important of Islamic economic doctrines: the creation of a level playing field, affording equal opportunities to all, and promoting social and economic justice. Moreover, the attainment of education in Islam is an important goal in itself; with "education" (and related words such as "knowledge") being the second most mentioned word in the *Qur'an*. Second, well-designed and universal labor training programs afford globalization benefits and support Islamic goals much in the same way as education. Third, access to healthcare must be provided to all. This will protect society from any labor abuses that may originate from domestic and foreign corporations. Fourth, an adequate and accessible social safety net must be developed. No matter how well education and labor training are designed and delivered, some members of society, such as the handicapped, the sick, and the aged, will be excluded and further marginalized by the strictly market-driven forces of globalization. Fifth, an effective tax system is an absolute necessity to address egregious income and wealth disparities and support government finances. Although *zakah* is the duty of all Muslims who have the ability to pay, it may be insufficient to meet the needs of society and to address an un-Islamic distribution of wealth. Sixth, countries seem to maximize their derived benefits from globalization to the extent that they have good institutions and policies, a statement that is strongly suggested by common sense and available empirical results. Thus, good institutions and governance in the areas of finance and banking, competition, and the rule of law will promote their economic performance and be strongly supportive of Islamic principles in areas such as creating a level playing field, honoring contracts, and eliminating corruption. Seventh, to achieve sustained economic growth, countries should adopt sound macroeconomic policies.

Are Islam and globalization compatible? The answer is evident. The broad theoretical and empirical effects of globalization are generally recognized. While the direction of the impact of globalization may not be predetermined and singular, but instead be country and case specific, it is evident that economic growth, income distribution, poverty, and much more, *could* be positively affected. For countries to benefit from globalization, they should adopt supportive policies and institutions to enhance the benefits and minimize the costs. Muslim countries are no different. Muslim countries can benefit from globalization, enhancing growth and mitigating adverse economic effects on large segments of their population. Economic and social progress and justice are at the core of Islamic teachings. Muslim countries can maximize their benefits from globalization if they should adopt Islamic principles of sound economic and social governance, policies that are suggested as supportive from both theoretical and empirical results of globalization. The seven areas in the previous paragraph would thus enable these countries to show superior economic performance, benefit from globalization, and achieve their Islamic goals of economic and social justice.

Shiller's (2003) vision of the future of conventional finance, to address issues such as income inequality and fairness, would only further reinforce the tendency for conventional and Islamic finance to converge in the future, with globalization as the vehicle.

Islamic countries could always benefit from faster economic growth, better income distribution, and reduced levels of poverty. If Islamic countries want to maximize these benefits from globalization and avoid a backlash from their disadvantaged citizens, they can do so by adopting better policies and institutions while embracing globalization. These policies, while affording them enhanced benefits from globalization, are similar to those that would promote economic and social justice as preached in Islam. Thus, not only should Islamic countries embrace globalization, but also the rapid pace of globalization may in turn force Muslim countries to adopt policies that are more Islamic in nature and content. Globalization may in fact push Islamic countries to be more Islamic by adopting policies that uphold economic and social justice and promote economic prosperity. Finally, we should note that Islam, a religion that has embraced all mankind and cultures, is itself global. Thus, Islam must be a positive force in supporting those globalization policies that will benefit all humanity and promote God's work on earth.

Endnotes

1 See *Qur'an* 6:108: "But do not revile those [beings] whom they invoke instead of God, lest they revile God out of spite, and in ignorance: for, goodly indeed have We made their own doings appear unto every community." And *Qur'an* 17:20: "All [of them]—these as well as those—do We freely endow with some

of thy Sustainer's gifts, since thy Sustainer's giving is never confined [to one kind of man]." (Shirazi, 2001)

2 See *Qur'an* 42:38: " . . . and whose rule [in all matters of common concern] is consultation among themselves . . . " All communal affairs *must* be conducted through mutual consultation. (Ul Haq, 1995)

3 The Prophet is reported to have said that "poverty may sometimes lead to *kufr* (a denial of God's teachings)" (Ul-Haq, 1995) and that "poverty is almost like disbelief in God." (Zaman, 1999)

4 The word *knowledge*, including its derivatives, is the second most repeated word in the *Qur'an* after *Allah* (God), and the Prophet is reported to have said "striving after knowledge is a sacred obligation/ religious duty for every Muslim." (Ul Haq, 1995)

5 Education and literacy training for children and adults were [primarily] provided by the state for free after the Prophet immigrated to Medina. (Ul Haq, 1995)

6 All men, according to the *Qur'an*, are obligated to financially support and care for their families. The *Qur'an* does not *require* women to generate an income and financially support their families. However, no Qur'anic verses speak against women working, earning a living, becoming financially independent, and/or financially supporting their families. All citizens are consistently urged to work and contribute to the economic and social development of society.

7 See *Qur'an* 9:105: "And say [unto them, O Prophet]: *Act!* And God will behold your deeds . . . " The Prophet is reported to have said that "to strive to earn a livelihood through the right means is an obligation after the duty of prayer" and "bread earned by one's own labor [or effort] is the best of all earnings." (Ul Haq, 1995) *Qur'an* 4:95: "Such of the believers as remain passive (literally, 'who sit at home')—other than the disabled—cannot be deemed equal to those who strive hard in God's cause with their possessions and their lives: God has exalted those who strive hard with their possessions and their lives far above those who remain passive."

8 See *Qur'an* 2:11: " . . . they are told, 'Do not spread corruption on earth' . . . "; *Qur'an* 2:205: " . . . and God does not love corruption . . . "; *Qur'an* 7:56: "do not spread corruption on earth after it has been so well ordered"; *Qur'an* 7:85: " . . . do not deprive people of what is rightfully theirs . . . "; *Qur'an* 11:111: "And, verily, unto each and all will thy Sustainer give their full due . . . " (Ul Haq, 1995)

9 Iqbal (1986). See *Qur'an* 4:33: "And unto everyone have We appointed heirs to what he may leave behind . . . give them, therefore, their share." (Ul Haq, 1995)

10 The terms *taxes* and *social spending* are used interchangeably throughout the *Qur'an*. See also *Qur'an* 59:7, which says that "it [wealth] may not be [a benefit] going round and round among such as you may [already] be rich." (Ul Haq, 1995)

11 See *Qur'an* 9:60: "The offerings given for the sake of God (*zakah*) are [meant] only for the poor and the needy, and those who are in charge thereof (who collect

the tax), and those whose hearts are to be won over, and for the freeing of human beings from bondage, and [for] those who are overburdened with debts, and [for every struggle] in God's cause, and [for] the wayfarer: [this is] an ordinance from God—and God is All-Knowing, Wise." *Qur'an* 70:24–25: " . . . in whose (the faithfuls') possessions there is a due share, acknowledged [by them], for such as ask [for help] and such as are deprived [of what is good in life]." *Qur'an* 51:19: "[But,] behold, the God-conscious . . . [would assign] in all that they possessed a due share unto such as might ask [for help] and such as might suffer privation." The Prophet is also reported to have said that "charity is *halal* (permitted) neither for the rich nor the able-bodied." (Ul Haq, 1995)

12 The Prophet is reported to have said: "Nothing makes a poor man starve except that which a rich person avails in luxury." See Mirakhor (2003a). In *Qur'an* 20:118–119, Adam is told: "Behold, it is provided for thee that thou shalt not hunger here nor feel naked, and that thou shalt not thirst here or suffer from the heat of the sun." The Prophet is reported to have said: "He is not a faithful who eats his fill while his neighbor [or fellowman] remains hungry by his side." (Mirakhor, 2003a)

13 See *Qur'an* 30:39: "And [remember]: whatever you may give out in usury so that it might increase through [other] people's possessions will bring [you] no increase in the sight of God—whereas all that you give out in charity, seeking God's countenance, [will be blessed by Him:] for it is they, they [who thus seek His countenance] that shall have their recompense multiplied! *Qur'an* 3:92: "[But as for you, O believers,] never shall you attain true piety unless you spend on others out of what you cherish yourselves; and whatever you spend—verily, God has full knowledge thereof." *Qur'an* 2:276: "Allah . . . will give increase for goods of charity." (Iqbal, 1986) *Qur'an* 2:177: "True piety does not consist in turning your faces toward the east or the west—but truly pious is he who believes in God, and the Last Day, and the angels, and revelation, and the prophets, and *spends his substance*—however much he himself may cherish it—upon his near of kin, and the orphans, and the needy, and the wayfarer, and the beggars, and for the freeing of human beings from bondage; and is constant in prayer, and *renders their purifying dues* (*zakah*) . . . it is they that have proved themselves true, and it is they, they who are conscious of God."

14 The Prophet is reported to have said: "The leader [or government] who has authority over people is a guardian and responsible for them." (Ul Haq, 1995)

15 When asked about *azm*—taking a particular course of action—the Prophet is reported to have defined it in this way: "It means taking counsel with the knowledgeable people (*ahl al ra'y*) and thereupon following them [therein]."

16 Verses reproving hoarding and the non-investment:
Qur'an 102:1–6: "You are obsessed by greed for more and more [comforts, material goods, greater power over fellow men and nature] until you go down to your graves . . . Nay, if you could but understand [it] with an understanding [born of certainty, you would indeed, most surely, behold the blazing fire [of hell]!"
Qur'an 104:1–9: "[Woe unto him] who amasses wealth and counts it a safeguard, thinking that his wealth will make him live forever! Nay, but [in the life

to come such as] he shall indeed be abandoned to . . . A fire kindled by God, which will . . . close in upon them in endless columns [overwhelming with despair as they belatedly realize their guilt]."

Qur'an 107:1–7: "Hast thou ever considered [the kind of man] who gives the lie to all moral law? Behold, it is this [kind of man] that thrusts the orphan away, and feels no urge to feed the needy . . . those who want only to be seen and praised, and, withal, deny all assistance [to their fellowmen]!"

(Ul Haq, 1995)

17 The Prophet is reported to have carried out such policies for housing and cultivation.

CHAPTER 3

Islamic Finance, Conventional Finance, and Globalization

3.1 The Development of Islamic Finance

The central proposition of Islamic finance is the prohibition of the type of transaction in which a rent is collected as a percentage of an amount of principle loaned for a specific time period without the transfer of the property rights over the money loaned to the borrower, thus shifting the entire risk of the transaction to the borrower. As the *Qur'an* prohibits debt-based contracts, it simultaneously ordains an alternative: in consonance with its systemic approach that as something is prohibited, an alternative is simultaneously ordained. The alternative to debt-based contracts is *al-bay'* (البيع: a mutual exchange in which one bundle of property rights is exchanged for another (see Lane, 2003; Al-Isfahani, 1992; Ibn Mandhoor, 1984; Al-Mustafaoui, 1995), thus allowing both parties to share production, transportation, and marketing, and as a result share the risk. It further allows both parties to exchange in order to reduce the risk of income of volatility and to allow consumption smoothing; a major outcome of risk sharing which increases the welfare of the parties to the exchange.

The emphasis on risk sharing is evident from one of the most important verses in the *Qur'an* in respect of economic behavior. The verse states: ". . . they say that indeed exchange (بيع) is like usury (*Riba*). But Allah has permitted exchange and has forbidden usury . . ." (2:275). This verse can be considered as the cornerstone of the *Qur'an*'s conception of economy since from it flows major implications of how the economy should be organized. One of these implications relates to the nature of these two contracts. Etymologically, the first *al-bay'* (بيع) is a contract of exchange of one commodity for another where the property rights over one good are traded for those of another. In the case of contracts of *riba*, a sum of money is loaned today for a larger sum in the future without the transfer of the property rights over the principle from the lender to the borrower. Not only does the lender retain property rights over the sum lent, but property rights over the additional sum paid as interest are also transferred from the borrower to the lender. The verse renders exchange and trade of commodities (and assets) the foundation of economic activity.

Important implications follow: exchange requires the freedom of the parties to contract. This, in turn, implies freedom to produce, which calls for clear and well-protected property rights that would permit production. Moreover, to freely and conveniently exchange, the parties need a place— that is, a market. To operate successfully, the market needs rules, norms, and procedures to allow: information to flow smoothly; trust to be established among buyers and sellers; competition to take place among sellers, on the one hand, and buyers, on the other; and transaction costs, as well as costs to third parties resulting from the adverse impact of exchange, to be reduced. Risk is a fact of human existence. Risks to income are important; when they materialize, they play havoc with people's livelihood. To reduce income risk is therefore welfare enhancing, lowering volatility to allow smoothing of consumption. This is accomplished by risk sharing and risk diversification, which are facilitated by trade and exchange. By relying on exchange, the *Qur'an* promotes risk sharing. Arguably, it can be claimed that through its rules governing just exchange, distribution, and redistribution, the position of the *Qur'an* on economic relations is entirely oriented toward risk sharing. This is perhaps the reason why, in the *Qur'an*, more emphasis is placed on rules governing exchange distribution and redistribution—to effect a balanced risk sharing—than on production.

It is clear that the objective is to promote risk sharing. But why? Here, an economic hermeneutic of the relevant verses placed within the systemic context of the *Qur'an* strongly suggests that risk sharing, along with other prescribed behavioral rules—for example, exhortation on cooperation (*Qur'an* 5:2)—serves to bring humans closer to unity, which in itself is a corollary of Islam's central axiom: the Unity of the Creation. An Islamic philosophic axiom declares that from One Creator only one creation can issue. The *Qur'an* itself unambiguously declares: "Neither your creation (was) nor your resurrection (will be) other than as one united soul" (*Qur'an* 31:28; see also 4:1; 6:99). In a series of verses, the *Qur'an* exhorts humans to take individual and collective actions to achieve social unity and cohesion and then strive to preserve and protect collectivity from all elements of disunity (for example, 3:103). Unity and social cohesion are so central among the objectives of the *Qur'an* for mankind that all conducts prohibited may be regarded as those that cause disunity and, conversely, those prescribed to promote and protect social cohesion. It is a natural consequence of such a system to require risk sharing as an instrument of social integration. Therefore, promoting maximum risk sharing is, arguably, the ultimate objective of Islamic finance. It is for this reason that Muslim scholars consider profit–loss sharing and equity participation as first best instruments of risk sharing (Iqbal and Mirakhor, 2007; Mirakhor and Zaidi, 2007).

Indeed, there is some evidence that stock market and social interaction are related (Hong et al., 2004; Huberman, 2001). One scholar who has recognized the full potential benefits of risk sharing for mankind is Shiller (2003). He points out that "[M]assive risk sharing can carry with it benefits far beyond that of reducing poverty and diminishing income inequality. The reduction of risks on a greater scale would provide substantial impetus to human and economic progress." Arguably, the most meaningful human progress would be achieved when all distinctions among human beings on the basis of race, color, creed, income, and wealth are obliterated to the point where humanity truly views itself as one. The *Qur'an* (4:1) unambiguously calls attention to the fact that, despite all apparent multiplicity, humans are fundamentally of one kind and rejects all bases for distinction between and among them except righteousness (*Qur'an* 49:13). This axiom applies to all dimensions of human existence, including in the fields of economics and finance. The objective of the unity of mankind could well be promoted by financial globalization since it has the potential of being the great equalizer of our time. It has the ability to unwind and unbundle, direct, analyze, and price risk, searching for the highest return. It can explore all risk–return to assets and the real rate of return, leading to greater risk sharing. It can do so across geographic, racial, national, religious, cultural, language, and time boundaries. In the process, it can level playing fields of finance and help remove barriers among people and nations. The same potential holds for Islamic finance if progress follows the trajectory envisioned by Islam, which specifies preconditions for the successful operation of financial arrangements within its framework firmly anchored on a network of norms and rules of behavior (institutions), prescribed for individuals and collectivities (Iqbal and Mirakhor, 2002). This network includes, but is not limited to, those institutions that modern scholarship considers crucial for financial development, integration, and globalization (Garretsen et. al., 2003).

Among the institutions prescribed by Islam are: (i) property rights, (ii) contracts, (iii) trust, and (iv) governance. The word "property" is defined as a bundle of rights, duties, powers, and liabilities with respect to an asset. In the Western concept, private property is considered the right of an individual to use and dispose of a property along with the right to exclude others from the use of that property. Even in the evolution of Western economies, this is a rather new conception of property that is thought to have accompanied the emergence of the market economy. Before that, however, while a grant of the property rights in land and other assets was the right to use and enjoy the asset, it did not include the right to dispose of it or exclude others from its use. For example, the right to use the revenues from a parcel of land, a corporate charter, or a monopoly granted by the state did not carry the right of disposing of the property. It is thought that the development of the market economy necessitated a revision of this conception of property, since it was thought that the right not to be excluded from the use of assets owned by another individual was not marketable; it was deemed impossible to reconcile this particular right with a market economy. Hence, of the two earlier property rights principles—the right to exclude others, and the right not to be excluded by others—the latter was abandoned and the new conception of property rights was narrowed to cover only the right to exclude others. In Islam, however, this right is retained without diminishing the role of the market as a resource allocation and impulse transmission mechanism within the framework (Iqbal and Mirakhor, 2007).

The first principle of Islamic property rights is that the Supreme Creator is the ultimate owner of all property and assets, but in order that humans can become materially able to perform duties and obligations prescribed by the Law Giver, they have been granted a conditional right of possession of property; this right is granted to the collectivity of humans. The second principle establishes the right of collectivity to created resources. The third principle allows individuals to appropriate the products resulting from the combination of their labor of these resources, without the collectivity losing its original rights either to the resources or to the goods and services by individuals. The fourth principle recognizes only two ways in which individuals accrue rights to property: (i) through their own creative labor; and/or (ii) through transfers—via exchange, contracts, grants, or inheritance—from others who have gained property rights title to a property or an asset through their labor. Fundamentally, therefore, work is the basis of acquisition of the right to property. Work, however, is performed not only for the purpose of satisfaction of wants or needs; it is considered a duty and an obligation required from everyone.

Similarly, access to and use of natural resources for producing goods and services is also everyone's right and obligation. So long as individuals are able, they have both the right and the obligation to apply their creative labor to natural resources to produce goods and services needed in the society. However, if individuals lack the ability, they no longer have an obligation to work and produce without losing their original right to resources. Therefore, an important principle called "immutability or invariance of ownership" constitutes the fifth principle of property rights in Islam (Iqbal and Mirakhor, 2007). The latter writes the duty of sharing into Islam's principles of property rights and obligations. Before any work is performed in conjunction with natural resources, all members of the society have an equal right and opportunity to access these resources. When individuals apply their creative labor to resources, they gain a right of priority in the possession, use, or market exchange of the resulting product without nullifying the rights of the needy in the sale proceeds of the product. As a result, the sixth principle imposes the duty of sharing the monetary proceeds after the sale of the property. This principle regards private property ownership rights as a trust held to effect sharing. The seventh principle imposes limitations on the right to dispose of the property—presumably absolute in the Western conception of property rights. Individuals have a severely mandated obligation not to waste, destroy, squander, or use property for unlawful purposes. Once the specified property obligations are appropriately discharged, including that of sharing in the prescribed amount and manner, property rights are held inviolate and no one can force appropriation or expropriation. This right is held so sacred that, even in relatively modern times, a rule had to be developed to accommodate emergency cases, such as the expropriation of land for public utility development; this legitimate violation is called "*ikrah hukmi,*" or "unpleasant necessity" (Iqbal and Mirakhor, 2007). Even in these unusual cases, action could be taken only after adequate compensation was paid to the owner.

While the above principles strongly affirm the people's natural tendency to possess—particularly products resulting from individual creative labor—the concomitant private property obligations give rise to the interdependence among members of society. Private initiative, choice, and reward are recognized but are not allowed to subvert the obligation of sharing. The inviolability of appropriately acquired private property rights in Islam deserves emphasis. As observed by a legal expert (Habachy, 1962), given the divine origin of Islam,

> . . . *its institutions, such as individual ownership, private rights, and contractual obligations, share its sacredness. To the authority of law, as it is understood in the West, is added the great weight of religion. Infringement of the property and rights of another person is not only a trespass against the law; it is also a sin against the religion and its God. Private ownership and individual rights are gifts from God, and creative labor, inheritance, contract, and other lawful means of acquiring property or entitlement to rights are only channels of God's bounty and goodness to man. . . . All Muslim schools teach that private property and rights are inviolable in relations between individuals as well as in relations with the state. . . . It is not only by their divine origin that the Muslim institutions of private ownership and right differ from their counterpart in Western system of law; their content and range of application are more far-reaching. . . . If absolutes can be compared, it can be*

*safely said that the right of ownership in Muslim law is more abso-
lute than it is in modern systems of law. . . . The Muslim concept of
property and right is less restricted than is the modern concept
of these institutions.*

In a terse, unambiguous verse, the *Qur'an* exhorts the believers to
"be faithful to contracts" (5:1). This command, buttressed by other verses
(2:282, 6:151–53; 9:4; 16:91–94; 17:34–36; 23:8), establishes the observance and faithfulness to the terms of contract as the central anchor of a
complex relationship between: (i) the Creator and His created order, including humans; (ii) the Creator and the human collectivities; (iii) individuals
and the state, which represents the collectivity; (iv) human collectivities; and
(v) individuals. The concept of contracts in Islam transcends its usual conception as a legal institution "necessary for the satisfaction of legitimate
human need." It is considered that the entire fabric of the Divine Law is contractual in its concept and content (Habachy, 1962). Contract binds humans
to the Creator, and binds them together. As Habachy suggests:

*This is not only true of private law contacts, but also of public
law contracts and international law treaties. Every public office in
Islam, even the Imamate (temporal and spiritual leadership of the
society), is regarded as a contract, an agreement (áqd) that defines
the rights and obligations of the parties. Every contract entered into
by the faithful must include a forthright intention to remain loyal to
performing the obligations specified by the terms of contract.*

The fulfillment of contracts is exalted in the *Qur'an* to rank it with the highest achievements and noblest virtues (2:172) (Habachy, 1962).

The divinely mandated command of faithfulness to the terms and conditions of contracts, and abiding by its obligations, is built on the equally
strong and divinely originated institution of trust (Iqbal and Mirakhor,
2007; Kourides, 1970). There is strong interdependence between contract and trust; without the latter, contracts become difficult to enter into
and costly to monitor and enforce. When and where trust is weak, laws and
complex, expensive administrative apparatuses are needed to enforce contracts. Perhaps this is why so much emphasis is placed on trust: to make
entering into and enforcing contracts less costly. Accordingly, the *Qur'an*,
in a number of verses, proclaims trustworthiness as a sign of true belief
and insists on remaining fully conscious of the obligation to ensure that
the intention to remain trustworthy in fulfilling the terms and conditions
precedes promises or entering into contracts. Conversely, untrustworthiness
and betrayal of trust are considered a clear sign of disbelief (2:27; 2:40;

2:80; 2:177; 2:282–83; 3:161; 4:107; 4:155; 6:153; 7:85; 8:27; 8:58; 9:12; 9:75; 9:111; 11:85; 13:20; 16:91; 16:94; 16:95; 17:34; 23:8). Moreover, the *Qur'an* makes clear that fulfilling the obligations of a contract or a promise is mandatory. In short, the *Qur'an* makes trust and trustworthiness, as well as keeping faith with contracts and promises, obligatory and has rendered them inviolable except in the event of an explicitly permissible justification (Iqbal and Mirakhor, 2007; Habachy, 1962). In addition, there are numerous prophetic sayings that supplement the Quranic verses on trust. For example, it is reported that the prophet (*pbuh*) was asked: "Who is a believer?" He replied: "A believer is a person to whom people can trust their person and possession" (Habachy, 1962). It is also reported that he said: "The person who is not trustworthy has no faith, and the person who breaks his promise has no religion." Also, "keeping promises is a sign of faith," and "there are three (behavioral traits) if found in a person, then he is a hypocrite even if he fasts, prays, performs big and small pilgrimages, and declares 'I am a Muslim': when he speaks, he lies; when he promises, he breaches; and when trusted, he betrays" (Payandeh, 1984; Iqbal and Mirakhor, 2007).

Other than the above, there are individual and collective behavioral rules and norms that strengthen the governance structure of the state and firms, including transparency, accountability, voice, and representation. Nevertheless, the three basic institutions—property rights, contracts, and trust—give a flavor of the strength of governance in Islam. The rule of law governs the behavior of state rulers no less stringently than that of individuals. As two Western legal experts (Anderson and Coulson, 1958) observe: "Islam is the direct rule of God. His Law, the *Shari'ah*, is the sole criterion of behavior," and "the authority of the temporal ruler is both derived and defined by this law." Under the rule of law, "the ruler is by no means a free agent in the determination of the public interest," and the decisions that the ruler makes "must not be arbitrary, but rather the result of conscientious reasoning on the basis of the general principles of the *Shari'ah* as enunciated in the authoritative texts." These legal experts also assert that, based on their consideration of Islamic legal texts, the command to observe contracts and covenants faithfully "appl[ies] to the ruler acting in a public capacity" just as severely as to individuals. "Indeed, when considerations of expediency and public interests are taken into account, they apply even with greater force to the actions of the ruler." Therefore, a breach of faith on the part of a ruler is more heinous in its nature and serious in its consequence than a similar breach by an individual. Importantly, they observe,

> . . . *just as the ruler has no special prerogative or exemptions as regards the substantive law, so he has none regarding the application of the law through the courts. Ideally, the jurisdiction of the*

Qādi *(the judge), the only person qualified to apply the* Shari'ah, *is comprehensive and exclusive. The principle that no one can be judge in his own cause is firmly established in the legal texts, and when personally involved, the ruler should submit to the jurisdiction of the ordinary* Qādi's *courts. . . . the ruler that breaks faith cannot shelter behind any claim of sovereignty from the dictates of the law which brooks no such plea.*

The same principles of governance under which a ruler or a state should function apply also to firms. Iqbal and Mirakhor (2004) argue that within the Islamic framework, a firm can be viewed as a "nexus of contracts" whose objective is to minimize transaction costs and maximize profits and returns to investors subject to constraints that these objectives do not violate the property rights of any party, whether it interacts with the firm directly or indirectly. In pursuit of these goals, the firm honors all implicit or explicit contractual obligations. As could be discerned from the discussions on contracts and trust, it is incumbent on individuals to preserve the sanctity of implicit contractual obligations no less than those of explicit contracts. By the same token, firms have to preserve the sanctity of implicit and explicit contractual obligations by recognizing and protecting the property rights of stakeholders, community, society, and state. Since the firm's behavior is shaped by that of its managers, it becomes their fiduciary duty to manage the firm as a trust for all stakeholders in ensuring that the behavior of the firm conforms to the rules and norms specified by the law (Iqbal and Mirakhor, 2004).

Even from the above rather cursory consideration, it should be clear that, once fully implemented, an Islamic institutional framework would support rapid financial development and encourage financial integration and globalization which, in turn, would promote risk sharing. The institutions ordained by Islam reduce uncertainty and ambiguity to ensure predictable behavior. Islam also prescribes rules regarding income and wealth sharing to promote income-consumption smoothing. Arguably, sharing of economic risks in society is of great concern to Islam. This is evidenced by the strong position taken by the *Qur'an* on distributive justice through *zakat*, an obligatory 2.5 percent of wealth, as well as additional exhortation for voluntary economic assistance to those less able; all of which are insurance against income risk. However, these institutions are exceptional by their absence in many, if not all, Muslim countries (Chapra, 2000). In the case of the Middle-Eastern and North-African (MENA) region, for example, Abed and Davoodi (2003) found that the rates of growth since the 1970s have not only been lower than those of developing countries as a whole, but have been twice as volatile as the average for developing countries.

They attribute this poor performance to the following factors: high population growth and low productivity; lagging political and institutional reforms; large and costly public sectors; an inefficient and inequitable educational system; underdeveloped financial markets; high trade restrictiveness; and inappropriate exchange rate policies.

It should be clear that poor governance, transparency, and accountability, an inadequate judicial system, and weak property, creditor, and investor rights have all played a role in the poor growth performance of the region; ills that could be treated with the legal and institutional developments prescribed by Islam. While this process has not had any impetus, a number of Muslim countries, in and out of the MENA region, have recently implemented macroeconomic and structural reform policies and have adopted international best-practice standards and codes. As a result, the economic performance of these countries has improved markedly, also helped by an increase in oil revenue. While adoption, implementation, and development of Islamic institutions may be slow, implementation of international best practice of transparency and accountability plus the development of an independent and effective judiciary and the reform of the legal system—to protect property, creditor, and investor rights, and to enforce contracts—along with the promotion of financial sector development could increase investment, employment, and income, leading to a reduction in poverty.

Nearly three decades ago, beginning with Ross (1976, 1978), the theory of finance showed that a basic instrument could be spanned into a large number (Huberman and Kandel, 1987; Huberman et. al., 1987; Bekaert and Urias, 1996; Fearson et. al., 1993). The wide range of innovations in instruments of the new finance since then has demonstrated the validity of this idea. Undoubtedly, the process of instrument design within the field of Islamic finance will gather momentum once it attracts the needed expertise. At the present time, this is the most important challenge of Islamic finance (Baldwin, 2002; Iqbal and Mirakhor, 1999). The lack of expertise has been the reason why, so far, financial engineering in designing new instruments has focused on fast-tracking a reverse-engineering process of redesigning some conventional vehicles. Not only does the process of instrument design need to accelerate based on the approved transaction modes, but also instruments paralleling Shiller's (2003) ideas on "macro markets" need to be invented; here, the potential is great.

For example, virtually all government deficit financing in Muslim countries is debt-based. To remedy this, Ul-Haque and Mirakhor (1999) proposed an equity instrument to be sold by governments with its rate of return indexed to the rate of return to domestic, Islamic countries, and international-Islamic equity markets, each with specified weights. The analytic arguments for this proposal were explained by Choudhry and Mirakhor (1997). The reason governments would want to raise funds is to supply social overhead capital, defense, health, and education. If the private sector was either unwilling or unable, it would fall on governments to undertake the needed investments and cover the related expenditure with usual government revenue. The shortfall would be covered by floating the equity instrument, which would be, in essence, an instrument backed by assets represented by either earlier bundles of social overhead capital already completed or in train—for example, roads, dams, hospitals, and the like. Since these are lumpy investments and their public goods nature provides a higher social return than investments undertaken by the private sector, the rate of return must be at least as high as the rate of return to be paid by the private sector when raising equity in the stock market. But, since domestic markets may experience volatilities to which government finance should not be exposed, Ul-Haque and Mirakhor suggested adding two other markets—the index of returns to all Islamic countries' stock returns, and the index of returns to Islamic equity funds in the West—to the index of returns to the domestic equity market. There are obvious advantages to this instrument; one being a vehicle for integration of equity markets across the world, while the other would be globalization of this instrument, forcing governments to compete for funds domestically, regionally, and globally, leading to efficiency gains.

3.2   The Development of Conventional Finance

Modern conventional finance as a separate field has a relatively short history in the field of economics. The importance of investment and, in turn, financing has long been recognized in economics. Financial markets were seen as important in affording savers the instruments to attract their savings, and a channel to allocate savings to investors, and to do this in the most efficient way. The health of financial markets was appreciated largely in accommodating the financing of the real economy. The importance of finance was perceived from this very narrow perspective. Thus, finance was not treated as an important and separate field of endeavor.[1]

The appreciation of risk was the important building block in the development of modern conventional finance. Early in the 20th century, Irving Fisher, a giant of economics, was one of the first to appreciate the importance of risk in the functioning of financial markets. In the 1930s, a number of renowned economists, including Keynes, Hicks, Marschak, and Kaldor, saw the importance of risk in the selection of a portfolio. But in their analysis and discussion, the role of risk was largely limited to affecting expected capital gains and speculative and hedging activities. This strain of analysis led to results covering the relationship of futures prices and expected spot prices (normal backwardation) and the price-stabilizing effect of speculation. John Burr Williams was a pioneer in going beyond this narrow view of the role of risk in seeing asset prices as intrinsically related to the discounted value of their future income stream.

Harry Markowitz saw in the early 1950s the critical role of risk in assessing future income streams. Based on these developments and on Von Neumann–Morgenstern's theory of expected utility, Markowitz developed what is today referred to as the portfolio theory; in essence, the trade-off between risk and return, with portfolio diversification reducing the overall risk of a portfolio. James Tobin expanded Markowitz's work by adding money (risk free) as an asset and attributing the different portfolio selections (money as the riskless asset and various combinations of risky assets) of individuals to differing attitudes toward risk. However, the practical application of the Markowitz–Tobin (M–T) approach was difficult, with the benefits of diversification only identified after estimating the covariance of returns for every pair of assets. To overcome this operational limitation, in the early 1960s, William Sharp and John Lintner developed the Capital Asset Pricing Model (CAPM); they showed that calculating a more limited number of covariances or betas—the covariance of every asset return relative to the market index—could duplicate the M–T approach. In the 1970s, Richard Roll's empirical work questioned the results of CAPM.

In the mid-1970s, Stephen Ross moved away from the risk–return comparison basis of CAPM and used pricing by arbitrage to develop his Asset Pricing Theory. He further suggested that arbitrage-based reasoning was the fundamental feature of all finance. This assertion is at least confirmed by the Black–Scholes–Merton option-pricing model and by the Modigliani–Miller Theorem. In the case of option pricing, if a portfolio of other assets can reproduce the return from an option, then the price of the option must be equal to the value of the portfolio; if not, there will be arbitrage opportunities. The Modigliani–Miller Theorem also uses arbitrage reasoning to examine the impact of corporate financial structure for arriving at a market value for a firm. If the production outlook of two firms (with differing financial structures) is the same, then the market value of the firms must be the same; if not, there is an arbitrage opportunity.

The second important development in the theory of modern finance was the Efficient Market Hypothesis. This endeavor was initiated by the empirical finding that commodities and asset prices behaved randomly. In the case of US stock prices, Alfred Cowles confirmed this unexpected result in the 1930s. However, economists could make little sense of this "worrisome" result until Paul Samuelson came up with the ingenious explanation that came to be known as the Efficient Market Hypothesis. Samuelson reasoned that asset prices had to be random; if not, arbitrageurs could exploit the opportunity to make a profit. For asset prices to behave randomly, all available and relevant information would have to be immediately translated into asset price changes in markets that behaved "efficiently." Eugene Fama, in 1970, further developed the theory and connected it to the Rational Expectations Hypothesis.

In sum, appreciation of the importance of risk, of arbitrage pricing, and of efficient markets is the relatively recent foundation of conventional finance. At its core, conventional finance is seen today as the management of risk (Shiller, 2003). At the same time, Islamic finance is built on the foundation that risk must be *shared* between parties in any endeavor, as opposed to being assumed solely by one party or the other. On the face of it, modern finance should provide practitioners of Islamic finance with additional tools to achieve their central goal of better risk sharing. Moreover, as Islam prohibits financial gain without the assumption of some measure of risk, it would appear that efficient markets and the random walk behavior of financial assets and commodities are implicitly, if not explicitly, assumed in Islamic teachings.

Today, even after years of rapid innovation, conventional finance only embraces risk management of private sector equity. As we noted in Chapter 2, Shiller (2003) has emphasized that risk management is still in the early stages of its development. Risk management, especially across borders, has a very long way to go. Future developments in risk management, as envisaged by Shiller, will dramatically reduce individual risk and increase economic output and welfare.

3.3 Islamic and Conventional Finance: The Impact of Globalization

What will be the effect of globalization on Islamic finance, on the one hand, and on conventional finance, on the other? The answer could be the asymptotic convergence of the two if: (i) global finance relied more extensively on equity or equity-like flows, on the one hand, and invention/innovation of a wider spectrum of risk-sharing instruments, on the other; and (ii) there was a similar process of innovations in Islamic finance in Muslim countries. That is, this asymptotic convergence between the two would be enhanced as global risk sharing is made more adaptable to the needs of investors through innovation and enhanced equity flows, and Islamic finance goes global with the growth and diversification of Muslim economies supported by innovations in Islamic finance and institutional reform.

Nearly five decades ago, Modigliani and Miller (1958) showed that, in the absence of frictions, firms' financial structure would be indifferent between debt and equity. In the real world, there are a number of frictions that bias financial structures in favor of debt and debt-based contracts. The two most important are tax and information. The tax treatment of equity returns and interest in industrial countries, which dominate the world of finance and the present structure of capital flows, is heavily biased against equities. Informational problems (information asymmetry and the related problems of moral hazard and adverse selection) also bias financial transactions in favor of debt or debt-based contracts. Legal–financial systems in advanced countries are also structured in such a way as to tilt in favor of debt and debt-based transactions. However, as financial market developments progress, legal and institutional developments across the world accelerate, and information technology advances, the informational problems diminish. Whether tax and legal treatment of equity versus debt will become less biased is a policy question. What *is* clear is that as informational problems decline, it will become increasingly difficult to maintain legal, institutional, and tax policy impediments to level the playing field between equity and debt. Consequently, it is not unreasonable to expect a process of decreasing dominance of the financial system by debt and debt-based instruments, which has not been without costs, including severe financial crises. This dominance has been a major part of the financial scene globally for so long that it is difficult to note that there was a period in the evolution of finance when equity and partnership were the dominant mode of transaction in the Middle Ages. As we discussed in Chapter 1, globalization and financial globalization are not irreversible. In the case of financial globalization, Rajan and Zingales (2003), for example, argue that there have been periods in history, specifically 1870–1913, when the degree of global financial integration was no less than the current degree. Yet, as a result of world wars, the stock market crash, and a worldwide depression, global integration not only ceased but also failed to resume until recently (Obstfeld and Taylor, 2003; Faria et al., 2006). The same catastrophic factors can explain an even earlier episode of reversal of financial integration during the Middle Ages.

Before the beginning of the 20th century, economic historians of the Middle Ages all but ignored the importance of trade and financial relations between Europe and the rest of the world, which had been crucial to the economic development of the West before the 15th century (Udovitch, 1967a and 1967b). Abu-Lughod (1994) contends that this was due to the belief held by the Eurocentric scholarship that globalized trade became relevant only after the "rise of the West" in the late 15th century. According to Abu-Lughod, an advanced globalized system of trade "already existed by the second half of the 13th century, one that included almost all regions (only the 'New World' was missing). However, it was a world-system that Europe had only recently joined and in which it played only a peripheral role." Abu-Lughod maps the growing global trade flows between AD 737 and 1478, demonstrating that trade flows first centered in Meso-potamia and spread rapidly over the next eight centuries throughout the then-known world to become global (Frank, 1990; Gills and Frank, 1994). Beginning with Postan (1928), economic historians have indicated that these trade flows were supported by a financial system sustained by an expanding risk-sharing credit structure based on *commenda* and *maona*. *Commenda* is identical to *mudarabah*, and *maona* partnerships are either *musharakah* or *mudarabah*, depending on the nature of activity undertaken by the partners (see Labib, 1969; Lane, 1944; Day, 2002; Udovitch, 1962; De Somogyi, 1965; Ehrenkreuz, 1959; Imamuddin, 1960; Tuma, 1965).

Postan's paper, based on his investigations in the vast commercial archives of the Middle Ages in England, was path-breaking as it demon-strated that: (i) economists and historians had, until then, underestimated the growth of the volume of credit in the Middle Ages; and (ii) the bulk of this credit was either *commenda* or *commenda*-like, joint risk-sharing part-nerships, even if they were "miscalled or modified" as loans (Postan, 1928, 1957). There is little doubt that the institutions of *commenda* and *maona* originated in the Islamic world (Udovitch, 1962, 1967a, 1967b, 1970a and 1970b). These institutions, along with financial instruments such as *hawala* and *suftaja*, were brought to Europe and to other regions. Jewish scholars and merchants brought them to the Jewish Diaspora (Fischel, 1933, 1937), and Islamic sources did the same via Spain through trade and scho-lastic borrowing (Mirakhor, 2003b). Professor Gotein of Princeton Univer-sity painstakingly researched the documents known as the Geniza[2] records and reached the conclusions (Goitein, 1954, 1955, 1962, 1964, 1967) that: (i) trade in the Middle Ages was both extensive and intensive, financed by risk-sharing partnerships; (ii) partnership was used in industrial, commer-cial, and public administration projects; (iii) the Mediterranean and Indian trade, as revealed by the Cairo Geniza, were largely not based on cash benefits or legal guarantees, but on the human qualities of mutual trust and friendship; and (iv) even a cursory examination of the Geniza material proves that lending money for interest was not only shunned religiously, but was also of limited significance economically.

Studying both the Geniza records and Islamic *fiqh* sources, Udo-vitch reaches the following conclusions: (i) "there is remarkable symme-try between the Hanafite legal formulations of the late-8th century and the documented commercial practices of the 11th and 12th centuries Geniza merchants" (Udovitch, 1962, 1967a, 1967b); and (ii) he reaffirms Gotein's conclusion that researching "the extensive commercial records of the Geniza, we found comparatively little evidence of usurious transactions" (Udovitch, 1970a and 1970b). Moreover, research by medieval historians demonstrated the extensive use of risk-sharing partnerships (Adelson, 1960; Arfoe, 1987; Ashtor, 1975, 1976, 1983; Byrne, 1920, 1930; Exenberger, 2004; Laiou, 2002a, 2002b; Lieber, 1968; Lopez, 1951, 1952, 1955).

While risk-sharing techniques continued to prevail in Europe until the mid-17th century, beginning in the mid-16th century, the institution of interest-based debt financing also began to be used more widely and extensively throughout Europe (Munro, 2003). The initial utilization of this method of financing and its dominance over risk-sharing methods can be attributed to a combination of several factors, including: (i) the demise of the scholastic prohibition of usury (Munro, 2003; Sauer, 2002); (ii) the appearance and rapid growth of fractional reserve banking, which led to specialization of finance by intermediaries who preferred to provide financing to agent-entrepreneurs at fixed interest rates based on contracts enforceable by law and the state in order to reduce monitoring and transaction costs; (iii) the inflow of vast amounts of gold and other riches into Europe from the colonies in the Americas and elsewhere, which reduced the incentive for the elite classes to continue financing trade on the basis of risk sharing, preferring fixed-interest debt contracts; (iv) the emergence of nation-states whose governments needed finance for wars or other state activities, but could not raise resources except by means of fixed interest rate contracts according to which an annuity was paid in perpetuity without the need for governments to repay the principal (Michie, 2007); and, most importantly, (v) the process of securitization in the 14th century, an innovation that created a revolution in mobilizing financial resources (Michie, 2007). It is likely, however, that the breakdown of trust in Europe and elsewhere was a major factor in the loss of dominance of risk-sharing finance by the end of the Middle Ages.

As mentioned earlier, risk-sharing finance is trust-intensive, and trade financing during the Middle Ages was based on risk sharing which, in turn, was based on mutual trust (Goitein, 1964). Recent research indicates that catastrophic and traumatic experience contributes to the breakdown of trust in a community and among its members (Alesina and La Ferrara, 2002). If so, the Middle Ages certainly witnessed enormous, continuous, and extensive traumas, including four crusades, three Mongol invasions, and numerous wars in Europe. In addition, the Bubonic plague of the mid-15th century spread rapidly throughout the then-known world along well-established and intensively traveled trade routes (Abu-Lughod, 1994).

It is well known that the full-scale adoption of a fixed-interest-based financial system, with a fractional reserve banking sector at its core, has a major deficiency; the system is inherently fragile (Minsky, 1982; Khan, 1987;

Posen, 2001). Toward the end of the 1970s and in the early 1980s, the existence of financial intermediaries, in general, and banks, in particular, was justified because of their ability to reduce transaction and monitoring costs, as well as to manage risk. However, minimal attention was paid to the reasons why banks operated on the basis of fixed, predetermined interest-rate-based contracts—that is, on a fixed interest basis that rendered the system fragile and unstable, requiring a lender of last resort to regulate it. Generally, interest rate theories explain the rate as an equilibrating mechanism between the supply of and demand for finance, which is a rate that prevails in the market as a spot price and not as a price determined *ex ante* and fixed, tied to the principal and the period covered by the debt contract. In an important paper, Bhattacharya (1982) argued that: ". . . with risk-neutral preferences, when the choice of risk level is unobservable, then any sacrifice of higher mean asset payoff constitutes an inefficient choice. The classical model of intermediaries existing to save on transactions/monitoring costs in asset choice does not explain why their liability structure should not be all equity." With the development and growth of information economics and agency literature, another explanation was added to the list of reasons for the existence of intermediaries; they served as delegated monitoring as well as signaling agents to solve the informational problems, including asymmetric information existing between principals and agents. Based on the findings of the developing field of information economics (see, in particular, Stiglitz and Weiss, 1981), it has been argued that adverse selection and moral hazard effects in a banking system operating on the basis of fixed-fee contracts in the presence of asymmetric information—particularly in cases where this problem is acute—means that some groups will be excluded from the credit market even when the expected rate of return for these groups may be higher than for those with access to credit. Furthermore, risk–return sharing contracts—for example, equity—are not subject to adverse selection and moral hazard effects. "[T]he expected return to an equity investor would be exactly the same as the expected return of the project itself" (Cho, 1986).

The fragility of a financial system operating on the basis of a fixed, predetermined interest rate was underlined by Stiglitz (1988), who argued:

> [I]nterest rate is not like a conventional price. It is a promise to pay an amount in the future. Promises are often broken. If they were not, there would be no issue in determining creditworthiness. Raising interest rates may not increase the expected return to a loan; at higher interest rates one obtains a lower quality set of applicants (adverse selection effect) and each one's applicants undertake greater risks (the adverse incentive effect). These effects are sufficiently strong that the net return may be lowered as banks

increase the interest rates charged: it does not pay to charge higher interest rates.

The findings of the new field of information economics strengthened the arguments of Minsky (1982) and others that a debt-based financial system with fractional reserve banking—operating with a fixed, predetermined interest rate mechanism at its core—is inherently fragile and prone to periodic instability. Stiglitz's findings underlined Minsky's arguments that, as returns to banks decline, unable to raise interest rates on their loans, they enter a liability-management mode by increasing interest rates on their deposits. As this vicious circle continues to pick up momentum, the liability management transforms into Ponzi financing and eventually bank runs develop (Posen, 2001). The last two decades of the 20th century witnessed a number of global bouts with financial instability and debt crises, with devastating consequences for a large segment of humanity, thus raising consciousness regarding the vulnerability and fragility of the financial systems, which are based, at their core, on fixed-price debt contracts. As previously emphasized, legal and institutional developments, along with good governance and the adoption of standards of best practice in transparency and accountability at the level of individuals, firms, and the state, buttressed by information technology advances, will mitigate the informational problems leading to lesser reliance on debt-based contracts.

3.4 Financial Stability and the Emerging Relationship between Islamic and Conventional Finance

Conventional finance is a debt-cum-interest based system. It is vulnerable to many sources of instability. Specifically, because credit expansion has no direct link to a real capital base it may become over-leveraged relative to capital. If credit finances consumption, it may deplete savings and erode capital and economic growth. The economy may exhibit unbacked credit expansion through the credit multiplier. The interest rate may deviate considerably from the unknown natural rate of interest and may cause speculative booms followed by asset busts. Speculative booms are accommodated by unlimited debt creation. When booms go bust, defaults ensue as debt was issued against multiplying financial assets that had no real collateral. In conventional finance, banks do not satisfy inherent balance sheet stability conditions, even in the presence of Basel II regulation. Banks are obliged by law to guarantee their nominal liabilities in full. In the case of asset losses, they have to cover these losses from their capital reserves, recapitalization, or government bailouts. Their cash flow has no real basis; consequently, banks may incur large income losses when actual cash flow falls dramatically short of expectations.

In Islamic banking there is no credit creation out of thin air. Under conventional banking, deposits at one bank can be instantaneously loaned out or used to purchase a financial asset and become reserves and a basis for a new loan at a second bank, thus contributing to purchasing power creation and the inflation of prices of goods and assets; such a step does not exist in Islamic banking. Deposits have to be re-invested directly by the bank in trade and production activities in order to create new flows of goods and services. New money flows arise from the proceeds of sales of goods and services. Money is not issued by the stroke of a pen, independently of the production of goods and services. Investment is equal to savings, and aggregate supply of goods and services is always equal to aggregate demand. There can be no bank run or speculation, as the source of credit for speculation, which is credit multiplication, does not exist. Tangible real assets that are owned directly by the financial institution cover its liabilities. Financial assets do not cover them. Risks for Islamic financial institutions are mitigated, as they relate essentially to returns from investment operations and not to the capital of these institutions—that is, the stability of Islamic banking and finance is contingent on 100 percent reserve banking.

In the next chapter, we start out by taking a detailed look at whether an Islamic financial system is theoretically more or less stable than the conventional system. Financial stability has become ever more important in the aftermath of the global financial crisis that started with the sub-prime meltdown. If an equity-based system is more stable, then in the future this could be an important force toward the convergence of the two financial systems. If equity becomes more important in conventional finance, then both will tend to converge, as they will increasingly share a common bond—namely, risk sharing.

We then take a detailed look at the changing nature and growth of international capital flows and the recent growth of Islamic finance to see what these developments portend for the future. We will argue that there is nothing magical about the recent historical prominence of debt financing. We will see that before the rise of debt financing, equity financing was pre-eminent but that a host of factors and developments catapulted debt financing to the forefront. In recent years, however, international capital flows have moved in favor of equity flows. The financial instability and turmoil that started in 2007 may also favor equity financing in the future. Bank failures and the leveraging of debt have made this crisis the worst in living memory, and with a likely significant impact on the real sector and economic growth for a number of years to come. At the same time, Islamic financial institutions have been relatively unscathed by the crisis, with their reputation intact and a steady stream of new clients. Islamic finance, based on risk sharing, has a much shorter history than conventional finance. But in just a few years, benefiting in part from conventional financial research and innovation, Islamic finance has expanded rapidly from a small base in Islamic countries and internationally. We briefly examine in the next chapter some historical developments and compare the recent and future evolution of conventional and Islamic finance.

Endnotes

1 For this section, we have followed the outline of, and relied on the assessment provided in: http://cepa.newschool.edu/het/schools/finance.htm.

2 Goitein (1964, p. 315) refers to "the so-called Cairo Geniza" as "a treasure of manuscripts written mainly during the Fatimid and Ayyubid periods and originally preserved in a synagogue in Old Cairo." Further, he indicates that "Geniza (pronounced: Gheneeza), as may be remarked in passing, is derived from the same Persian word as Arabic '*Janazah*,' burial, and has almost the same meaning. It is a place where discarded writings were buried so that the name of God, which might have been written on them, might not be discarded. Thus, Geniza is the opposite of an orderly archive." He adds: ". . . the documents discussed in this paper, albeit mostly written in Hebrew characters, are in Arabic language." There are a number of Geniza centers of scholarship in the US and the UK (Imad, 2005).

CHAPTER 4

Recent Developments in Conventional Finance, Financial Globalization, and Islamic Finance

4.1 Introduction

The financial crisis that started with the collapse of the sub-prime real estate market in the United States in 2007 has not yet played itself out, but one thing is certain: in the months and years ahead, the conventional financial system, a system that is heavily based on debt financing and leveraging, will come under intense scrutiny. In our opinion, if research shows that the conventional financial system is inherently unstable, which we believe it will, then there will be a push toward one that is more stable. This could, in turn, provide an opportunity to take a closer look at the properties of an Islamic financial system. While a theoretical examination of stability is important, the actual flow of funds and trends in financing may also provide certain insights as to the ongoing evolution of the global financial system.

Since 1990, the world has witnessed a dramatic and rapid change in the structure of financial markets and institutions. Progress in the theory of finance, rapid innovation in the practice of finance, revolution in information technology, deregulation and liberalization, and institutional reform have all changed the nature of financial relations, leading to the emergence of the "new finance." As a result, the cost of finance has been reduced, and investment in many instruments matching different risk–return profiles has been made possible, leading to better risk sharing among market participants worldwide. Financial transactions have become more at arm's length, allowing broader participation in deeper and expanded markets. This, in turn, has expanded the number of participants in financial markets, dispersed ownership, and spread risks (Rajan, 2005). Islamic finance is a much later arrival on the global financial scene and has more recently benefited from innovation. The questions are whether conventional and Islamic finance are evolving generally in the same direction, and what forces may shape their future development and how.

4.2   The Role of Financial Systems and the Stability Characteristics of the Conventional Financial System

A financial system is a collection of institutions that facilitate transactions between financial resources and their users, providing support for the real sector of the economy to convert primary resources into production for final use (Fry, 1995). In other words, these institutions intermediate between surplus financial units and investors in the real sector of the economy. Because uncertainty regarding the future is a fact of life, there are risks intrinsic to those that provide financing. It is believed that, generally, surplus fund holders wish to avoid risk, while entrepreneurs are by nature risk takers. Investment projects can fail due to no one's fault. But they can also fail because of fraud, misrepresentation, negligence, and the provision of either incomplete or wrong information. These issues arise due to an informational problem referred to as asymmetric information. Asymmetric information exists when any one party to a transaction has important information regarding the details of the transaction, which the other party does not possess. It can appear as adverse selection or moral hazard. The first appears when the wrong transaction is selected because of hidden or inadequate information. Moral hazard is a concept that originated in the insurance field and refers to the tendency of the insured to make less effort in avoiding risks than they would if they had no insurance. In financial transactions, the concept refers to a situation where the entrepreneur seeking financing intends to use the fund differently than stated to the financier, who has neither sufficient information regarding the entrepreneur's intention nor control over the behavior of the entrepreneur to mitigate the risk of moral hazard. This leads to the need for monitoring mechanisms that ensure the entrepreneur behaves according to what was agreed upon. The associated costs are referred to as monitoring costs (Fry, 1955, pp. 305–12).

It is thought that because of monitoring costs, surplus fund holders prefer debt contracts to sharing the risk of the project through equity participation. In a debt contract, a borrower promises to repay the principal plus an additional sum, the interest, over a stipulated time frame. This, in effect, cuts off the relationship between the project for which funds are needed and its financing, since a debt contract establishes the legal right of a lender to receive more money in the future in exchange for a given amount of principal today—it is an exchange of spot money for more future money—regardless of the outcome of the project undertaken by the investor–entrepreneur.

Indeed, if the risks of informational problems and associated monitoring costs are priced into the loan contract, then all risks are shifted to the entrepreneur. One explanation given for the existence of financial intermediaries is that, due to informational problems and associated monitoring costs, it is easier for lenders to delegate their management to a third party, such as a bank, which is thought to be more efficient and benefits from economies of scale in collecting information on borrowers as well as monitoring them.

There are ways in which lenders remedy informational problems. For instance, they ration lending by charging higher interest rates. This remedy mechanism has adverse consequences. First, it rations out risky, but potentially successful projects; and, second, it leads to a paradox that, as the lender raises interest rates beyond a certain point, its expected income declines as borrowers reduce or terminate their demand for loans. A second method is for lenders to ask for collateral—that is, an asset of the borrower whose property rights over that asset are automatically transferred to the lender in case of default. Third, lenders include both positive and negative clauses in the contract. The former requires, among other actions, a minimum amount of capital to be put up by the entrepreneur. It also requires periodic reports and/or inspections as part of the contract. The negative clauses prohibit certain actions on the part of the borrower, including restrictions on uses of the borrower's income, transfer of assets, and prior authorization from the lender before specified financial operations. Sometimes, the borrowers themselves try to signal, at times at heavy costs, their trustworthiness as well as the soundness of the projects they are undertaking. They may, for example, pay for insurance that protects the lenders in case of project failure and/or against the risk of default. Much of the financial structure of modern economies consists of interest-based debt contracts.

Another chief characteristic of modern financial economies is the overwhelming presence of a credit system. The difference between debt and credit is that, while a debt contract can assume a one-time event between a lender and borrower, credit is based on a longer-term relationship of trust between a borrower and a lender, as the name implies; credit is derived from the Latin word "*credo*" (I believe). Economic historians suggest that credit, in its modern sense, began with commercial banking (Ferguson, 2008). However, if credit is taken in its broadest meaning—that is, a loan for productive activity—economic historian Sidney Homer (1963, pp. 17–24) traces the origin of credit as far back as 5000 BC, when "capital and credit became important and provided a main impetus toward human progress."

In modern times, *credit* refers to an established debt relationship between a financial institution and its borrowing client. If, however, one considers credit as the provision of financial resources to facilitate investment and production, loan agreements based on interest rates are not the only means of credit relations. Such a relationship can be based on the provision of rewards, not on fixed money return on principal, as in a debt contract, but contingent on a project's outcome—that is, the expected value of the project. In other words, the risks of the project are shared. A debt contract is a fixed nominal obligation with a certain maturity date. A share contract does not have these features. Moreover, a share is not redeemable. Such a contract does not have the maturity constraint of the debt contract and, provided a market exists, shares obtained through provision of financing can be sold in case of liquidity need. Thus, contingent payoff, non-redeemability, maturity, liquidity, and risk sharing are characteristics that distinguish a share contract from a debt contract. An advantage of share contracts is that, while monitoring of the investor-entrepreneur and the project may impose costs on the shareholders, because their incomes depend only on the expected value of the project, rather than the probability of default as in a debt contract, shareholders need not face the risk of moral hazard or adverse selection.

There are other forms of mobilizing finance that, presumably, avoid, or at least minimize, informational problems. These include securitization, leasing, and factoring. The first de-links the repayment of a loan from the performance of the borrowing firm by creating an independent entity called special purpose vehicles (SPV), which buy some assets with predictable revenue streams, such as account receivables, from the firm. Because the risk of the assets owned by the SPV is different from and less than the risk of the original firm as a whole, the SPV can issue new securities that are backed by the underlying assets (called asset-backed securities, or ABS), which it owns. Because of better credit quality of the underlying assets, the SPV can mobilize funds at lower cost. Moreover, the SPV can, at lower cost, enhance the credit quality of its securities. Such techniques of credit enhancement include partitioning the securities into senior tranches, which are repaid as the first claimants of assets and cash flows in case of default, and junior or subordinate tranches which claim residual assets and cash flows after senior tranches are paid. An SPV, or its parent firm, can create a cash reserve account to cover some losses in case of default and/or buy insurance to guarantee payoffs as a means of credit enhancement. Securitization liquefies existing assets to allow the firm to acquire other assets and/or pay off expensive debt.

In leasing, a firm (the lessor) allows another party (the lessee) the use of an asset it owns in exchange for periodic payment. The lessor retains the legal ownership of the asset while the asset is generating income flow for the lessee. Therefore, the leased asset serves as collateral as well as a source of income generation. Factoring allows a firm to sell its accounts receivable to a specialized credit agency or a bank at a discount, thereby increasing its own liquidity. While securitization has mostly relied on debt instruments, such as asset-backed commercial paper (ABCB), an SPV could potentially issue shares allowing greater risk sharing. As was mentioned, the existence of informational problems in debt markets leads to inefficiencies stemming from attempts by lenders to protect themselves. An important inefficiency is credit rationing and high interest rates, which penalize unfairly low-risk projects or those with potentially high returns. Equity or risk-sharing contracts avoid this inefficiency; however, where and when the level of trust is low, shareholders' costs of monitoring the entrepreneur and the project, and efforts to become informed, may not be negligible (Stiglitz, 1987; Stiglitz and Weiss, 1992; Greenwald and Stiglitz, 1990; and Baltensperger, 1978).

The informational problems that plague the debt market exist between financial institutions and their clients. Among these institutions, commercial banks are highly susceptible to informational problems in their relationships with their clients as well as in their relations with the central bank. In all market-based financial economies, the banks operate on the basis of fractional reserve, where they are required to maintain a fraction of the deposits in readily available liquid form to meet unexpected and sudden large withdrawals. While such reserves are considered as an instrument of controlling informational problems under normal circumstances, in the face of sudden shocks, the failure of one bank potentially becomes contagious for other banks (as banks lend to other banks) and financial institutions generally. Such a possibility creates a systemic risk for the financial system and for the economy as whole. Moreover, because the financial system, in general, and the banking system, in particular, facilitate and operate, along with the central bank, the country's payments system, the failure of the financial system can spell financial and economic disaster for the society as whole. To stop the contagion effect of a banking crisis from spreading, governments, through the central bank, guarantee deposits up to some maximum level. This is referred to as deposit insurance. Additionally, during normal times, the commercial banks are allowed to use the central bank as their own bank to alleviate short-term liquidity constraints by discounting financial assets at the central bank. Moreover, the central bank can step in and save banks in whose case liquidity problems (due to bad decisions, fraud, mismanagement, and so on.) threaten to convert into solvency problems. In this way, the central bank acts as "a lender of last resort."

The central bank "bails out" these institutions to mitigate the risk of contagion and the broader threat to the payments system. The disadvantage of deposit insurance and bailouts is that they give rise to moral hazards, because if expectations form that a bank or an important financial (or even non-financial) institution is considered "too big to fail," this encourages undue risk taking on the part of market players. Through its intervention, the state uses public funds to rescue private lenders unable to service their debts, thus avoiding the collapse of the credit market and threats to the payments system while, at the same time, creating a moral hazard problem which encourages speculative behavior within the financial system, including within the banking system.

The fractional reserve system molds out of its banks powerful creators and destroyers of credit; for small changes in their monetary base, the banks can expand credit by a multiple amount (Krichene and Mirakhor, 2008). Central banks exploit this ability of the banking system through monetary policy to contract or expand credit, depending on the result they wish to achieve, using bank credit channels. The banking system's ability to create credit is used to help the economy expand or contract—that is, it is used counter-cyclically. Within a financial system, which operates overwhelmingly with interest-based debt contracts as well as a fractional reserve banking system, there is a mechanism that operates in the opposite direction—that is, it has pro-cyclical effects—and is called leveraging. The concept refers to using equity capital to attract and secure loans that are many times larger than the amount of equity. In a modern financial system, generally all financial institutions—banks and non-bank financial institutions—are highly leveraged. And, leverage works through the balance sheet of leveraged institutions. To illustrate how this mechanism operates, consider, as a simplified example, the balance sheet of a commercial bank.

Commercial banks and other financial intermediaries are generally very sensitive to changes in anticipated risks and in asset prices, and manage their balance sheets continuously and actively. Their sensitivity to changes in the price of their assets is particularly acute when their net worth reacts to changes in asset prices through an accounting procedure called "marked-to-market," meaning that the value of assets on their balance sheet is continuously adjusted as market prices of these assets change (regardless of their initial price when put on the balance sheet). The guidance to a leveraged institution for active management of its balance sheet is the concept of value at risk (VaR), defined as the numerical estimate of a financial firm's worst-case loss and is indicated by V. Any loss beyond this worst case can only occur with a benchmark probability p. Usually, a financial intermediary, a bank, is required to maintain equity capital, E, to meet total value at risk for a total asset of A on its balance sheet, such that $E = V \times A$. Leverage is defined as the ratio of total assets to equity capital—that is: $L = \dfrac{A}{E} = \dfrac{1}{V}$, so that there is an inverse relationship between the leverage ratio and value at risk. The implication is that as the value at risk declines, which happens when asset prices increase during an upswing in financial markets, the leverage ratio increases, meaning that the unit can take on more debt or become more leveraged. For commercial banks, this means higher credit creation precisely when credit should contract. Therefore, leverage acts pro-cyclically (Adrian and Shin, 2008).

The leverage ratio of commercial banks in the United States is estimated at around 10 (9.8), much lower than those of the investment banks, estimated at about 20–25 (Greenlaw et. al., 2008). A commercial bank's assets are composed of the securities it holds, including the loans it has extended; its liabilities include the deposits of its clients, as well as its equity capital.

A simplified balance sheet of a commercial bank can be presented as shown in Table 4.1.

TABLE 4.1　Simplified Balance Sheet of a Commercial Bank

Assets	Liabilities
1. Securities	1. Clients' deposits
2. Loans to clients	2. Equity capital

To simplify this further, combine the asset side and assume the balance sheet totals $100 where the assets are financed by $90 worth of debt (whose price is assumed constant) and $10 worth of equity capital, so that the leverage ratio is $\frac{100}{10} = 10$, which the bank considers as its target leverage ratio—that is, in case of increases or decreases in the value of its assets, it adjusts its balance sheet to restore the target leverage ratio. Assume now that the price of assets declines by $1, so that:

Assets	Liabilities		Assets	Liabilities
100	90 = D	asset price declines by $1	99	90 = D
	10 = E	$\longrightarrow$		9 = E
100	100		99	99

As a result of a decline in the asset price, the leverage ratio changes $\longrightarrow L = \dfrac{A}{E} = \dfrac{99}{9} = 11$, requiring a balance sheet adjustment to restore the target leverage ratio. This means that the balance sheet has to contract, since $L = \dfrac{A}{E} \rightarrow 10 = \dfrac{A}{9} \rightarrow A = 90$. The way the balance sheet is adjusted to restore the target leverage ratio is for D, debt (deposits), to decline by 9 $\longrightarrow$

Assets	Liabilities
90	81 = D
	9 = E
90	90

An asset price reduction of $1 leads to a contraction in credit extended by the intermediary of $9.

Under normal circumstances, the intermediaries adjust their balance sheet to restore their target leverage ratio. In times of financial market distress, however, when pessimism leads to panic, the intermediaries increase their target leverage ratio, leading to substantial contraction in their balance sheet and, therefore, in credit. This results in a credit crunch and is the result of de-leveraging.

The reverse of this process is at work when asset prices increase. To illustrate, return to the initial balance sheet and assume an increase in asset prices of $1.

Assets	Liabilities		Assets	Liabilities
100	90 = D	asset price increase by $1	101	90 = D
	10 = E	$\longrightarrow$		11 = E
100	100		101	101

As a result, the leverage ratio has changed: $L = \dfrac{A}{E} = \dfrac{101}{11} = 9.2.$ To restore the target leverage, $10 = \dfrac{A}{11} \to A = 110.$ Thus, the balance expands by adjusting the level of debt (credit):

Assets	Liabilities
110	99 = D
	11 = E
110	110

In times of a rapid increase in asset prices, intermediaries expand their balance sheet by increasing credit by a multiple of the increase in their asset prices. If optimism about a buoyant asset market leads to euphoria, then the intermediaries lower their target leverage ratios or/and move, if possible, some of their assets off balance sheet. The latter lowers the numerator of the leverage ratio, allowing the intermediary to expand credit to restore its target leverage ratio. In a buoyant asset market these developments lead to increased demand for assets, forcing prices to increase beyond the level justified by the fundamentals of the asset itself—that is, a bubble will be created. As Greenlaw et. al. (2008, pp. 29–30) suggest:

> *Leverage targeting entails upward-sloping demands and downward-sloping supplies. The perverse nature of the demand and supply curves is even stronger when the leverage of the financial intermediary is pro-cyclical—that is, the possibility of feedback, then the adjustment of leverage and of price changes will reinforce each other in an amplification of the financial cycle. If greater demand for the asset tends to put upward pressure on its price, then there is the potential for feedback in which stronger balance sheets trigger greater demand for the asset, which, in turn, raises the asset's price and leads to stronger balance sheets. The mechanism works in reverse in downturns. If greater supply of the asset tends to put downward pressure on its price, then weaker balance sheets lead to greater sales of the asset, which depresses the asset's price and leads to even weaker balance sheets. The balance sheet perspective gives new insights into the nature of financial contagion in the modern, market-based financial system. Aggregate liquidity can be understood as the rate of growth of aggregate balance sheets. When financial intermediaries' balance sheets are generally strong, their leverage is too low. The financial intermediaries hold surplus capital, and they will attempt to find ways in which they can employ their surplus capital. In a loose analogy with manufacturing firms, we may see the financial system as having "surplus capacity." For such surplus capacity to be utilized, the intermediaries must expand their balance sheets. On the liabilities side, they take on more short-term debt. On the asset side, they search for potential borrowers that they can lend to. Aggregate liquidity is intimately tied to how hard the financial intermediaries search for borrowers.*

It should be recalled that the fractional reserve banking already gives the financial intermediaries the power to create (and destroy) credit (therefore, money) out of thin air (Krichene and Mirakhor, 2008). In this way, booms and contractions are magnified. As shown above, balance sheet adjustment and leverage reinforces this power substantially, to the point of making credit creation out of nothing appear extraordinarily helpful in stimulating economic activity. However, in referring to this phenomenon, Maurice Allais (1987) asserts that: "in reality, the 'miracles' performed by credit are fundamentally comparable to the 'miracles' an association of counterfeiters could perform for its benefit by lending its forged banknotes in return for interest. In both cases, the stimulus to the economy would be the same, and the only difference is who benefits."

On the other hand, an Islamic banking system has two types of banking activity. First, there is deposit banking, which is for safekeeping and payment purposes. This system operates on a 100 percent reserve requirement, and fees may be collected for this type of banking service. Second, there is the investment banking system, which operates on a risk and profit-sharing basis with an overall rate of return that is positive and determined by the economy's growth rate.[1]

The Islamic model is referred to as the "two-windows" model, which also features demand and investment accounts but takes a different view from the "two-tier" model on reserve requirements. The two-windows model divides the liabilities side of the bank balance sheet into two windows, one for demand deposits (transaction balances) and the other for investment balances. The choice of the window would be left to depositors. This model requires 100 percent reserves for demand deposits but stipulates no reserve requirement for the second window. This is based on the assumption that the money deposited as demand deposits is placed as *amanna* (safekeeping) and must be backed by a 100 percent reserve. These balances, belonging to the depositors, do not carry with them the innate right for the bank to use them as the basis for money creation through fractional reserves. Money deposited in investment accounts, on the other hand, is placed with the depositor's full knowledge in risk-bearing projects and thus no guarantee is required. In this model, as in the other, depositors may be charged a service fee for the safekeeping services rendered by the bank. The bank may manage a certain portion of current and investment accounts to be used for offering interest-free loans to deserving and needy segments of the community. In this way, the responsibility for selecting and managing interest-free loans is delegated to the bank by the depositors, since the bank may prove to be a better distributor due to its having superior information.

This form of intermediation corresponds closely to the understanding the early Muslims had of banking and investment practices, which by the mid-eighth century had developed a variety of credit institutions and instruments such as checks (*ruqa*), documents of debt transfer (*hawala*), and bills of exchange (*suftaja*). Banking services, including currency exchange transactions, were performed by merchant bankers, and investment activities through profit sharing were accomplished through direct finance. As was understood by Muslim scholars and merchant bankers alike, a contract based on Islamic law severely restricted the use of deposits for most purposes. This is in contrast to the concept of deposits in the West, where the depository institution not only keeps the deposits but also has a right to use them for a variety of commercial purposes. The Islamic conception of property rights imposes severe restrictions on the use of someone's property placed in another's safekeeping.

Conventional banking is a debt-cum-interest based system. It is vulnerable to instability because credit expansion has no direct link to a real capital base and it may become over-leveraged relative to capital. In Islamic banking there is no credit creation out of thin air. Deposits have to be re-invested directly by the bank in trade and production activities and create new flows of goods and services. New money flows arise from the proceeds of sales of goods and services. Money is not issued by the stroke of the pen, independently of the production of goods and services. Investment is equal to savings, and aggregate supply of goods and services is always equal to aggregate demand. Tangible real assets that are owned directly by the institution cover the liabilities of the financial institution. Financial assets do not cover them. Risks for Islamic financial institutions are mitigated as they relate essentially to returns from investment operations and not to the capital of these institutions. The stability of Islamic banking and finance is based and contingent on 100 percent reserve banking.

Even if it is assumed that the credit-creating power of the financial intermediaries is beneficial, it is clear that such power also has potentially harmful effects on economic activity. Because this power operates through interest-based debt contracts and instruments, it dictates the costs of finance needed for investment; thus, while de-linking financing from underlying productive investment and assets (since it provides money for financing today for more money in the future, regardless of the outcome of the project), the price of the debt contract (interest rate) establishes a benchmark for acceptable rates of return on investment projects in the real sector. Thus, the interest rate on money lent today for more money in the future rules the rate of return to the real sector. Indeed, the financial sector of a modern economy exercises a dominating role over its production sector. Thus, disturbances in the financial sector are automatically transmitted to the production sector, affecting employment and income in the whole economy. Governments concerned with economic growth, employment, and the severity of the impact of financial fluctuations on the level of economic activity focus on this aspect of the relationship between the financial and the real sector. They manipulate the rate of interest charged by financial intermediaries on the credit they extend to entrepreneurs; thus, they indirectly influence the rate of return in the real sector. They do this through monetary policy. An active monetary policy places limits on the credit expansion or contraction power of financial intermediaries. This is done by making it easy, or hard, for these institutions to access the resources of the central bank or create an incentive for them to become more or less liquid through the sales of government securities, which constitute a significant part of intermediaries' assets. Thus, to check a downward movement in the level of economic activity, central banks administer easy monetary policy. To check an upward movement in the level of economic activity, fearing inflation, central banks administer tight monetary policies.

Additionally, because financial intermediaries, particularly commercial banks, manage the economy's payments system and because of the deposit insurance system, which the government makes available to the intermediaries, the state is justified in regulating and supervising the behavior and performance of financial intermediaries. Regulation is composed of a set of rules imposed on these institutions to ensure the safety and security of their resources. Supervision ensures that the institutions continuously abide by these rules. One characteristic of regulatory frameworks is that rules are developed in response to past abuses or transgressions not foreseen by previous rules; they are, therefore, *ex post* frameworks. Given the dynamism of profit-seeking behavior, financial institutions are constantly in search of ways and means of circumventing the rules of the regulatory framework. Regulators are always playing a catch-up game. This behavior, referred to as the search for regulatory arbitrage, becomes particularly intense when financial markets become buoyant.

There are times in which monetary policy becomes passive and the regulatory-supervisory framework exercises forbearance in the face of changes in the financial system that could potentially pose serious risks to the economic system. This could occur either in response to political pressure or due to an underlying ideological orientation of policy makers. Focusing on the latter, policy makers and regulators may have an abstract thought in mind which constitutes the model upon which they base their own model of behavior. That is, their underlying model, which becomes the basis of the model that the policy maker follows, is a model of the policy maker's model. One such model is derived from a major school of economic thought that believes markets left to themselves, with minimal government intervention, are capable of producing the best results for the economy as a whole. This line of thought, known as neoclassical economics, dates back to the classical economists, but its analytic underpinnings were provided in the mid-20th century by the work of Arrow and Debreu (1954) who demonstrated the existence of a general equilibrium for a competitive economy under a set of assumptions that included perfect information, complete markets, no transaction costs, and no role for monetary factors. Under these assumptions, equilibrium would prevail in the economy instantaneously, with all resources—including labor—fully employed.

Within the same general framework, two other propositions were developed in the second half of the 20th century that formed the intellectual underpinnings (or the model of the model of the policy maker) for an ideology of passive monetary policy and regulatory forbearance. The first, mentioned in Chapter 3, was the Modigliani–Miller Theorem (1958, 1963), which addressed the question of the optimal capital structure of the firm—that is, the best combination of sources of financing investment: equity, debt, and internal funds (undistributed profits or retained earnings). The theorem stated that in a perfect capital market, a firm's value depends on the profitability of the assets that investment generates and not on *how* such investments were financed. This implies that a firm should be neutral between sources of financing. This is referred to as the Modigliani–Miller Neutrality Theorem.

The second proposition was developed within the neoclassical framework in the 1970s and is referred to as the Efficient Markets Hypothesis (Fama, 1970). It suggests essentially that competitive prices contain all the information required for rational economic decision making. The implication of this hypothesis for the real sector of the economy is that, given that prices include all the needed information, the price mechanism has the capability to allocate resources in such a way as to achieve maximum output. For the financial sector, this hypothesized efficiency simply means that, regardless of time and space considerations, asset prices are always and everywhere established by the demand for and supply of assets about which suppliers and consumers have made rational decisions, because the prices of these assets contain all the information required for such decisions. Therefore, the prevailing asset prices are the correct ones reflecting the true value of assets. If asset prices change, it is because new information regarding the assets themselves has become available. In other words, the market as a whole has the correct view of asset prices that reflect the underlying fundamental values of assets. Even if each individual participant in the market may have an inaccurate estimate of the asset values, as a group market participants (including investors, dealers, lenders) will not over- or underestimate the fundamental values of assets.

The Efficient Market Hypothesis would imply no overconfidence, or bubbles, in the market as a whole. Therefore, no matter how wildly asset prices swing, such fluctuations are markets' responses to changes in the underlying fundamental characteristics of the assets themselves, reflecting the scarcity or oversupply of the assets in the market. Asset price bubbles—when the market prices deviate substantially from the price justified by the underlying fundamentals—are a natural reaction of the market. Some consider bubbles as beneficial because they stimulate the mobilization of resources for investment in the assets whose prices are rapidly rising. Moreover, no attempt should be made to stop rising asset prices because, even if bubbles burst, the net effect for society is positive and because rising bubbles are difficult to predict in the first place (Gross, 2007).

The perfect market paradigm, and the attendant notions of existence of a competitive equilibrium, neutrality of capital structure (that is, debt-to-equity ratio), and the Efficient Market Hypothesis, all of which were developed between 1950 and 1970, assume perfect rationality on the part of market participants, making decisions with perfect information in a market in which every risk, every commodity, and every contingency is fully identifiable (no uncertainty) and can be represented by a tradable market instrument. That is, it was assumed for every, and all, contingencies that a tradable security was available—in other words, the market is complete. Moreover, the market is assumed to be a frictionless market without transactions or information costs. Further, the market is fully liquid; trade can take place instantaneously, and financial resources pose no constraints as participants can borrow instantaneously and without limit. Such a market ensures the optimal allocation of resources for maximum output. It is also efficient, as prices adjust instantaneously and appropriately to any new information. This information cannot be predicted ahead of its appearance; it is random, and once it appears everyone will have it. And market prices adjust quickly to the random information; therefore, prices also change randomly, leaving no room for anyone, including dealers and traders, to earn income from trading in new information. Most importantly, in such a market, risks are spread uniformly among the participants and because insurance to cover all risks is available to every market participant.

It is important to note that, while rigorous mathematical models demonstrate the existence of equilibrium for competitive markets under the above assumptions, the stability of such equilibriums is much more difficult to demonstrate. It turns out that relaxation of the underlying assumptions renders the competitive market equilibrium erratic and unstable. Nevertheless, and despite the unrealistic nature of its assumption, the efficient market is considered as an ideal paradigm and standard that all market economies should aim to achieve. In this light, volatility and turbulence are caused by shocks that the market experiences because of information imperfection (the informational problems discussed earlier) and/or market incompleteness (not enough security instruments for all contingencies). The ideology of adherence to the efficient market paradigm becomes a model of the model based on which policy is formulated. All financial innovations represent progress toward market completeness, and all volatilities (including the formation and the implosion of bubbles) are attempts by the market to adjust to new information.

Believing in such a system, market intervention may have negative consequences for the economy. Therefore, the best course of action is a passive policy and regulatory forbearance. Thus, the then chairman of the board of the central bank of the United States (the Federal Reserve) considered new financial innovations, such as derivatives, as (i) a means of "dispersion of risk to those willing and able to bear it," and (ii) as instruments that would prevent "cascading failures" (Greenspan, 2002). The implication of the latter is that new instruments make it possible to spread risk around and away from the commercial banks; therefore, the risk of contagion in the banking system ("cascading failures") will be mitigated. The chairman's view of using active monetary policy to target bubbles also reflects the underlying ideology. As late as December 12, 2007, in an op-ed page article in the *Wall Street Journal*, Greenspan remarked:

> *After more than a half-century observing numerous price bubbles evolve and deflate, I have reluctantly concluded that bubbles cannot be safely defused by monetary policy or other policy initiatives before the speculative fever breaks on its own.*

Given the history of the deregulation movement in the United States since the early 1980s, Greenspan's reference to "other policy initiatives" should not be difficult to understand. The basic idea is that because asset price bubbles are illusive and impossible to spot until they burst, monetary policy should not target rising asset prices in a particular sector since any pre-emptive action to do so runs the risk of derailing the whole economy (Kohn, 2006). Since the underlying model of the policy maker's model is the efficient market paradigm, regulation would be administered with the "light touch" as monetary policy. (For a readable account of the unrealism of the efficient market paradigm, see Cooper, 2008.) It was only after the crisis was in full swing that Greenspan acknowledged that the efficient market was a flawed paradigm. Robert Skidelsky stated in *New York Magazine* on December 12, 2008:

> *Among the most astonishing statements to be made by any policymaker in recent years was Alan Greenspan's admission this autumn that the regime of deregulation he oversaw as Chairman of the Federal Reserve was based on a "flaw": he had overestimated the ability of a free market to self-correct and had missed the self-destructive power of deregulated mortgage lending. The "whole intellectual edifice," he said, "collapsed in the summer of last year." What was this "intellectual edifice"? As so often with policymakers, you need to tease out their beliefs from their policies. Greenspan must have believed something like the efficient market hypothesis, which holds that financial markets always price assets correctly. Given that markets are efficient, they would need only the lightest regulation. Government officials who control the money supply have only one task—to keep prices roughly stable.*

Greenspan, of course, was not alone in thinking that interventions to deflate a bubble may do more harm. For example, as late as February 29, 2008, the president and chief executive officer of the Federal Reserve Bank of Chicago, in a speech before the US Monetary Forum, asked: "Should a policymaker deflate a bubble before it becomes problematic?" He then answered: "I am skeptical that we can identify bubbles with enough accuracy and know enough about how to act to say that we wouldn't have more failures than success..." Furthermore, as former chairman Greenspan (2004) noted, "in order to make sure you burst a bubble, you have to attack it aggressively, because if your attack fails, it just gets bigger. And there are big risks to the real economy." Similar sentiments were expressed by the president of the European Central Bank in Singapore on June 8, 2005 in a speech titled "Asset Price Bubbles and Monetary Policy."

4.3   A Different Explanation for the Financial Crisis of 2007

The conventional view holds that the emergence of the financial crisis of 2007 was due to a number of factors, including: extraordinarily high liquidity; rapid pace of financial engineering which innovated complex, opaque, and difficult-to-understand financial instruments significantly ahead of what the market could digest; informational problems caused by lack of transparency in asset market prices, particularly in the market for structured credit instruments; outdated, lax, or absent regulatory-supervisory oversight which encouraged excessive risk taking; faulty risk management and accounting models; and the emergence of an incentive structure that created a complicit coalition composed of financial institutions, real estate developers and appraisers, insurance companies, and credit rating agencies whose actions led to a deliberate underestimation and underpricing of risk.

The conventional view suggests that mitigating the risk of emergence of similar financial crises in the future requires: (i) "efficient," rather than "more," regulations and supervision that avoids excesses in risk taking; (ii) prudentially higher capital requirement or collateralization to reduce leveraging; (iii) improving risk management to focus on market and systemic risk, rather than the risk to individual institutions; (iv) designing and adopting an improved system of due diligence by financial institutions and financial assets and instruments; (v) designing and adopting an improved system of liquidity management by institutions participating in the financial market that would mitigate liquidity risk—that is, the chance that a holder of an asset may not be able to sell it quickly; (vi) designing and establishing a last resort liquidity provider that can buy assets from liquidity-stressed market participants and hold in order to infuse liquidity into the market until the market returns to normalcy; (vii) creating an incentive system for banks to bring on board and consolidate off-balance sheet items to which they have extended (explicit or implicit) guarantees and credit lines; and (viii) revising the marked-to-market accounting rule to avoid enforcing and accelerating the downward pressure on asset prices in times of liquidity stress.[2]

There is an alternative view, which sees crises as endogenous, endemic to financial capitalism. More specifically, instability and crises are inherent in a financial system where the predominant mode of financing is interest-based debt contracts and credit. According to economic historians, from its very beginning, profit seeking for the purpose of wealth accumulation has characterized capitalism and distinguished it from other economic systems. At the heart of the financial wealth-creating institutional framework of financial capitalism is a system of debt–credit creation centered in the commercial banking subsystem that places a multiple of the deposits of many depositors at the disposal of borrowers of money capital. In essence, every deposit expands into a multiple of itself to become loans (credit) in the hands of borrowers (Krichene and Mirakhor, 2008). In the process, the banks make money off the interest rates they charge on the money they lend for more money in the future. Part of the borrowed money finances new investments, part finances purchases of financial assets, and the rest finances current consumption. The only part of the created credit that helps in the expansion of the economy is the part that is borrowed to finance investment, which provides the future flow of income to validate the debt obligation that made the financing of investment possible.

It is worth noting that, contrary to the common view, consumption today validates the debt obligations incurred for financing of past investments. A fall in consumption represents a failure to validate payment obligations made in the past. For validation of past and present obligations, investment and consumption must grow. Debt and credit, however, grow or decline for reasons different from those for which investment and production grow; there is no direct connection between credit expansion and investment in the real sector (for production). There is an indirect connection between them through the interest rate mechanism. Financial institutions (banks and non-bank financial intermediaries) set interest rates for loaning money. These institutions are only tangentially interested in the real rate of returns to an investment project, and that only as a signal that payment obligations will be validated. To ensure that this will be the case, lenders ask for collateral. As such, a financial system becomes more sophisticated, and more dynamic ways and means will be sought through innovations to financialize as many commodities and real assets as possible. The process of financialization, it is argued, expands access to finance, thus reducing the force of financial constraint. The financialization process transforms illiquid real economic resources into asset classes that are traded in various asset markets. If and when a financial sector is dominated by interest rate-based debt contracts, the financialization process creates more and more debt as it expands throughout the economy, converting equity in real assets into debt. This was the case in the early stages of the housing boom in the US, where excess liquidity and low interest rates created an incentive for homeowners to cash out equities built up in their homes through refinancing. The cashed-out equity supported a consumption boom.

It is noted that securitization, ongoing over the past three decades, is part of the general process of financialization. While it is quite conceivable that financialization (or securitization) could be just as easily equity based, the dominant force of socio-political factors and the power structure have created incentives for debt-based financialization. The result has been rapidly growing corporate debt-to-equity ratios and household debt-to-income ratios; acceleration of dominance of the financial sector relative to the real sector; income transfer from the real sector to the financial sector; deterioration of income distribution and increased income inequality; and changes in the orientation of the US economy from a saving–investment–production–export orientation to one of borrowing–debt–consumption–import (Palley, 2007).

This reorientation has transformed economic productive activities such that they resemble the activities of a casino, as Keynes remarked, or those of a racetrack, both of which use real resources but produce no real output (Hirshleifer, 1971). Such an economy produces "rolling bubbles" in financialized assets. As one bubble bursts, finance moves to another. Such has been the case over the past three decades, as bubbles were created and then imploded in the emerging market debt, dotcom, real estate, and commodities markets. In none of these was investment in real productive activities the primary objective of debt and credit expansion. Expectations of higher prices of the financial assets attracted participants in droves to create bubbles. That this would happen was analytically demonstrated as early as the 1980s. For example, Flood and Gerber (1980) demonstrated that rational individuals participate in asset price bubbles if they have expectations of rising asset prices. Growth in liquidity, low interest rates, higher leverage, and rapidly expanding credit, combined with regulatory-supervisory forbearance and passivity, accelerate the emergence and growth of bubbles.

Growth in the volume of debt in the US over the past three decades has been the defining characteristic of the process of financialization. Palley (2007) estimates that the total credit-to-GDP ratio grew from 140 percent to 328.6 percent of GDP between 1973 and 2005, while the mortgage debt-to-GDP ratio grew from 48.7 percent to 97.5 percent over the same period.

Household debt-to-GDP grew from 45.2 percent in 1973 to 94 percent in 2005. Palley also presents data demonstrating that not only has financialization led to rapid expansion of debt, but it has also contributed to adverse "changes in the functional distribution of income, wage stagnation, and increased income inequality…" (Palley, 2007). In the Modigliani–Miller theorem of neutrality of the corporate financial structure (represented by the debt-to-equity ratio), it is argued that how a firm finances its investment is irrelevant to its value. However, within the US financial system, there is an incentive structure in place that biases the financial structure in favor of debt. The US tax code gives interest payments a more favorable treatment than dividends and profits. Moreover, corporations can use debt and interest payments to reduce other claims (workers) on its income stream. Additionally, the rate of return on equity capital of the firm increases through debt financing, which allows it to expand leverage.

According to Palley (2007), "corporations as well as consumers have been encouraged to adopt a cult of debt finance. To reinforce the process of progressive reliance on debt finance, asset price inflation provides consumers and firms with collateral to support debt-financial spending. Borrowing is also supported by steady financial innovation that ensures a flow of new financial products, allowing leverage and widening the range of assets that can be collateralized" (Palley, 2007). A theoretical foundation of justification of financialization has been the framework developed by Arrow and Debreu (1954). In this model, financial assets represent contingent claims, not those resulting from *ex ante* fixed-return debt contracts. That is, claims are validated if a future contingent state materializes. These contingent claims result from financing of investment in the real sector. When a firm finances an investment in the real sector by issuing an *ex ante* fixed-return debt, the result is not a state-contingent claim—that is, it does not depend on the outcome of the investment project for which financing was obtained. The debt contract requires repayment on the date specified by the contract regardless of the outcome of the project. In effect, the financing bears no relation to the real investment. While it is true that the investor undertaking the project must compare the rate of return to the project to the rate of interest specified by the debt contract, the financing itself (that is, the lender, amounts borrowed, the debt contract, and the rate of interest charged) is, in effect, decoupled from the real sector investment. Thus, the rate of interest specified in a debt contract, which is essentially a promise to pay more money in the future for an amount of spot money, dominates the rate of return to investment in the real sector without the financing itself having an organic relation to that investment.

While in the early stages of the growth of the debt-dominated financial system there is a tenuous relationship between financing and real sector investment through the conduit of an entrepreneur's comparison of the expected rate of return to the investment project and the rate of interest, as financialization proceeds and debt securitization grows in sophistication, the relationship becomes progressively less important. As the financial sector grows to dominate the real sector, layer upon layer of securitization thins the connection between the two, to the point where an inverted pyramid of debt is supported by a very narrow base, real sector output and assets. The overwhelming dominance of the financial sector over the real sector can be discerned by noting that the ratio of global financial assets to the world's annual output of goods and services grew from 109 percent in 1980 to 316 percent in 2005. Similarly, while the total world GDP was about US$48 trillion in 2006, the value of global financial assets in the same year was US$140 trillion (nearly three times as much). As of 2007, the global liquidity market was estimated to be 12.5 times as large as global GDP. Financial derivatives constituted 80 percent of this liquidity. As Lim (2008, p. 13) suggests, a point has been reached "where what happens in the financial markets affects, or perhaps dictates, what happens in the real economy. It is the case of the tail wagging the dog."

In short, the alternative explanations of financial crises view them as internally generated instability episodes that inevitably arise from the basic debt–credit–interest rate relations. Where a financial system is dominated by interest-based debt and credit contracts, a fundamental "conflict between guaranteeing return of capital while also putting that capital at risk is a key channel through which financial instability can be, and recently has been generated" (Cooper, 2008). Fractional reserve banking and its close relatives in the form of money market funds and other financial innovations operated by highly leveraged institutions ensure that the credit (and debt) creation process amplifies manifold. This takes place through the mechanism of the money–credit multiplier within the fraction reserve banking system, and through leverage ratios within the banking system as well as other highly leveraged financial institutions. Credit multiplies in the upswing phase of a financial cycle, when financial asset market price bubbles emerge, and is rapidly destroyed in the downswing phase of the cycle when bubbles burst. "In money markets, as with most debt markets, the way to earn highest rates of interest is to make loans for the longest possible periods to the lowest quality, least reliable investors. The pressure for high money market yields, therefore, encourages fund managers toward a high-risk lending strategy. But this strategy runs into direct conflict with the money market fund's commitment to give back all of the investor's money, plus interest earned, without the risk of losses" (Cooper, 2008).

What is true of money market funds is much more forcefully true of other highly leveraged financial institutions such as hedge funds, special purpose vehicles, structured investment vehicles (SIVs), and others. The paradox of a debt-dominated, dynamic financial system is that, as it innovates layer upon layer of debt-based financial instruments, the real (productive) sector of the economy, which ultimately has to generate income streams to validate all the repayments of financial capital plus interest rates stipulated *ex ante* in the debt contracts, shrinks in size relative to the size of the financial markets. As noted by Lim (2008), the global size of financial assets in 2007 was 12.5 times larger than global GDP! That such an inverted pyramid would eventually collapse under its own weight seems inevitable. Additionally, debt contracts essentially pit *ex ante* fixed and guaranteed payment commitments against an expected but uncertain future income stream from the underlying investment in the real sector to validate the payment of principal and interest stipulated in the debt contract. It is no wonder, then, that Keynes referred to such a system as a "casino."

The warning signs of such an eventual implosion had been around long before the recent crisis. Indeed, five years before the event, it was observed (Mirakhor, 2002) that:

> *While the financial innovations of the 1990s in the conventional system have led to mobilization of financial resources in astronomical proportions, they have also led to equally impressive growth of debt contracts and instruments. According to the latest reports, there are now US$32 trillion of sovereign and corporate bonds alone. Compare this (plus all other forms of debt, including consumer debt in industrial countries) to the production and capital base of the global economy, and one observes an inverted pyramid of huge debt piled up on a narrow production base that is supposed to generate income flows that are to serve this debt. In short, this growth in debt has nearly severed the relationship between finance and production. Analysts are now worried about a "debt bubble." For each dollar worth of production, there are thousands of dollars of debt claims.*

The succeeding five years made this picture far more ominous as debt grew further, with its growth rates dwarfing the rate of expansion of the global production base. For example, by 2007, credit default swaps alone had grown in size to more than US$50 trillion, compared to a total US GDP of US$14 trillion.

The view that a financial system dominated by credit and debt contracts is prone to instability and eventual collapse has been around since the 19th century. But a more recent debate dates to the years of the Great Depression when the view found forceful expression in the writings of eminent economists, such as Irving Fisher and Henry Simons (see Krichene and Mirakhor, 2008) in the US and Keynes (1930, 1936) in the UK. The recognition that the fractional reserve banking system, in which credit multiplier and leverage ratio mechanisms were operative, was the source of credit instability led American economists, including Fisher and the Chicago Group (including Simons, Frank Knight, and other members of the economics faculty in the University of Chicago), to propose the reform of the US banking system to require banks to maintain reserves equal to 100 percent of their deposits. While the proposal was not enacted into law (by some accounts due to the political pressure of the banking lobby; see Phillips, 1995) at the time, the proposal has resurfaced from time to time in a variety of other forms, such as "narrow banking," "collateralized banking," and others (see Bossone, 2002; Phillips, 1992a, 1992b, 1995; Konstas, 2006; Minsky, 1994; Pierce, 1991; Spong, 1993; Scott, 1998; Garcia et. al., 2005; Wallace, 1996; Kobayakawa and Nakamura, 1999). The more recent discussions of the 100 percent reserve banking proposals focus on the moral hazard and costs of deposit insurance and lender of last resort functions, which central banks have to establish in order to cover deposits in the fractional reserve banking in case of defaults, and on the advantage that the proposed reform will have in imposing discipline on credit creation within the system.

Whereas these American economists saw the fractional reserve banking system and its power of credit creation as a source of financial instability, Keynes saw another (deeper) "villain of the piece": the role of interest and the rentiers who demanded it. Keynes saw this role as so detrimental to the economy that, in his book *The General Theory of Employment, Interest and Money* (1936), he called for steps to be taken toward the "euthanasia of rentiers." The issue of interest rate as rent was important enough to Keynes that he devoted a good part of the book to the topic (particularly Chapters 12, 17, and 23, which are among the most neglected parts of the book).

A careful reading of the *Treatise on Money* as well as the *General Theory* makes clear that Keynes did not believe that there is either a theoretical explanation or an economic justification for the existence of an *ex ante* fixed (or even variable) interest rate payment that (along with the principal) was guaranteed by a debt contract. His own liquidity preference theory explained why the rentiers were demanding an *ex ante* return on money they loaned, rather than providing a justification (theoretical or economic) for the existence of such a rate. Nor has any theory emerged subsequently that can explain or justify such a rate as an integral part of a coherent economic model (see Iqbal and Mirakhor, 1986). In fact, Keynes himself develops a theoretical edifice in terms of the concept of "own rate of interest" to suggest that any commodity in the spot market will have a rate of return in its term in the future market, which may be zero, positive, or negative, but most certainly not fixed *ex ante* as was the case with a rate of interest on money demanded by the rentier. Moreover, throughout his writings, Keynes emphasized that the future is uncertain—in the Knightian (in reference to the work of Frank Knight) sense; an uncertainty not reducible to risk to be insured. In such a world, rates of return to assets could not be known *ex ante*. Whereas the marginal efficiency of capital (the rate of return on real sector investment) is determined within the real sector of the economy, the *ex ante* fixed rate of interest on money is "determined by psychological and institutional conditions" (Keynes, 1936, pp. 202, 217).

While Keynes did not advocate outright elimination of rates of interest by direct government intervention, he did consider that it is quite possible for the interest rate to converge to zero "within a single generation," making "capital goods so abundant that the marginal efficiency of capital is zero." He saw this as the "most sensible way" of "gradually getting rid of many of the objectionable features of capitalism. For a little reflection will show what enormous social changes would result from a gradual disappearance of a rate of return on accumulated wealth. . . . Though the rentier would disappear, there would still be room, nevertheless, for enterprise and skill in the estimation of prospective yield about which opinions could differ. For the above relates primarily to the pure rate of interest apart from any allowance for risk and the like, and not to the gross yield of assets, including the return in respect of risk" (Keynes, 1936, p. 221). Clearly, Keynes made a distinction between return to entrepreneurial and financial resources willing to take risks, which would be contingent on the outcome of the real-sector investment undertaken by the entrepreneur and financed by the risk taker investor, and an *ex ante*-determined rate of interest on money required by the rentier in order to part with liquidity. The latter he considered "the villain of the piece."

The *Treatise on Money* was published in 1930 when economic deterioration was picking up momentum and becoming the Great Depression. Shortly after the publication of *Treatise*, a scholar named H. Somerville published a short article in the December 1931 issue of the *Economic Journal* that prompted a debate on issues covered in *Treatise*, including saving, investment, taxes, debt, credit, interest rate, usury, and scholastic thought. Somerville argued, "one of the unexpected consequences of Mr. Keynes is a vindication of the Canonist attitude to interest and usury." By "Canonist," Somerville was referring to a system of thought expounded by scholastic scholars (also called Churchmen or Schoolmen) of the Middle Ages who, in combining faith and reason, explained many religious precepts of Christianity. The most famous of these scholars was St. Thomas Aquinas. In his book *History of Economic Analysis* (1954), Joseph Schumpeter, after discussing the economic thoughts of the Greeks and Romans, claimed that an intellectual gap of 500 years existed following the contribution of Greco-Roman thought to economics and scholastic thought, and referred to this as "the Great Gap." Schumpeter states that, as far as economics is concerned, "we may safely leap over 500 years to the epoch of St. Thomas Aquinas (1225–74) whose *Summa Theologica* is in the history of thought what the South-Western Spire of the Cathedral of Chartres is in the history of architecture" (pp. 73–74). In a paper presented in 1983, Mirakhor offered evidence that such a gap (great or otherwise) never existed. He traced the thoughts of scholastic scholars, including economic thinking, to the Islamic world and its scholars whose writings and thoughts were transmitted to the scholars of the Middle Ages via a variety of channels (see Mirakhor, 1983 and 2003b for a fuller discussion). Among the economic thoughts of scholastics was the prohibition of interest charges on money loaned. By claiming that the position Keynes took in his *Treatise* on the question of saving without investing, but demanding a reward anyway, vindicated the scholastic view on prohibition of interest, Somerville triggered a heated debate in the *Economic Journal* between December 1931 and March 1932 when the Great Depression was in full swing. Particularly controversial was Somerville's claim (1931, pp. 647–48) that:

> *It is an inescapable conclusion from the Keynesian analysis that interest is the villain of the economic piece. Not that Mr. Keynes suggests the possibility of abolition of interest. According to his theory, interest could be too low and might require to be raised in the general interest: this would be in circumstances when prices were advancing too rapidly. Leaving aside for a moment the old question whether interest is necessary to evoke saving, the only use that Mr. Keynes can see for interest is as a depressant in times of over-activity.*
>
> *The orthodox doctrine has related interest closely to profits as if the two progressed or declined together. Mr. Keynes shows them as antagonists. Interest upon money is simply an added cost upon capital goods and therefore a deduction from profit and a burden upon enterprise. Socialist theory assails interest even more destructively than does Mr. Keynes, but socialist theory also assails profit, whereas Mr. Keynes salutes profit as the engine that drives the car of progress.*

It is worth noting that by the "orthodox doctrine," Somerville does not mean the "Canonists" but the acceptable body of economic thought of his own day. The above remarks indicate that he is not a socialist, a popular school of thought of the time. He makes his own position clear (p.647):

> *The cardinal point made by Mr. Keynes is the distinction between Saving and Investment, between the saving of money and its conversion into capital-goods. Saving without investment is not a service to production, and the saving of money does not by itself cause any conservation of products, but their waste, or their disposal at lower prices and the slowing down of productive activity. . . . From the point of view of the general economy it might be better to spend on production than on consumption, but certainly the worst thing is the sterile saving of money. The saving is sterile from the standpoint of community, though it may be profitable to the individual who, apart from any interest earnings, may watch his idle money grow in purchasing power through the fall in general prices. In such conditions, it is a matter to be deplored that holders of money are able to get interest by bank deposits. Interest only encourages socially wasteful saving and discourages socially desirable investment. To this extent, therefore, and in such conditions, interest is anti-social. Mr. Keynes urges the lowering of interest, even the abolition of interest on bank deposits, as proper policy to be pursued when trade is below par.*

He also reiterated that the position of the Canonists on the impermissibility of interest as usury did not extend to profits earned as a result of risk taking. This is the point of convergence of the views of the Canonists on interests and profits with those of Keynes. He stated (p. 648):

> *. . . the Canonists never quarreled with payments for use of capital, they raised no objection to true profit, the reward of risk, ability and enterprise, but they disputed the identification of the lending of money with the investment of capital and denied the justice of interest as a reward for saving without investment. . . . The Canonist principle was that sharing in trade risks made an investor a partner, a co-owner of capital, not simply a money lender, and gave a title to profit.*

To support his understanding of the scholastic position on interest and profit, Somerville referred to William Ashley's *Economic History*, one of the leading textbooks of the time on the subject (see Mirakhor, 1983), particularly *Book II* of Ashley's text, in which it is asserted that "until the beginning of the 16th century it was the constant teaching of the Canonists that to *bargain for a fixed reward, or dividend, upon the capital invested, whatever the fortunes of business might be*, made the contract usurious." Somerville concluded his article by suggesting (p. 649):

> *There may be reasons for thinking that the world will go back to the early Canonist doctrine. The classical argument that interest is necessary to evoke saving wears a different aspect when we appreciate that saving does not necessarily mean investment. The saving of money may actually diminish investment, and interest is deterrent to investment. If we could ensure, as the Canonists tried to do, that saving should be rewarded only when it was also investment in capital-goods, we should have gone far to stop the master-evil that Mr. Keynes has revealed to us, of saving exceeding investment.*

Somerville's potent argument that, based on his understanding of Keynes's main thesis in the *Treatise*, the cause of underemployment and inherent instability in a money-capitalist system is the fact that in such a system, where debt contracts dominate investment financing, without government intervention, there is no way to guarantee equality of saving and investment, and that the interest rate is the mechanism responsible for this state of affairs, brought an immediate response. Three of the four papers published in the March 1932 issue of the *Economic Journal* (by Edwin Cannan, B.P. Adarkar, and B.K. Sandwell) under the heading "Notes and Memoranda: Saving and Usury: A Symposium," were highly critical of Somerville, accusing him of: misunderstanding either the Canonists' position, or that of Keynes, or both; "misconceptions" of saving and investment; and "hostility to personal ownership" (pp. 123–35). The fourth paper was by Keynes himself (Keynes, 1932, pp. 135–37) who was supportive of Somerville in terms of the latter's understanding and presentation of Keynes's arguments in the *Treatise* and of the position of the Canonists. Keynes's article focused primarily on Edwin Cannan's paper (pp. 135–36):

> *. . . Prof. Cannan agrees with Mr. Somerville that if saving is conceived as mere refraining from expenditure, or if it is conceived as saving up money, "the case against interest as a consequence of saving is black." But, he continues, "the answer is that interest is not, in fact, obtained as a consequence of saving in either of these two senses. No one gets a penny of interest in consequence of merely refraining from expenditure; no one gets a penny of interest in consequence of having merely saved up money." I wish I could agree with him in attributing this natural justice to the economic system, but I am sure it is not so. Prof. Cannan has, I think, overlooked a vital aspect of the argument in my* Treatise on Money *wherein it differs from what I was brought up to believe and continued to believe until recently.*

The point is this. The answer to the question whether there is an increment of wealth corresponding to the saving of an individual seldom depends, as Prof. Cannan claims, on what he does with the money which represents that part of income which he refrains from spending on current consumption. In particular, the answer does not depend, as Prof. Cannan seems to suggest, on whether he "hoards" the money by increasing his cash or uses it to buy a security or some other capital asset. He may use his savings to buy a bond, and yet there may be no increment of capital wealth coming into existence as a result of his saving. I have argued in my Treatise *that the causes which determine the increment of capital wealth are only contingently and indirectly connected with those which determine the amount of individual savings. If an increment of saving by an individual is not accompanied by an increment of new investment—and, in the absence of deliberate management by the Central Bank or the Government, it will be nothing but a lucky accident if it is . . . then it* necessarily *causes diminished receipts, disappointment and losses to the other party, and* the outlet for savings of A will be found in financing losses of B.

Thus, when an individual saves, his savings must *be balanced by the creation of either an asset or a debt (or a loss paid for by an asset changing hands). But, as a rule, it lies entirely outside the power of the individual saver to determine which it is to be, and whether the result, or rather the accompaniment, of his saving is to be an asset or a debt. What he has done is to make possible the creation of an asset without a rise in price level. But failing a simultaneous increment of new investment, either by good management or by a lucky accident, then his act of saving will* cause *an equal loss to someone else; a debt will be created or an asset will change hands, but there will be no increment of wealth.*

Does Prof. Cannan hold that if an individual increases his bank-deposit by "saving up" money out of income, there necessarily results an increment of wealth to the community? If so, this is a view with which I have tried to join issue in my Treatise on Money; *if not, he has failed to meet the point.*

Now when an act of saving merely results, however unintentionally, in a loss to someone else, it is of an anti-social tendency, and the subsequent payment of interest to the saver—for pace *Prof. Cannan, debts have to pay interest just as much as assets—is a burden which, if accumulated with time, may become insupportable.*

> *That is why, without contesting anything in Mr. Adarkar's note, I nevertheless agree with Mr. Somerville that it is this social evil, to the possibility and theoretical explanation of which I drew attention in my* Treatise, *which probably lay behind the doctrine of the Canonists.*

The implication is clear: it is interest-debt that is a "social evil" and the "villain of the piece" of the explanation for unemployment, fragility, and ultimately the inherent instability of debt-based financial capitalism. Without the institution of interest, unspent income would find its way to investment in exchange for a reward contingent on the outcome of the real sector investment, for which savings provided financing. Emboldened by the support his views received from Keynes, Somerville produced another note for the June 1932 issue of the *Economic Journal*, in which he mounted a well-argued attack on the institution of interest. The centerpiece of this argument focused on the fact that the economics profession had not produced a satisfactory theory or explanation of why an *ex ante* fixed interest had to be paid on debt. One by one, he refuted the existing explanations and restated the Canonists' position on usury, again demonstrating the convergence of this view to that of Keynes with considerable more clarity (Somerville, 1932, pp. 322–23):

> *Canonist legislation prohibited all interest . . . but freely allowed profits even to sleeping partners. . . . Interest was forbidden, while profit was allowed, because interest arose simply from a loan of money and profit from an investment of capital. . . . In striking at interest on money loans, the Canonists were striking at saving-without-investment apart from that which consists in the simple hoarding of currency. At the same time, they were positively encouraging, both by their prohibition of interest and their allowance of profit, investment in the sense of the production of capital goods. . . .*
>
> *Money-lending without investment was recognized practically and theoretically as a social evil in the fourteenth century. Mr. Keynes's "Saving without Investment" is correctly translated as money-lending without investment, it being understood that savings deposits are regarded as lending. . . . The lending of money necessarily involves a debt, and it never by itself constitutes an asset. . . . The great support which Mr. Keynes gives to the Canonists, I take to be this: his strong distinction between saving and investment shows that it is theoretically wrong to treat money as representative capital and lending as investment. Interest is the price paid for the use of money[;] it is not the yield of capital.*

Keynes went on to expound his ideas on the issues raised in *The Economic Journal Symposium* in his *General Theory* with greater clarity. In Chapter 23, he makes the following remarks regarding the Canonists' position on usury *(Keynes, 1936, p. 352)*:

> *I was brought up to believe that the attitude of the Medieval Church to the rate of interest was inherently absurd, and that the subtle discussions aimed at distinguishing the return on money-loans from the return to active investment were merely Jesuitical attempts to find a practical escape from a foolish theory. But I now read these discussions as an honest intellectual effort to keep separate what the classical theory has inextricably confused together, namely the rate of interest and the marginal efficiency of capital. For it now seems clear that the disquisitions of the schoolmen were directed toward the elucidation of a formula which should allow the schedule of the marginal efficiency of capital to be high, whilst using rule and custom and the moral law to keep down the rate of interest.*

These remarks seem to validate Somerville's conception of convergence between the view of scholastic scholars on interest and profit and those of Keynes. Be that as it may, in the *General Theory*, Keynes makes the point forcefully that interest rates, through their role in creating a wedge between saving and investment, create conditions under which the system becomes inherently unstable. In his concluding remarks (Chapter 24), Keynes suggests (p. 376):

> *I feel sure that the demand for capital is strictly limited in the sense that it would not be difficult to increase the stock of capital up to a point where its marginal efficiency had fallen to a very low figure. This would not mean that the use of capital instruments would cost nothing, but only that the return from them would have to cover little more than their exhaustion by wastage and obsolescence, together with some margin to cover risk and the exercise of skill and judgment. . . . Now, though this state of affairs would be quite compatible with some measure of individualism, yet it would mean the euthanasia of the rentier, and, consequently, the euthanasia of the cumulative oppressive power of the capitalist to exploit the scarcity value of capital. Interest today rewards no genuine sacrifice, any more than does the rent of land. . . . But whilst there may be intrinsic reasons for the scarcity of land, there are no intrinsic reasons for the scarcity of capital.*

He viewed the "euthanasia of the rentier" as a gradual process, one that "will need no revolution." This will happen when "a somewhat comprehensive socialization of investment will prove the only means of securing an approximation to full employment; though this need not exclude all manner of compromises and devices by which public authority will cooperate with private initiative" (Keynes, 1936, p. 378). Thus, there would be "an increase in the volume of capital until it ceases to be scarce, so that the functionless investor will no longer receive a bonus . . . " (Keynes, 1936, p. 376).

Keynes believed that financial capitalism left to its own devices is inherently unstable. At the core of his thought are the real phenomena of saving and investment processes. Coming basically from two different subsectors of the real economy, consumer and business, their coordinated behavior is subject to uncertainty. That, even under the best of circumstances, their equality is not always assured is the core of his explanation of the inherent instability of the system. The existence of a financial system dominated by *ex ante*–fixed interest-based debt contracts makes achieving sustained full employment equilibrium difficult, if not impossible. The essence of his prescription for achieving stability and full employment in such an economy was socialization of capital investment that would allow diminished scarcity of capital and the eventual "euthanasia of the rentier," to ensure that all savings would be channeled to productive employment-creating investment.

In Chapter 24 of his *General Theory*, Keynes argued that interest rewards no genuine sacrifice, and its compounding, which leads to wealth accumulation at an accelerated pace, ensures that wealth and income distribution in society is tilted toward the rentier. The end result is unemployment, poverty, and deprivation. Thus, he argued that the chief "evils" of modern financial capitalism were its inability to provide full employment and its strong tendency to generate an arbitrary and inequitable distribution of income and wealth. Through his call for the "euthanasia of the rentier," he linked both these "evils" to their underlying mutual cause: the institution of interest.

One of the most perceptive, productive, and brilliant followers of Keynes was Hyman Minsky. Minsky pushed forward the frontiers of "classical Keynesian" thought to produce valuable insights into the workings of the financial capitalist system. Like Keynes before him, Minsky considered such a system inherently unstable, believing that if the financial system is dominated by *ex ante*–fixed interest-based debt contracts, the structure itself becomes a source of amplification of disturbances. His major contribution is known as the Financial Instability Hypothesis (Krichene and Mirakhor, 2008; Mirakhor, 1985). This hypothesis contains two main propositions. The first proposition states that there are two financing structures: one promotes stability, the other instability. The second proposition states that in the financial system of money capitalism, stability is not sustainable because, during prosperity, stability contains the seeds of its own instability; that is, "stability is destabilizing." A simple rendition of the first proposition is to say that the more a financial structure (debt-to-equity ratio) tilts toward debt, the greater the fragility of the system. This is what happens, according to Minsky, to the financial structure of the economy through time. In a period of prosperity, there are large payoffs to borrowing used to finance activity in areas and sectors of the economy with profitable opportunities. Initially, businesses are conservative and finance their activities through equity finance and/or from their own internal funds. And, if they borrow, they do so only if their future income streams are sufficient for them to meet the payment commitment stream (principal and interest) over the lifetime of the contracted debt. Minsky terms this "hedge finance."

The financial system dominated by this type of financing (mostly equity and internal funds with some debt commitments that are validated comfortably by an underlying income stream) is consistent with stability. However, as profit opportunities intensify during prosperity, there are higher rewards for borrowing as enterprises take on greater risk. Thus, more and more firms and other participants tilt their financial structure toward debt and increased leverage and become "speculative" units. That is in response to what they see as profitable opportunities and an expectation of exploiting them. These firms overwhelm the financial structure with debt to the point where their income stream becomes insufficient to pay the principal. Although speculative units pay interest when due, they have to rollover the principal at maturity. According to Minsky, matters do not rest here. Firms continue to borrow to the point where their financial structure is made of debt commitments, which can be validated by more borrowing to pay both the principal and interest. Minsky referred to these units as "ponzi units," and to their financing as "ponzi finance." He believed that, during the prosperity phase of a business cycle, capitalist economies tend to become progressively more fragile as their financial structure changes from hedge (little or no debt) to speculative and ponzi finance (Minsky, 1986).

The pivotal element of Minsky's Financial Instability Hypothesis is debt. So important is this element that he considered his hypothesis as a "theory of the impact of debt on system behavior." There are two forces that push debt financing to higher and higher levels in the upward phase of the cycle. First, market participants borrow more and more because asset price increases validate their expectations, which was the foundation of their increased borrowing in the first place. Moreover, as prices increase, the value of their collateral increases and with it their creditworthiness, allowing them to borrow more. Second, banks and other highly leveraged financial institutions expand credit and push lending in two ways: (i) as prices of assets increase, their balance sheets expand, allowing them to extend more credit; and (ii) they find new ways and means of credit expansion through financial innovation. These financial intermediaries are, after all, what Minsky called "merchants of debt." They are constantly searching for ways and means of expanding their balance sheets. Thus, the debt structure continues to be extended throughout the financial system and beyond to the whole economy.

Minsky was an astute student and observer of capitalism. He saw it as a dynamic system that is constantly evolving. Within it, there are a number of dialectical processes and feedback loops at work that make issues of instability, unfair distribution, and unemployment structural problems of the system. In this he was following Keynes. And, like Keynes, he thought that the dialectic forces within the system would lead it into disaster if the system were left to its own devices. There were ways in which the system could be stabilized, and Minsky believed the solution was a "big government," big enough that its expenditure would be a stabilizing force and serve as an "employer of last resort" and a "big central bank" to serve as an effective lender of last resort. Additionally, Minsky called for a dynamic regulatory system that would be constantly ahead of the curve, to minimize the likelihood of regulatory arbitrage (see Minsky, 1986).

Many observers of the recent crisis have found Minsky's diagnosis of past crises, and his prediction and explanation of potential turbulences, as insightful and enlightening (see Whalen, 2008; Wray, 2008). He warned of growing fragility in the system, debt buildup in the household and business sectors, and the adverse potential of securitization, debt globalization, and wrong-headed government policies. He placed great stress on the adverse impact of the ongoing ideologically based deregulation that began in the early 1980s. Following his death in 1996, a number of his colleagues, former students, and other followers carried on this tradition, analyzing the unfolding events in the financial sector using his Financial Instability Hypothesis. In a number of papers published between 1996 and the onset of the crisis in 2007, these scholars warned of an impending disaster as they observed the growing debt and fragility in the system.[3] They saw the phenomenon of bubbles forming, inflating, and bursting not as isolated incidences arising from external factors, but as "rolling bubbles"—symptoms of growing financial fragility that would eventually lead to full instability. (George Soros, too, had seen these bubbles as part of a "super bubble" of growing debt and credit (Soros, 2008).) Minsky had observed the growing fragility of the US financial system since 1966, where a bubble's boom and bust in one asset market was followed by the formation and implosion of another bubble in a different asset market. He attributed these booms and busts—the emerging market debt crisis, and the LTCM, dotcom, housing, and commodities bubbles—to liquidity and credit expansion, followed by the bailing out of major players by the government. As financialization helped to create one asset market after another, expanding liquidity and credit in search of yield created one bubble after another.

4.4 Islamic Financial System and Lessons from the Recent Crisis

Over the past few decades, a consensus has emerged that expansion of credit and debt is detrimental to the stability of developing economies. For example, the IMF advised its developing country members that in order to mitigate the risk of instability, such as occurred in the emerging markets in 1997, they should: (i) avoid debt-creating flows, especially short-term flows; (ii) rely mostly on foreign direct investment as external financing; (iii) ensure, if they must borrow, that their external debt is never larger than 25 percent of GDP and that their debt obligations are not bunched toward the short end of maturities; (iv) ensure that their economy is producing large enough primary surpluses to meet their debt obligations; (v) ensure that their sovereign bonds incorporate clauses (such as majority action, initiation, and engagement clauses) that make debt workouts and restructurings easier—that is, ensure that the risk-sharing mechanisms associated with their debt obligations will help them avoid moral hazard; (vi) ensure that domestic corporations have transparent balance sheets, follow marked-to-market accounting, and have financial structures that are biased more heavily toward equity and internal funding and are not heavily leveraged; and (vii) ensure that their domestic financial institutions are regulated and supervised efficiently, are not highly leveraged, follow prudent credit policy, and are highly transparent. The IMF strongly prescribed periodic audits by its members of the soundness and stability of their financial sectors. While a majority of the members complied, some of its major shareholders, notably the US, repeatedly refused such diagnostic audits. The global economic crisis proved that major countries were as much in need of the IMF's financial policy prescription as, if not more than, the developing countries. While financial turmoil in developing countries is usually largely contained in these countries, the US crisis has affected the global financial system.

Be that as it may, it is now clear that financial systems dominated by interest-based debt contracts are prone to financial fragility and instability. Nevertheless, other than Keynes and his most ardent followers, few notable economists, if any, have actually proposed outright elimination of *ex ante*–fixed interest-based debt contracts in practice. However, the workings and implications of such debtless systems have been investigated in the form of theoretically modeled systems such as pure "stock market" economies and "cash-in-advance" systems.

One of the earliest analytically elegant models of a stock market economy was developed by Lloyd Metzler (1951), who investigated the economic implications of an economic system in which private wealth is in only two forms: "money (including demand deposits) and common stock, and that all common stock involves appropriately the same degree of risk." Metzler further assumed that "the central bank is legally authorized to buy and sell the common stock held by the owners of private entity or stock and that this common stock constitutes the only non-monetary asset of the banking system." The Metzler model further assumed a closed economy, and that the labor supply was fixed and all means of production, other than labor, were produced at constant returns to scale. With these assumptions, Metzler defined a "rate of interest" as "nothing more than the yield of the stock, and this yield, in turn, is the ratio of the income earned by the stock to its market price" (Metzler, 1951). It is clear that this "rate of interest" is not the same as the customary *ex ante*–fixed interest rate on borrowed money stipulated in a debt contract. For one thing, Metzler's "interest rate "is determined by the earnings and price of the stock," clearly an *ex post* concept. Second, unlike the customary *ex ante*–fixed debt-contract interest rate, where the total interest paid is tied to the amount of money loaned, Metzler's rate was based on the performance of the stock in the market and the earnings from the investment activity that issued the stock; again, an *ex post* rather than an *ex ante* concept. Metzler then proceeded to drive the equilibrium conditions for such a system and to investigate its stability characteristics.

Sensing that Metzler's model was a reasonable first approximation of an Islamic financial structure, since it assumed away the existence of a debt instrument, Mohsin Khan (1986) constructed a simple version of the Metzler model that demonstrated how the system produces a saddle point—that is, the equilibrium is stable. He suggested that the:

> *. . . Islamic model of banking, being based on principles of equity participation, . . . may well prove to be better suited to adjusting to shocks that result in banking crises and disruption of the payments mechanism of the country. In an equity-based system that excludes predetermined interest rates and does not guarantee the nominal value of deposits, shocks to asset positions are immediately absorbed by changes in the value of shares (deposits) held by the public in the bank[;] therefore, the real values of assets and liabilities of banks in such a system would be equal at all points in time.*

Khan and Mirakhor (1988) structured a different model to show that monetary policy is not impaired in such a system. Both these models were closed-economy models. Zaidi and Mirakhor (1988) constructed an open-economy general equilibrium model to investigate the implications of the operation of an Islamic financial system, particularly the effects on the economy's capacity to adjust to disturbances and on international capital flows. They concluded that monetary policy is effective for stabilization purposes and that disturbances to asset positions are absorbed efficiently in an Islamic financial system. These models focused on the financial sector without directly involving the real sector of the economy. Mirakhor (1990) constructed a model that incorporated some of the characteristics of the above models and features of some well-known models, as well as insights from the works of researchers who had extended Metzler's model in new directions. The latter research had demonstrated that a fully equity-based system has desirable features that improve the shock-absorption adjustment capacity of the economy—that is, such a system is more stable than a debt-based system, as it adjusts rapidly to shocks (see, for example, Shane, 1984; Cole, 1988). Like the Metzler–Khan model, the model in Mirakhor's paper assumed only two assets: money and shares; but, unlike the former model where the rate of return was given as the ratio of the return to stock and its market price, Mirakhor's model derived a rate of return from the real sector, thus providing an interactive process between the financial sector and the real sector which provided the rate of return to the former sector. The equilibrium conditions in the short and long run for both closed- and open-economy models were derived. The paper then investigated the stability of the equilibrium and the process of adjustment of the system to shocks.

In summary, standard economic analysis can demonstrate the stability of an Islamic financial system and its resilience to shocks, at least in theory. The intuition behind this conclusion is that, unlike a debt-based system, there is a one-to-one mapping of the financial structure onto the underlying real sector assets. There is neither the problem of mismatching household savings and finance for investment, nor of mismatching maturities. Risks of loss are shared between the surplus fund holder and the entrepreneur. There is no opportunity to expand credit and leverage beyond what can be supported by the real sector output (Krichene and Mirakhor, 2008). It has already been remarked that conventional analysis has demonstrated that, in the case of share contracts, the informational problems that are characteristic of a debt-based system do not exist, thus making risk-sharing, equity-based financing more efficient. All of this has been demonstrated by standard analysis in a conventional system. But each financial system operates within an institutional framework that facilitates its efficient operations. If the elements of that framework are impaired, the efficiency of the system is adversely impacted. The stability characteristics demonstrated by the above-mentioned theoretical papers are generated within a conventional institutional framework. Even so, the superior stability characteristics of a non-interest-based equity system, as compared to an interest-based debt system, have been demonstrated. Scholars, some of whose works were briefly reviewed above, have argued that it is the predominance of debt that is responsible for the inherent instability of a debt-based market economy. The point being that it is, at least theoretically, possible to envision a non-interest-based financial structure within a conventional system. What makes for a truly Islamic system, however, is not only the prohibition of interest— although this is an important element—but the institutional framework within which the system has to operate. Without its institutional underpinnings—a platform of behavioral rules—Islamic finance becomes indistinguishable from a conventional system with financing being provided through sharing rather than debt contracts.

The institutional framework—what Douglass North calls the "institutional scaffolding"—that Islam provided for the operation of its economic and financial system strengthens the stability of the system. The elements of this "scaffolding" come directly from the *Qur'an* with additional explication and operationalization from the *Sunnah* of the Messenger (*pbuh*). This framework includes, inter alia, sanctity of contract (explicit and implicit); property rights; trust; rules of behavior in governance; existence of markets; rules regarding allocation, production, and distribution of resources, income, and wealth; rules governing the behavior of market participants; and rules regarding post-market distribution. (See Iqbal and Mirakhor, 2007; and Askari et. al., 2009, for a more detailed discussion of the elements of the institutional framework of Islam.) There can be little doubt that with such a strongly rules-based framework that includes faithfulness to contracts and a strong prohibition against dealing with interest, lying, cheating, and fraudulent activities, the financial system of Islam would be transparent, efficient, and informationally trouble-free. For example, consider the implications of full operationalization of only one element of Islam's institutional scaffolding— that is, the first verse of Chapter 5 of the *Qur'an*—the rule on faithfully abiding by the terms and conditions stipulated by a contract to which one is a party. Its full implications are astounding. No one would need fear that a contract would not be performed as a result of lying, cheating, fraud, or negligence. Imagine the efficiency gains in such a system; no monitoring costs, no risk of moral hazard or adverse selection, and minimal cost of transaction in contracting.

While there are many individuals whose behavior corresponds to the rules specified by the institutional framework of Islam, the scaffolding in its entirety is not yet fully in place in even a single Muslim country. Until such time as Islamic rules of behavior are fully operationalized, the available institutional framework in Muslim societies will have to be organized to ensure that people's behavior does not distort, dislocate, or exploit other members of society. It is in this context that the recent crisis holds valuable lessons for Islamic finance. As discussed earlier, there are two explanations of how the crisis developed. One view holds that crises are endemic to a financial system that is debt denominated, and where contracts are made on the basis of money now for money later without much consideration of relations to real sector activities. Such a system creates an incentive structure for rapid expansion of credit and debt, through leverage, and the emergence of asset price bubbles. As market players in such a system, financial institutions are "merchants of debt."

As rising asset market prices validate round after round of rising profit expectations, these "merchants of debt" are encouraged to increase leverage, through financial innovation, expand credit, and, in turn, encourage their clients to tilt their financial structure ever more toward debt, thus making it more and more fragile. When asset market prices reach a limit of increase and interest rates rise due to fear of inflation, some of these debt obligations are not validated. Because of the complexity and interrelated nature of financial markets, the failure to validate a few large debt payment obligations creates a rapid contagion effect as more and more portfolios in the market become contaminated. As Soros has observed, bubbles have a built-in asymmetric nature. It takes a lot longer for them to emerge, but they implode in short order. As the authorities bail out major participants from the disastrous impact of one asset market bubble implosion, lowering interest rates to minimize the impact on the real economy and other asset markets, and higher liquidity, innovations create new asset classes to which liquidity in search of yield migrates. The result is a "rolling bubble," except that each bubble is larger and packs a greater force than the one before it.

Soros suggests the emergence of an immense "super bubble" within which smaller bubbles are created and then busted. Such was the case in the US financial system as bubbles rolled from emerging markets debt, to the dotcom, real estate, and commodities markets. At each turn, bailouts, low interest rates, inflow of funds from emerging markets, and financial innovations created a powerful source of funds in search of yield, which poured into the new asset classes. The first view holds that these results were predictable and were predicted as financial fragility (greater reliance on debt) was reinforced. This view holds that the "ideologically based aversion to regulation" that prompted the "deregulation revolution" of the last quarter-century in the US, as well as in other advanced economies, created an incentive structure for accelerating the rapidly paced, debt-based financial innovations which, in turn, were powerful stimulants to the emergence of the consumer–business debt binges.

The more conventional view, on the other hand, tends to downplay the idea of a "super bubble" and "rolling bubble," as well as the thesis on the inherent instability of a debt-based financial system. It treats bubbles in isolation, each having different reasons for their emergence, but mostly due to the "irrational exuberance" of market players. It further holds that bubbles cannot be predicted; therefore, attempts by policy makers to target rising prices in a given asset market may well have an adverse impact on economic growth. Moreover, this view argues that risk taking is an essential element of the dynamism of a market economy; and that, therefore, too much regulation that thwarts risk taking will harm economic growth. Financial innovations are necessary to the dynamic of risk taking, and it is to be welcomed as it helps to complete markets and, thus, increase efficiency. Asset price increases are a natural response of the market to investment opportunities, and bubbles are the result of an overly exuberant response by market participants to profit opportunities. Sooner or later, market forces will dampen the over-exuberance and bubbles will disappear. As indicated earlier, the former chairman of the US Federal Reserve was one policy maker who espoused such a view, although he recently admitted that this view is based on a faulty theoretical model.

The major lesson of the recent crisis for Islamic finance, especially at this juncture in its evolution, is the need for the design and development of a comprehensive and dynamic regulatory–prudential–supervisory framework, uniquely designed for an Islamic financial system. Such a framework, properly designed, will satisfy the requirements of any existing regulatory framework anywhere in the world and goes beyond them to ensure the stability of the system. Theory has demonstrated the stability of an equity-based, risk-sharing financial system. Moreover, theory can also demonstrate, easily and comfortably, that the institutional framework (rules of behavior) of Islam, within which its financial system must operate, reinforces to a high degree the stability and efficiency of the financial system. In practice, however, and as long as the institutional framework is not fully in place, an Islamic financial system can fall victim to the same adversely designed incentive structure as the conventional system, particularly because, presently, Islamic finance is operating in an institutional framework which is basically that of the conventional system. The mere declaration of prohibition of *ex ante*–fixed interest-based debt contracts by fiat, but without any effort at implementation of the supporting institutional framework, will not accrue the benefits of properly structured Islamic finance to the population; in fact, it may do harm by creating a sense of complacency in society. Creating a non-interest-based system side-by-side with a conventional system within an institutional framework that is basically designed to support the latter system has both benefits and costs. Which of the two dominates is an empirical question. However, from pure intuition, the benefits would seem to overwhelm the costs in the long run, when all possible benefits are considered, because it will permit an orderly evolution of Islamic finance.

In either case, a properly designed regulatory–prudential–supervisory framework seems essential to the orderly development and evolution of Islamic finance. Such a framework will have to be uniquely designed to distinguish it from that of a conventional system, in that it has to structure its incentive system to include both negative elements (*don'ts*), that specify prohibited behavior, and positive elements (*do's*) that encourage and enforce recommended behavior. Such a framework will have to be comprehensive, covering all transactions, and all financial instruments and institutions operating in the system, without exception. One of the most damaging elements of the US regulatory system was that a larger segment of the financial markets and institutions had little or no regulatory–prudential–supervisory oversight. Moreover, the regulatory framework was fragmented. In an Islamic financial system there are no interest-based debt contracts; financial innovation can proceed only as it relates to equity and trade-based transaction. (Both areas provide ample opportunity for financial engineering.) Nevertheless, the risk of inappropriate, ostensibly trade- or equity-based, but actually debt-like, instruments that are highly collateralized to enhance their credit rating may not be easily avoidable. The soundness and appropriateness (from an Islamic doctrinal point of view) of some of the reverse engineered financial instruments innovated in recent years has been a matter of debate among scholars. (See recent papers by Dr. Najatullah Siddiqi on this issue; see also Mirakhor and Zaidi, 2007; Chapra, 2007; Hassan, 2007.) It is the responsibility of an appropriately designed regulatory oversight to ensure that such risks are mitigated. Moreover, such a framework will have to be unified under one regulatory umbrella. The artificial segmentation of the financial markets into the money and capital markets for regulatory purposes was one of the most damaging aspects of the regulatory framework in the US, in which the regulatory authority was segmented between various agencies—the Federal Reserve, the Comptroller of Currency, and the Securities and Exchange Commission, states and their regulatory apparatus, and the commodities market with its regulatory–supervisory rules. Given the rapidly paced financial innovation, the line of demarcation between money markets, capital markets, and all sorts of financial asset markets is blurred. In an Islamic financial system, segmentation of regulatory authority is even less logical because of the nature of a system that promotes nearly a one-to-one interaction between real sector and financial activities.

The properly designed regulatory oversight for Islamic finance will have to be uniform—that is, its standards must apply uniformly to all Islamic financial institutions, transactions, and instruments everywhere globally across all jurisdictions. The reason being that the systemic risk of a failure of one financial institution or instrument is far greater for Islamic finance than for its conventional counterpart because of the potentially magnified reputational damage for the entire system, particularly at this juncture of the evolution of Islamic finance. Because profit-seeking motivation currently drives financial sector innovations, there are strong incentives to create instruments and ways and means of regulatory arbitrage. An appropriately designed regulatory framework for Islamic finance will have to have sufficient built-in flexibility and dynamism to allow it to stay ahead of the innovation curve, in order to minimize the risk of regulatory arbitrage. An appropriately designed regulatory framework, which is comprehensive in the sense that it also unifies alternative systems and is administered globally, requires a universal mandate to enforce its rules and standards everywhere. Such a mandate requires all governments in countries where Islamic finance is in operation to extend it to the unified global regulatory agency for the development of oversight standards of Islamic financial institutions, transactions, and instruments. Given the design and implementation of such a framework, even governments of non-Islamic countries where Islamic finance operates should have no difficulty with such a mandate because they, too, are primarily concerned with the safety and security of all financial institutions operating within their borders.

No less an ardent supporter of free markets than Lionel Robbins once remarked: "the pursuit of self-interest, unrestrained by suitable institutions, carries no guarantee of anything but chaos" (Robbins, 1952). A regulatory framework is the most important of "suitable institutions." While important in the conventional system, it is crucial for an Islamic financial system at this nascent stage of its development, and given the present sensitivities, because of the heavy costs of materialization of reputational and systemic risks of the failure of even one Islamic financial institution or instrument. Consequently, the most important lesson of the recent crisis for Islamic finance is an urgent need for the design, development, and implementation of a comprehensive, unified, uniform, global, and dynamic regulatory–prudential–supervisory framework. Such a framework of standards needs a unified administrative agency to uniformly and globally enforce the rules of the framework across jurisdictional boundaries. This requires the agency to have a legislatively-based mandate to enforce implementation of its standards and its oversight rules. Clearly this is a most serious challenge, but one that must be met because, at the present stage of its development, Islamic finance is embedded in an institutional framework that was designed to support a conventional financial system and in which innovations replicate instruments designed for a conventional system through "reverse engineering." In such a system, there is no assurance that financial bubbles and their boom and bust cycles can be avoided. Because materialization of such events has significant reputational risk for Islamic finance, to a degree that may abort its further development, the design and implementation of an appropriate regulatory framework, as described above, is urgently needed.

4.5 Summary

Over the past few decades, a consensus has emerged that the rapid expansion of credit and debt (leveraging) is detrimental to financial stability. In fact, rapid credit creation is a necessary, but insufficient, condition for instability. Financial stability is further threatened by wholesale financial deregulation. The absence of thoughtful financial supervision, regulation, and enforcement is a threat to any financial system, both conventional and Islamic.

In conventional banking, due to fractional reserve banking, financial intermediaries are given the power to create (and destroy) credit (therefore, money) out of thin air. In this way, booms and contractions are magnified. Balance sheet adjustment and leverage reinforces this power substantially, to the point of making credit creation out of nothing appear beneficial for stimulating economic activity. Conventional banking is a debt-cum-interest based system. It is vulnerable to instability, because credit expansion has no direct link to a real capital base and may become over-leveraged relative to capital. Commercial banks are very sensitive to changes in anticipated risks and asset prices, and they therefore manage their balance sheets continuously and actively. Their sensitivity to changes in the price of their assets is particularly acute when their net worth reacts to changes in asset prices through "marked-to-market" accounting.

Whereas notable American economists such as Frank Knight and Henry Simons saw the fractional reserve banking system and its power of credit creation as a source of financial instability, Keynes saw a deeper villain in the mix. Keynes saw interest as being so detrimental to the economy as to call for steps to be taken to ban it. A careful reading of the *Treatise on Money*, as well as the *General Theory*, makes clear that Keynes did not believe that there is either a theoretical explanation or an economic justification for the existence of an *ex ante* fixed (or even variable) interest rate, payment of which (along with the principal) was guaranteed by a debt contract.

In Islamic banking, differentiated by its 100 percent reserve banking, there is no credit creation out of thin air. Deposits have to be re-invested directly by the bank in trade and production activities and create new flows of goods and services. New money flows arise from the proceeds of sales of goods and services. Money is not issued by the stroke of a pen, independently of the production of goods and services. Investment is equal to savings, and aggregate supply of goods and services is always equal to aggregate demand. Tangible real assets that are owned directly by the institution cover the liabilities of the financial institution. Financial assets do not cover them. Risks for Islamic financial institutions are mitigated, as they relate essentially to returns from investment operations and not to the capital of these institutions. The stability of Islamic banking and finance is based and contingent on 100 percent reserve banking. Still, supervision and regulation are critical for a smooth functioning of the Islamic financial system. The properly designed regulatory oversight for Islamic finance will have to be uniform in its application to all Islamic financial institutions, transactions, and instruments everywhere globally across all jurisdictions. The reason being that the systemic risk of a failure of one financial institution or instrument is far greater for Islamic finance than for its conventional counterpart because of the potentially magnified reputational damage for the entire system, particularly at this juncture of the evolution of Islamic finance.

Endnotes

1 Mirakhor (2003a); Iqbal and Mirakhor (2007).
2 For details of the conventional view of the crisis and its causes, see various documents of the International Monetary Fund (IMF) 2006–07, including *World Economic Outlook*, *Global Financial Stability Report*, and *Finance and Development*; and various publications (including speeches by governors and chairmen) of the Federal Reserve System, the Bank for International Settlements, and the European Central Bank.
3 See various working papers and policy briefs of the Levy Economics Institute of Bard College, available online.

CHAPTER 5

Empirical Trends in Conventional and Islamic Financial Globalization

In previous chapters, we have argued that a major embodiment of global ization is the enhanced flow of capital across borders. In this chapter, we argue that the conventional debt-based financial system has characteristics that make it susceptible to bubbles and is theoretically unstable. This instability has, as in the case of the 2007 crisis, spread rapidly across national borders. Our reasoning behind the financial crisis of 2007 would indicate that, in the future, more reliance may be placed on equity, compared to debt, in the conventional financial system. This should encourage a convergence between Islamic and conventional finance.

We now turn to market capitalizations and capital flows to see whether actual market developments afford any insights as to the future course of Islamic and conventional finance.

5.1 Trends in Conventional Financial Globalization

Between 1991 and 2000, gross capital flows (the sum of the absolute value of capital inflows and outflows) among industrialized countries expanded by 300 percent, the bulk of which was due to the rise in foreign direct investment and portfolio equity flows—both rising by 600 percent—while bond flows over the same period increased by 130 percent (Evans and Hnatkovska, 2005). Over the same period, both stocks and flows of capital movements increased substantially, especially in relation to the volume of domestic GDP and the size of financing markets. More recent data (Table 5.1 and Figures 5.1, 5.5, and 5.8) show that, after the market turbulence in 2000–02, these trends resumed, with FDI and portfolio equity flows assuming a larger share of the total flow. The largest increase in FDI in 2006 was in the emerging European markets and the Middle East.

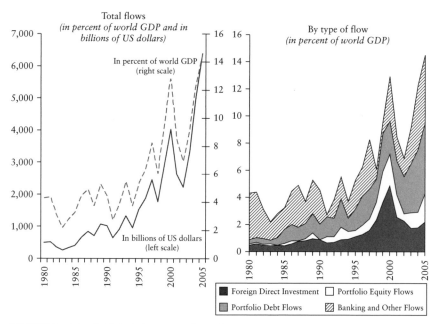

FIGURE 5.1 Total Global Cross-Border Inflows, 1980–2005
Source: IMF (2007a).

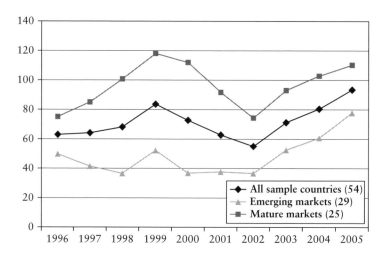

FIGURE 5.2 Equity Market Capitalization, 1996–2005 (percent of GDP)
Source: IMF (2007a).

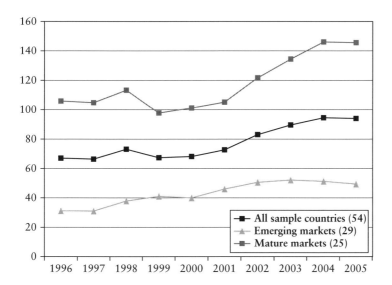

FIGURE 5.3 Bond Market Capitalization, 1996–2005 (percent of GDP)
Source: IMF (2007a).

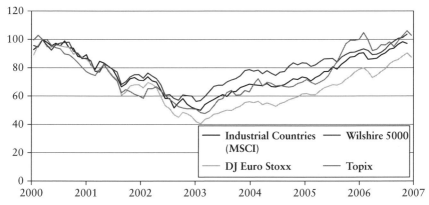

FIGURE 5.4 Equity Markets, 2000–06
Source: IMF (2007b).

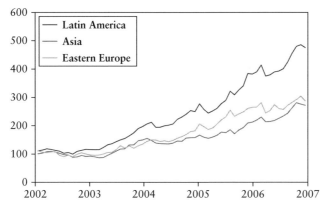

FIGURE 5.5   Portfolio Equity and FDI Emerging Equity Markets, 2002–07
Source: IMF (2007b).

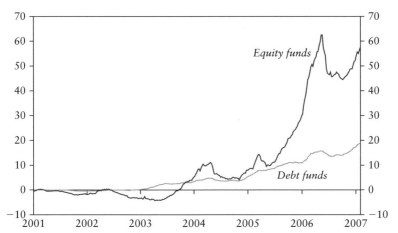

FIGURE 5.6   Cumulative Net Flows to Emerging Market Funds, 2001–07
(US$ billion)
Source: IMF (2007a).

TABLE 5.1 Emerging Market and Developing Countries: Net Capital Flows[1]

	1996–98	1999	2000	2001	2002	2003	2004	2005	2006
Total									
Private capital flows, net[2]	159.3	74.6	56.7	70.2	88.3	173.3	238.6	257.2	255.8
Private direct investment, net	142.3	177.4	168.6	182.8	152.2	165.3	190	266.3	266.9
Private portfolio flows, net	60	60.1	11.4	−80.5	−90.9	−12.1	25	29.4	−76.3
Other private capital flows, net	−43	−162.9	−123.4	−32.1	26.9	20.1	23.5	−38.5	65.2
Official flows, net[3]	20.2	22.4	−34.2	6.6	2.3	−44.5	−57.8	−122.6	−143.8
Change in reserves[4]	−72.6	−98.2	−131.2	−120.6	−198.9	−358.9	−508.2	−590.1	−738.4
Memorandum									
Current account[5]	−72.1	34.4	123.5	86.8	132.3	229.4	299.7	511.6	638.5
Africa									
Private capital flows, net[2]	6.5	8	−4.2	2.2	0.9	2.7	12.3	18.3	20.2
Private direct investment, net	5.8	8.6	7.6	23.1	13.5	15.4	16.8	27	19.1
Private portfolio flows, net	5	9.1	−1.8	−7.9	−1.6	−0.5	5.4	4.1	18.5
Other private capital flows, net	−4.3	−8.7	−10	−13	−11	−12.2	−9.8	−12.8	−17.4
Official flows, net[3]	5	4.1	7.7	6.5	8.6	6.4	4.3	−1.8	−3.8
Change in reserves[4]	−4.2	−0.4	−12.8	−9.7	−5.5	−11.4	−32.7	−42.3	−48.4
Central and Eastern Europe									
Private capital flows, net[2]	27.4	36.3	38.7	10.9	54	52.5	74.7	117.5	121.1
Private direct investment, net	14.9	22.7	24.1	24	24.1	16.2	34.5	50.1	65.8
Private portfolio flows net	1.7	5.3	3.1	0.4	1.7	6.5	26.9	20.9	8.1
Other private capital flows, net	10.8	8.3	11.6	−13.4	28.3	29.9	13.3	46.4	47.1
Official flows, net[3]	−0.5	−2.4	1.6	6	−7.5	−5	−6.6	−8.3	−4.9
Change in reserves[4]	−8.8	−12.1	−6	−3	−18.5	−11.5	−13.6	−48.2	−21.2
Commonwealth of									
Independent States[4]									

(Continued)

TABLE 5.1 (*Continued*)

	1996–98	1999	2000	2001	2002	2003	2004	2005	2006
Private capital flows, net[2]	−5.3	−13.5	−27.6	7.2	15.8	17.9	7.7	37.6	65.7
Private direct investment, net	5.5	4.7	2.3	4.9	5.2	5.4	12.9	14.4	33.1
Private portfolio flows, net	2.2	−0.9	−10	−1.2	0.4	−0.5	8.1	−3.1	13.9
Other private capital flows, net	−13	−17.3	−19.9	3.5	10.2	13	−13.4	26.3	18.8
Official flows, net[3]	−1	−1.8	−5.8	−4.9	−10.4	−8.9	−7.3	−22.1	−32.6
Change in reserves[4]	5.1	−6.4	−20.3	−14.5	−15.1	−21.8	−53.8	−75.6	−126.9
Emerging Asia[7]									
Private capital flows, net[2]	36.9	−1.9	4.5	23.5	25.4	69.2	142.5	69.7	53.9
Private direct investment, net	56	70.9	59.8	52	52.6	73.1	68	105.8	102.4
Private portfolio flows, net	16	54.1	19.6	−50.2	−60.1	7.8	11.2	−8.1	−99.4
Other private capital flows, net	−35.1	−12.7	−74.8	21.6	32.8	−11.6	63.4	−27.9	50.9
Official flows, net[3]	5.9	8.5	−10.9	−12	4.1	−16.6	−7	−2.8	−9.8
Change in reserves[4]	−45.1	−84.8	−59.1	−85.4	−154.3	−234.3	−339	−284.1	−365.6
Middle East[8]									
Private capital flows, net[2]	11.8	−3.8	−10	−5.5	−19.4	4.7	−12	−19.9	−15.5
Private direct investment, net	7	4.4	4.9	12.3	9.7	17.8	8.8	17.6	12
Private portfolio flows, net	0.5	−8.6	−1.2	−13.5	−17.4	−14.9	−14	−14.9	−5
Other private capital flows, net	4.3	0.4	−13.7	−4.3	−11.6	1.8	−6.8	−22.5	−22.5
Official flows, net	5.2	8	−20.5	−14.2	−9.8	−24.6	−32.5	−57.1	−75
Change in reserves[4]	−8.1	−2	−31.2	−11.6	−3.1	−33.7	−45.7	−106.6	−129.7
Western Hemisphere									
Private capital flows, net[2]	82	48.5	55.2	31.9	11.5	26.2	13.3	33.9	10.4
Private direct investment, net	53.1	66.1	70	66.5	47.2	37.5	49.1	51.4	34.5

Private portfolio flows, net	34.6	1	1.7	−8.1	−13.9	−10.5	−12.5	30.5	12.4
Other private capital flows, net	−5.7	−18.6	−16.5	−26.5	−21.8	−0.9	−23.3	−48	−11.6
Official flows, net[3]	5.6	6.2	−6.4	25.2	17.4	4.3	−8.7	−30.4	−17.7
Change in reserves[4]	−11.4	7.4	−1.8	3.5	−2.4	−36.2	−23.4	−33.4	−46.5
Memorandum									
Fuel exporting countries									
Private capital flows, net[2]	−5.4	−27.2	−57	−12.7	−11.2	12.7	−14.9	−6.8	−2.6
Other countries									
Private capital flows net[2]	164.8	101.8	113.6	82.9	99.5	160.6	253.4	264	258.4

Source: IMF 2007(b).

[1] Net capital flows comprise net direct investment, net portfolio investment, and other long- and short-term net investment flows, including official and private borrowing. In this table, Hong Kong SAR, Israel, Korea, Singapore, and Taiwan Province of China are included.

[2] Because of data limitations, flows listed under "private capital flows, net" may include some official flows.

[3] Excludes grants and includes overseas investments of official investment agencies.

[4] A minus sign indicates an increase.

[5] The sum of the current account balance, net private capital flows, net official flows, and the change in reserves equals, with the opposite sign, the sum of the capital account and errors and omissions. For regional current account balances, see Table 25 of the Statistical Appendix.

[6] Historical data have been revised, reflecting cumulative data revisions for Russia and the resolution of a number of data interpretation issues.

[7] Consists of developing Asia and the newly industrialized Asian economies.

[8] Includes Israel.

Empirical evidence suggests that the composition of capital flows matters a great deal. Equity flows (portfolio equity flows + FDI + venture capital) promote better risk sharing, reduce volatility, and strengthen stability (Bekaert, 2000; Bekaert and Lundblad, 2006; Kose et. al., 2006; Albuquerque, 2003; Alfaro et. al., 2005). There is a substantial body of evidence that these flows, especially FDI, are positively associated with economic growth (Levchenko and Mauro, 2006). FDI is considered an important channel for transfer of technology and organizational knowledge (Borensztein et. al., 1998; Ayyagari and Kosova, 2006). Over the past few decades, stock markets too have shown increasing vitality and rapid growth. The development of stock markets increases the rate of saving and leads to growth in investment, while enhancing its quality. Stock markets diversify the investor base while distributing risks across investors, which, in turn, increases the resilience of the economy to shocks (IMF, 2007a, 2007b). As mentioned earlier, the composition of capital flows has a significant influence, with FDI and equity flows exerting a great stabilizing influence on the economy's vulnerability to shocks and financial crises. It has been demonstrated that greater reliance on debt flows exposes a country to a higher probability of sudden stops of international capital flows and to financial crises (Frankel and Rose, 1996). A growing body of research has demonstrated the positive impact of stock market development on economic growth (Henry, 2000a; Stulz, 2005).

There is mounting evidence in the last decade that many developing countries have implemented reforms that promote legal and institutional development. They have improved governance, transparency, and accountability, and have adopted regulatory and supervisory standards of best international practice in accounting and data reporting. They have also stabilized their economy with sound macro policies and debt management. Some have even borrowed or rented additional credibility by cross-listing their domestic corporate shares in more advanced markets (Doidge et. al., 2004; Edison and Warnock, 2006; Karolyi, 2004). As a result, they have received increased capital inflows, with FDI and portfolio equity flows constituting a major portion of these flows (IMF, 2007a; Dehesa et. al., 2007; also see Table 5.1 and Figures 5.1, 5.7, and 5.8).

In addition to the evidence that many developing countries have improved their legal institutions and governance, there is some indication that the three paradoxes mentioned earlier—demonstrating the divergence between theory and empirics of financial globalization—are beginning to lose strength. Lucas (2000) points out that the 21st century will witness a reversal of the widening inequality among nations. His assertion is based on an analysis of a Solow-type neoclassical model with global capital mobility, assuming that all countries have access to the same technology and institutions

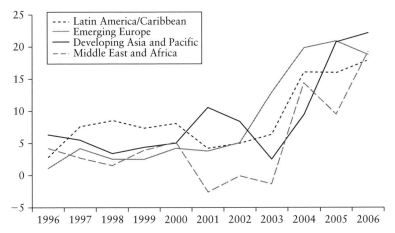

FIGURE 5.7   Emerging Markets: FDI Outflows by Region, 1996–2006 (US$ billion)
Source: IMF (2007b).

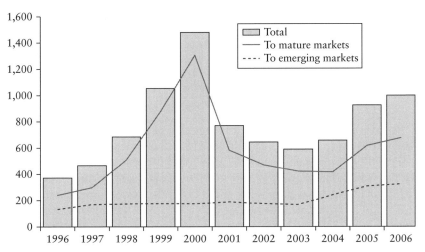

FIGURE 5.8   Global FDI Inflows, 1996–2006 (US$ billion)
Source: IMF (2007b).

as well as to market-friendly economic policies. In this case, the "Lucas paradox"—that capital did not move from rich countries to poor ones—will no longer hold, and a "catch-up" process will rapidly narrow the income gap among countries. Lucas contends that more capital will move to developing countries, which is reasonable as they adopt policies and institutional infrastructure that will reduce their risk premium on investment.

Developing countries' adoption of the set of policies and institutions—sound macroeconomic policy, best-practice international standards of transparency, accountability, and good governance, as well as legal institutions that protect investors, creditors, and property rights, and enforce contracts—will reduce the risk premium (Ju and Wei, 2006). It is not unrealistic that, as their financial sectors develop and international financial integration proceeds, assets of identical risk will command the same expected return, irrespective of spatial or domicile differences. Moreover, data from 2000 show the increasing flow of capital to developing countries (Table 5.1 and Figure 5.7). In recent years, equity flows to emerging markets have been stronger than bond flows, and equity market capitalization stronger than bond market capitalization (Tables 5.2 to 5.5, Figures 5.6 to 5.11). Micro data are also beginning to reveal a perceptible shift of household assets portfolio allocation toward greater risk-sharing instruments. The data on the composition of households' financial assets in Europe, the United States, and Japan between 1995 and 2003 (Table 5.6) demonstrate that in the Euro area, the European Union, and the US, households allocated a larger portion of their portfolio to risk-sharing instruments. While comparable figures are not available in other areas, similar behavior could be expected as policy, institutional, legal, and financial development progress in developing countries. Considering the Lucas paradox, Alfaro et. al. (2005) concluded that "institutional quality is the leading causal variable" in explaining the paradox based on their empirical study.

Recent empirical evidence also suggests that, since 2001, there has been a systematic decline in home bias, at least in US equity investments (IMF, 2007a; Ammer et. al., 2006; Aurelio, 2006; Kho et. al., 2006). There has also been some empirical evidence that social capital—especially trust, institutional and legal developments, as well as greater transparency and availability of information—may, at least tentatively, explain the equity premium puzzle (O'Hara, 2004; Lorenz, 1999; Lopez-de-Silanes et. al., 1997; Helliwell and Putnam, 1995; Berg et. al., 1995; Ashraf et. al., 2005; Dasgupta and Serageldin, 1999). The last decade has witnessed a growing body of empirical research demonstrating that finance, particularly risk-sharing instruments such as equity, is trust-intensive; therefore, in societies where the level of trust was high, financial sectors were deeper and more developed. In particular, this literature indicates that there is a high correlation

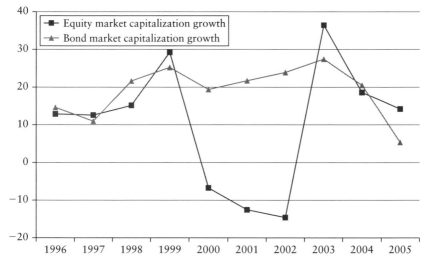

FIGURE 5.9   Equity and Bond Market Capitalization Growth: All Sample
Countries, 1996–2005 (percent)
Source: IMF (2007a).

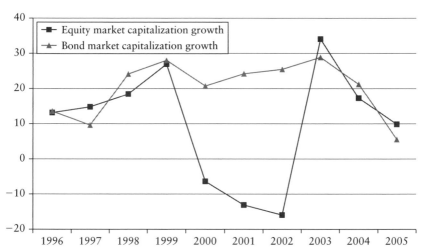

FIGURE 5.10   Equity and Bond Market Capitalization Growth: Mature Markets,
1996–2005 (percent)
Source: IMF (2007a).

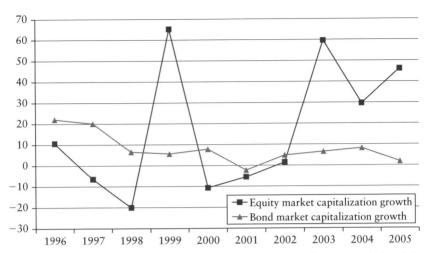

FIGURE 5.11   Equity and Bond Market Capitalizaton Growth: Empirical Trends in Conventional and Islamic Financial Globalization, 1996–2005 (percent)
Source: IMF (2007a).

TABLE 5.2   Equity Market Indices, 2002–06

	End of period Billions of US dollars				
	2002	2003	2004	2005	2006
World	792.2	1,036.3	1,169.3	1,257.8	1,483.6
Emerging Markets	292.1	442.8	542.2	706.5	912.7
Latin America	658.9	1,100.9	1,483.6	2,150.0	2,995.7
Asia	140.4	206.4	231.6	286.2	371.5
Europe, Middle East and Africa	108.4	163.9	222.7	300.3	361.1
	Period of Change				
World	−21.1	30.8	12.8	7.6	18.0
Emerging Markets	−8.0	51.6	22.4	30.3	29.2
Latin America	−24.8	67.1	34.8	44.9	39.3
Asia	−6.2	47.1	12.2	23.5	29.8
Europe, Middle East and Africa	4.7	51.2	35.8	34.9	21.3

Source: IMF (2007a).

TABLE 5.3 Equity and Bond Market Capitalization in Nominal Dollars, 1996–2005 (percent growth)

	1996	1997	1998	1999	2000	2001	2002	2003	2004	2005
Equity market capitalization growth										
All sample countries	12.9	12.6	15.1	29.2	−6.7	−12.5	−14.6	36.4	18.6	14.2
Emerging markets	10.7	−6.5	−20.1	65.2	−10.7	−5.5	1.5	59.7	29.7	46.1
Mature markets	13.1	14.8	18.4	26.9	−6.4	−13.1	−16.0	34.0	17.2	9.8
Bond market capitalization growth										
All sample countries	14.6	11.0	21.6	25.2	19.4	21.7	23.9	27.4	20.5	5.4
Emerging markets	22.1	20.0	6.6	5.7	7.8	−2.2	4.8	6.6	8.2	1.9
Mature markets	13.5	9.6	24.1	28.0	20.7	24.2	25.5	28.9	21.2	5.6

Source: IMF (2007a).

TABLE 5.4 Equity and Bond Market Capitalization, 1996–2005 (percent growth)

	1996	1997	1998	1999	2000	2001	2002	2003	2004	2005
Equity market capitalization										
All sample countries (54)	63.0	64.1	68.2	83.6	72.7	62.8	55.0	71.2	80.4	93.4
Emerging markets (29)	49.8	41.5	36.6	52.2	36.9	37.7	36.6	52.4	60.8	77.8
Mature markets (25)	75.1	85.0	100.7	118.1	112.0	91.7	74.3	93.0	102.9	110.3
Bond market capitalization[1]										
All sample countries (54)	67.1	66.4	73.1	67.4	68.2	72.7	83.1	89.6	94.5	94.0
Emerging markets (29)	31.2	31.1	37.9	41.0	40.0	46.0	50.6	52.1	51.2	49.3
Mature markets (25)	105.9	104.7	113.3	97.8	101.1	105.1	121.7	134.4	146.0	145.5

Sources: Datastream; S&PIFC Emerging Market Database; and World Federation of Exchanges.
[1] Domestic and international bonds.

TABLE 5.5 Equity and Bond Market Capitalization as percent of GDP, 1997–2005 (percent growth)

	1997	1998	1999	2000	2001	2002	2003	2004	2005
Equity market capitalization growth									
All sample countries (54)	1.8	6.4	22.6	-13.0	-13.6	-12.4	29.4	13.0	16.1
Emerging markets (29)	-16.7	-11.8	42.7	-29.3	2.2	-2.8	43.1	16.0	28.0
Mature markets (25)	13.2	18.5	17.2	-5.1	-18.1	-18.9	25.1	10.6	7.2
Bond market capitalization growth									
All sample countries (54)	-1.0	10.1	-7.8	1.2	6.6	14.3	7.8	5.5	-0.5
Emerging markets (29)	-0.4	21.9	8.2	-2.5	15.0	9.9	3.0	-1.7	-3.7
Mature markets (25)	-1.1	8.2	-13.7	3.4	4.0	15.8	10.4	8.7	-0.3

Source: IMF (2007a).

TABLE 5.6 Household Portfolio Allocation to Equity—International Comparisons, 1995 and 2003

	Share and other equity	of which: mutual funds shares	Share and other equity	of which: mutual funds shares
	1995		2003	
Portugal	25	7	27	9
Belgium	29	9	29	16
Denmark	23	7	17	9
Germany	19	7	22	12
Spain	31	11	39	13
France	35	12	36	10
Italy	20	4	35	17
The Netherlands	20	5	11	4
Austria	6	4	16	10
Finland	5	1	41	5
Sweden	30	7	40	12
United Kingdom	20	4	16	5
Euro area (9)	24	8	29	11
European Union (12)	23	7	26	9
United States	46	5	48	10
Japan	14	2	11	2

Source: Cardoso and da Cunha (2005).

between trust and development of the financial sector (Calderon et. al., 2002; Guiso et. al., 2004). Importantly, if the level of trust is high, more reliance is placed on risky assets, such as equity. People invest a larger portion of their wealth in stocks, use more checks, and have access to greater amounts of credit than in low-trust societies. Over the last decade, a number of researchers have demonstrated the impact of trust on economic performance (Knack and Keefer, 1997; Glaeser, 2000; Zak and Knack, 2001; Zak, 2003; Beugelsdijk et. al., 2004). In 1974, Arrow had suggested that trust "is an important lubricant of a social system. It is extremely efficient; it saves a lot of trouble to have a fair degree of reliance on other people's word" (Arrow, 1974). Fukuyama (1996) asserts that the general level of trust—an important component of social capital (Coleman, 1988, 1990; Glaeser et. al., 1999; Alesina and La Ferrara, 2002)—was a strong explanatory factor in the economic performance of industrial countries; the high level of trust was reinforced in these societies by strong institutions.

A recent empirical paper (Guiso et. al., 2005) demonstrates low trust as a crucial factor in explaining the low level of stock market participation—that is, the equity premium puzzle. Based on the analysis of cross-country data, the paper suggests that where the level of trust is relatively high, investment in equity in general, and in the stock market in particular, is relatively high as well. Moreover, the paper asserts that in low-trust countries, equity participation depends on observance of the rule of law and the existence of legal institutions that protect property, creditor, and investor rights, and those that enforce contracts. It suggests that in low-performing economies not only is the level of trust low, but property and investor rights are poorly protected, and legal contract enforcement is weak. The policy implication for these economies is to strengthen legal institutions, improve transparency, accountability, and governance—in both the private and public sectors—and to provide the public with a greater amount of information on risk sharing in general, and equity markets in particular. The growing body of empirical evidence over the last two decades has focused on the existence (or the lack) of strong institutions as a powerful factor explaining cross-country differences in economic performance. Recent research has underlined that the same legal and institutional factors are responsible for financial sector development and its ability to integrate with global finance, which would strengthen economic performance.

In sum, the general indication is that there is globally a move in favor of equity participation in comparison to debt. This market development will be further reinforced by measures that increase the level of trust and by better and more transparent institutions.

5.2 Growth in Islamic Finance

Islamic finance has experienced rapid growth,[1] especially over the last decade, despite its analytic underpinnings, in modern economic and financial terms, having been explained only a little over two decades ago (Khan, 1987). There is no accurate estimate of the size of the market at present, but it is certain that it is nowhere near its potential. Just as is the case with financial globalization, Islamic finance has realized only an insignificant fraction of its risk-sharing capacity; of the 15 basic modes of available transactions, only a few have been used widely and even then only a few instruments have been innovated based on these transaction modes (Iqbal and Mirakhor, 2002).

In 2007, *The Banker* compiled a list of the 500 top Islamic institutions, including Islamic banks, Islamic windows, Islamic investment banks and insurance companies.[2] According to this report, the global total of *Shari'ah*-compliant assets grew at an impressive rate of 29.7 percent in 2007

TABLE 5.7   Islamic Finance Assets, 2006–07 (US$ million)

Region	2007	2006	% Change
GCC	178,129.55	127,826.55	39.4%
Non–GCC MENA	176,822.17	136,157.64	29.9%
MENA total	354,951.72	263,984.19	34.5%
Sub-Saharan	4,707.98	3,039.32	54.9%
Asia	119,346.46	98,709.56	20.9%
Australia/Europe/America	21,475.72	20,300.24	5.8%
Global total	500,481.88	386,033.33	29.6%

Source: The Banker (2007).

compared to the previous year, to reach US$500.4 billion. Although this size is relatively small compared to the US$74,232.2 billion in total assets managed by the top 1,000 conventional banks worldwide, the rapid growth in Islamic institutions is almost double the growth rate of 16.3 percent for conventional banks.

Globally, the MENA (Middle East and North Africa) region accounts for the largest share (70.9 percent) of total *Shari'ah*-compliant assets, followed by Asia with a market share of 22.7 percent. Within MENA, market share is split almost evenly between the GCC (Gulf Cooperation Council, consisting of Bahrain, Kuwait, Oman, Qatar, Saudi Arabia, and the United Arab Emirates) states with 35.6 percent and the non-GCC MENA states with 35.3 percent. Table 5.7 shows the size and growth rate of assets under management by the top 500 Islamic financial institutions as compiled by *The Banker* (2007). An interesting observation is that the top 15 countries by the size of Islamic assets include a non-Muslim country—the United Kingdom—at tenth place, with *Shari'ah*-compliant assets of US$10.4 billion, mainly due to successful operations by HSBC Amanah, with total assets of US$9.7 billion.

Islamic banking—consisting of commercial and investment banking—is one of the oldest sectors of Islamic finance. Although Islamic banking has firm roots in the Middle East, it also has a presence in South and East Asia. Bahrain in the Middle East and Malaysia in East Asia are trying to establish themselves as financial centers for Islamic finance and thus offer special incentives for Islamic banks. Islamic banking assets in Bahrain grew from US$1.3 billion to US$8.0 billion at the compounded annual growth rate (CAGR) of 28.99 percent from 1998 to 2005. Similarly, Islamic banking assets in Malaysia grew from US$19.4 billion to US$31.5 billion at a CAGR of 17.48 percent from 2002 to 2005.[3]

TABLE 5.8 Islamic Banking Market Share by Country, 2006 (percent)

Saudi Arabia	19.54
Bahrain	18.97
Malaysia	16.30
Kuwait	14.64
UAE	14.39
Qatar	3.79
Egypt	2.83
Iran	2.82
Switzerland	1.86
Jordan	1.73
Bangladesh	1.24
Indonesia	1.11
Pakistan	0.35
United Kingdom	0.25
Palestine	0.09
Yemen	0.06
Rest	0.03

Source: ISI Analytics (2007). This list excludes Sudan, where the total banking system conforms to *Shari'ah*.

Table 5.8 shows the percentage market share of total Islamic banking assets of various countries as of 2006.

Compared to Islamic banking, *Shari'ah*-compliant capital markets are relatively new. During the early stages of development, capital market activities were limited to syndicated financing and Islamic funds. One main reason was the absence of a *Shari'ah*-approved structure that was tradable in the market. Therefore, the initial focus of capital market activities was on fund management, especially during the boom in the world equities markets. Islamic funds were introduced in the late 1980s and early 1990s. These funds were a portfolio of different asset classes, such as funds specializing in commodities, equities, and Islamic instruments such as leases (*ijarah*). For equities, special screening filters were defined to satisfy the requirements of *Shari'ah*. For example, shares of those companies that dealt with interest-based income, or carried extensive debt in their capital structure, or engaged in activities that were not "socially responsible"—such as alcohol production or gambling—were excluded from the fund.

Islamic funds have enjoyed considerable success, but not all investors were willing to invest in the risky equities asset class. Typical investors in Islamic banks were looking for less-risky securities where the principal is protected and the security offered a steady stream of cash flow. In short, investors were looking for a security that is *Shari'ah*-compliant but has the risk/return characteristics of a conventional fixed-income security—that is, a bond. Meanwhile, conventional finance witnessed an explosion of securitization of assets, ranging from accounts receivables to mortgages. Considering that Islamic finance promotes securities linked to an asset, and considering the success with securitization in conventional finance, it was inevitable that a security in the form of an Islamic bond—called *sukuk*—was designed, which became an immediate success. Within a short period of time, several different structures of *sukuk* had been introduced into the market.

Figure 5.12 shows the rapid growth of the market from approximately US$1 billion in 2002 to US$47 billion in 2007. The volume of new issuances almost doubled from 2006 to 2007, but did not grow significantly in 2007. Only 207 *sukuk* were issued globally in 2007, compared to 199 in 2006 and 89 in 2005.[4] Some observers attribute this slow growth in issuance to turmoil in the financial markets due to the sub-prime crisis. However, while the number of issues did not increase significantly, the average issuance size of *sukuk did* increase. Of course, *sukuk* issuance was also hit by the global recession as a result of the financial crisis in 2008.

A diverse range of structures was issued during 2007 and included structures based on *Bai' Bithaman Ajil* (BBA), *istisna'*, *mudharabah*, *ijarah*, *musharakah*, and *wakala* contracts. Table 5.9 lists *sukuk* issuances by various countries and sectors. It is interesting to note that whereas in conventional markets, sovereign bond issuance dominates the market, in the case of the *sukuk* market, 79.2 percent of issuances were by the corporate sector, with Malaysian corporations being the most active. This not only shows that sovereign entities have yet to exploit this market, but also is indicative of the fact that when it comes to structuring a *sukuk*, sovereign entities have

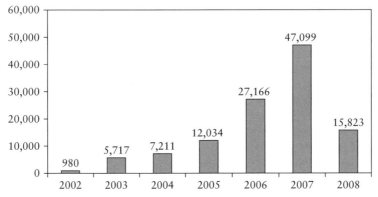

FIGURE 5.12   Global *Sukuk* Issuance, 2002–08 (US$ million)
Source: IFIS.

fewer options compared to corporations, which have more tangible assets to securitize.

The global slowdown and financial crisis in leading industrial economies also impacted on the *sukuk* market, and a drastic downturn in issuance of *sukuk* was observed in 2008 (see Table 5.10). It is clear that total issuance dropped from US$47 billion in 2007 to US$16 billion in 2008. Although the global recession was the primary reason, the *sukuk* market also experienced a negative impact as a result of the statement issued by AAOIFI which raised questions about certain market practices and *sukuk* structures.

Table 5.10 lists the top 10 investment banks that acted as lead managers for the issuance of *sukuk* in 2008. It is clear that the list is dominated by the leading conventional investment banks. Of the top 10, only four banks— Malaysian-based CIMB Islamic, Aseambankers Malaysia, Bank Negara, and Dubai Islamic Bank—are local as well as Islamic; the rest are Western banks. There are several reasons conventional banks play such a leading role. First, conventional banks are more experienced and knowledgeable about financial engineering and structuring transactions. Second, conventional banks have more sophisticated sales channels to market the issues. There is a growing trend of conventional investors investing in *sukuk*, as they see better value. Third, conventional banks are working more aggressively to capture this growing field, especially in GCC countries.

Growth in the *sukuk* market led to the development of the *Sukuk* Index by Dow Jones Indexes and Citigroup Corporation in 2006. An index plays a critical role in portfolio management as it serves as a proxy for the mar-

TABLE 5.9 *Sukuk* Issuance by Country and Sector, 2007

Country	Sovereign	Corporate	Quasi-Sovereign	Total
Bahrain	617	400		1,017
Brunei Darussalam	222			222
Cayman Islands		100		100
Indonesia	81	113		193
Kuwait		993		993
Malaysia	3,777	22,752		26,529
Pakistan	339	725		1,065
Qatar		450		450
Saudi Arabia		4,350	1,333	5,683
Sudan		130		130
United Arab Emirates	3,425	7,292		10,717
Total	8,461	37,306	1,333	47,100
Percentage	18.0%	79.2%	2.8%	

Source: IFIS.

TABLE 5.10 *Sukuk* Issuance, 2008

By Country/Region	Amount in (US$ million)	Percent of Regional Market	Percent of Global Market
United Arab Emirates	5,995.91	66	38
Saudi Arabia	1,873.74	21	12
Bahrain	890.58	10	6
Qatar	300.90	3	2
Total GCC Issuance, 2008	9,061.13	100	57
Malaysia	5,870.01	90	37
Indonesia	678.1	10	4
Brunei Darussalam	31	0	0
Total SEA Issuance, 2008	6,548.11	100	41
Pakistan	214.48	-	1
Total Sukuk Issuance, 2008	15,823.72		

Source: IFIS.

TABLE 5.11 Islamic Bonds Bookrunners/Lead Managers League Table, 2007

Ranking	Bookrunner/Lead Manager	Amount (US$ million)	Issues
1	CIMB Islamic	1,716.87	30
2	HSBC Amanah	1,385.42	21
3	JP Morgan	1,077.00	2
4	Calyon	1,016.60	2
5	Aseambankers Malaysia	844.92	25
6	Dubai Islamic Bank	814.75	5
7	Citigroup	741.51	12
8	Barclays Capital	645.38	3
9	Bank Negara Malaysia	626.95	1
10	Standard Chartered Bank	497.36	9

Source: IFIS.

ket and is used as a benchmark by portfolio managers to measure their performance. The Dow Jones Citigroup *Sukuk* Index includes *sukuk* with a minimum issue size of US$250 million, minimum maturity of one year, and a minimum rating of BBB–/Baa3 by the leading rating agencies.

In the Islamic funds domain, property funds have recently gained popularity and interest among investors in the Middle East and Europe. In addition, there are Islamic real estate investment trusts (REIT) which invest their portfolios in listed real estate securities—subject to *Shari'ah* compliance—that own and operate real estate such as residential, commercial, and

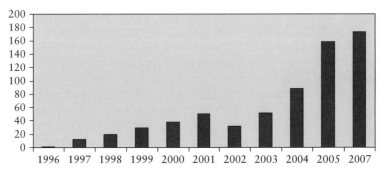

FIGURE 5.13 Growth of Islamic Equity Funds, 1996–2007 (US$ billion)
Source: ISI, Falaika.

retail properties, storage facilities, warehouses, and car parks.[5] Although the number of Islamic funds available on the market has expanded in recent years (see Figure 5.13), most are relatively small in terms of size. For example, approximately 50 percent of the funds have less than US$50 million of assets under management. A significant segment of Islamic funds is concentrated in equity investment (see Figure 5.13), mainly because this is relatively easy to set up and a conventional equity mutual fund can apply the filter and construct such funds. However, there are gaps across other asset classes, including sector-specific funds and fixed-income funds.[6]

In 1998, the FTSE Group launched the first series of Islamic equity indices, the FTSE Global Islamic Index Series (GIIS). The GIIS are a subset of the FTSE All-World Index group, which includes stocks from 29 countries. The FTSE has 15 Islamic indices; classification is based on industry (10 indices) and region (Global, Americas, Europe, Pacific Basin, South Africa). This was followed by the first Dow Jones Islamic Market Index (DJIMI) in 1999, created to track the performance of companies whose activities are consistent with *Shari'ah* principles. More recently, Standard & Poor's has also introduced similar indices. The performance of all these indices is regularly monitored and reported.

Whereas financial engineering in conventional finance was driven by breakthroughs in financial theory, financial engineering in Islamic finance has been driven by the innovative application of *Shari'ah* rules. *Shari'ah* scholars have worked closely with the practitioners to develop products demanded by the market. In its early days, financial engineering was limited to the development of a product for a financial intermediary such as an Islamic bank; however, with the development of capital markets the focus of product development has shifted more toward marketable securities.

A relevant example is the introduction of *sukuk*, which have become an overnight success. There are more than 10 different structures of *sukuk*, and the instrument has been welcomed by both Islamic and conventional market players. Following the success of *sukuk*, there has been more financial engineering activity in customized and structured products.

Despite the above-mentioned obstacles, Islamic financial engineering is taking place in several Western institutions that have extensive market and financial engineering knowledge and experience in order to capture market share. Most such activities are taking place through "wrapping" in the form of structured deposits, funds, or bilateral contracts. While these products are labeled as *Shari'ah* compliant, details of the structures are often not available publicly. Below are some examples of recent applications of financial engineering:

- Deutsche Bank (DB) has offered a structure that enables DB to issue *Shari'ah*-compliant securities linked to a wide range of asset classes, such as commodities, fixed-income, and money market funds with a range of different payoffs, such as capped and leveraged returns. These securities are also transferable at market value, which enhances market liquidity. Through this instrument, investors deposit funds with DB which are invested in *Shari'ah*-compliant securities, such as shares selected from a Dow Jones Islamic benchmark, and both investors and DB exchange promises (*wa'd*) to sell the securities at predetermined levels. The net effect is that, from an economic aspect, the *wa'd* arrangement amounts to an outperformance put or call option, even though such options are not normally considered to be *Shari'ah* compliant.[7]
- Standard Chartered Bank, Malaysia has introduced several hedging instruments that are *Shari'ah* compliant. For example, the Islamic Profit Rate Swap (IPRS) was introduced to assist in the management of profit rate risks. A profit rate swap is a mechanism structured to allow bilateral exchange of profit streams using two parallel and back-to-back Islamic marked-up sale (*murabahah*) transactions. In simple IPRS, a series of *murabahah* sale and purchases are conducted, allowing parties to swap or exchange profit rates from fixed to floating rates, or vice versa. In another version, called Islamic Cross-Currency Swap (ICCS), the same mechanism is applied for the purpose of cross-currency swaps. The pricing of all these Islamic hedging solutions depends on the expected rate of profit, which is agreed upon by the bank and the client. The period of the swap ranges from one to five years.[8]
- Deutsche Bank executed the first Islamic Collar Profit Rate Swap with Dubai Islamic Bank (DIB) in October 2007. The transaction was over

US$500 million in notional size, and is the largest such structure executed in the Islamic markets. The transaction was customized to the needs of DIB, which had specific hedging requirements that could not be achieved through plain-vanilla Islamic profit rate swaps. DB worked with DIB and their *Shari'ah* teams to design an off-balance-sheet profit rate swap with caps and floors to provide the desirable protection for DIB.[9]

An insurance conforming to *Shari'ah* is known as *takaful*, literally meaning "mutual guarantee," and is designed based on solidarity and cooperation among members. Unlike Islamic finance, the *takaful* business did not spread rapidly. The primary reason was a division of opinion among *Shari'ah* scholars with respect to the legitimacy of underwriting an event in the future, which was considered similar to speculation and thus gambling. Such an objection was particularly applicable to underwriting life insurance, which was considered totally unacceptable as it involves gambling and uncertainty, and goes against the Islamic concept of predestination (*qadar*).[10] Due to this internal debate, the *takaful* industry did not take off smoothly; however, over time, some of the internal *Shari'ah* issues have been resolved and a consensus has emerged on the permissibility of including business losses and—to a lesser extent—loss of life.

Even after one convincingly argues that insurance does not amount to gambling, the issue is raised of how to invest premium funds in a manner that is compliant with *Shari'ah*—that is, investments without involving *riba*. Unlike conventional insurance underwriters, *takaful* companies did not have access to liquid money and capital markets to construct efficient portfolios of fixed-income securities with desirable risk/return profiles. Therefore, during the early stages of development of Islamic finance, *takaful* companies had difficulty in placing funds in liquid securities. As the market for *Shari'ah*-compliant products is expanding, this constraint has become a lesser issue.

The first *takaful* entity was established in 1979—the Islamic Insurance Company of Sudan—followed by Malaysia in 1984, before spreading to Saudi Arabia and other Middle East countries. The *takaful* industry has been growing at a rate of 10–20 percent per annum, compared to the global average growth of the conventional insurance industry of 5 percent per annum. A large number of *takaful* companies exist in the Middle East, the Far East, and even in some non-Islamic countries. Re-*takaful* business has also been developed in Malaysia, Bahrain, Saudi Arabia, and the United Arab Emirates.[11]

The *takaful* industry has witnessed high growth in recent years (see Table 5.12). The total gross premiums underwritten by *takaful* companies were

TABLE 5.12   Islamic Insurance (*Takaful*) Market, 2002–06

Year	Size (US$ million)	General *Takaful*	Family *Takaful*
2002	1,396	98%	2%
2003	1,648	98%	2%
2004	1,749	98%	2%
2005	1,980	98%	2%
2006	3,000	98%	2%

Source: ISI Analytics (2007).

worth US$530 million in 2000; this rose close to US$3 billion by the end of 2006.[12] As of 2005, there were 82 companies engaged in *takaful* business. Of these, 77 were dedicated *takaful* companies and five were offering *takaful* products through Islamic windows. There were also eight companies engaged in re-*takaful* business.[13] In terms of market share, as of 2005, South and East Asia held 56 percent of the market, followed by the Middle East with 36 percent, Africa with 7 percent, and Europe, the United States, and others with a 1 percent share. Industry growth is forecast to be maintained at approximately 15 percent until 2015.[14]

Islamic finance is gradually being introduced in countries that are not Muslim. Although Western financial centers and financial intermediaries have always played an important part in executing and innovating Islamic transactions, such activities have been mostly carried out in the private sector and in a discreet fashion. By early 2000, this trend began to change, and several non-Muslim countries began to take an interest in the emerging market. This can be attributed to several factors, such as booming oil revenues leading to the accumulation of investible funds looking for attractive investment opportunities, increased awareness of regulatory issues relating to Islamic financial intermediaries, the desire to tap into alternative funding resources by sovereign and corporate entities, an increasing Muslim population in Western countries interested in *Shari'ah*-compliant financial products, and Western financial institutions seeing profitable opportunities in Islamic finance. These developments have motivated Western countries, most notably the UK, to adopt regulations that afford Islamic finance and Islamic financial products an equal footing with conventional finance. Islamic finance going global is evidenced by the wide distribution of subscribers investing in *sukuk*, as shown in Table 5.13. *Sukuk* issued by institutions based in Malaysia, Saudi Arabia, and the United Arab Emirates are held in significant portions by investors in Asia, Europe, and the United States.

TABLE 5.13 Global Investor Base for *Sukuk* (percent)

	Middle East	Asia	Europe	United States
Malaysia *sukuk*—2002	51.0	30.0	15.0	4.0
State of Qatar *sukuk*—2003	72.0	11.0	14.0	3.0
IDB *sukuk*—2004	32.0	35.0	26.0	7.0
Emirate Airlines *sukuk*—2005	59.6	8.4	32.0	

Source: Ismael (2007).

5.3   Convergence or Divergence?

There are numerous developments and factors that point to a future convergence of the two financial systems. These include the present unprecedented turmoil in the conventional financial markets resulting in a more careful examination of financial stability, the theoretical and observed instability features of the conventional financial system, the increasing recognition that equity capital flows are more stable and supportive of stable financial development and growth, the growth of Islamic finance beyond the borders of Muslim countries, relatively higher flows of equity capital across borders, and significant surplus capital in several oil-rich Islamic countries who may be increasingly demanding Islamic financial products. Opportunities in developed economies due to depressed asset prices, and extra liquidity in Islamic financial markets, will also play a role in further globalization of Islamic finance.

In the next chapter, we look at the issues involved in designing and developing an Islamic financial system, before taking up the issue of financial convergence in more detail in Chapter 7.

Endnotes

1 See *Financial Times* report, "Islamic Finance," May 24, 2007, for estimates of the growth, size, and potential of Islamic finance.
2 The list of 500 Islamic institutions includes 292 commercial banks (both fully Islamic and those offering Islamic windows or selling Islamic products), 115 Islamic investment banks and finance companies, and 118 insurance companies, adding to a total of 525 institutions from which the top 500 list was drawn.
3 ISI Analytics (2007).
4 Islamic Financial Information Services (ISI Analytics, 2007).
5 ISI Analytics (2007).
6 Ernst & Young (2007).

7　Deutsche Bank.

8　Aziz (2007). Please note that many structures that are acceptable in the Malaysian market may not be acceptable in the Middle Eastern market.

9　www.db.com/presse/en/content/press_releases_2007_3654.htm?month=3.

10　According to Saleh (1992), the proponents of the contract of insurance argue that gambling and insurance have distinct features. In the case of the former, a gambler pursues, through unlawful means such as betting and wagering, risks that could be easily avoided if he so wanted. As for insurance, the insured person seeks protection from danger over which he has no control. Moreover, gambling has very detrimental social effects, whereas insurance is very desirable and sometimes vital for trade and commerce.

11　Ayub (2007).

12　Ernst & Young (2007); IRTI and IFSB (2006).

13　ISI Analytics (2007).

14　Ibid.

CHAPTER 6

Key Considerations in Developing an Islamic Financial System

Financial globalization influences the design of a financial system and the development of financial markets. Financial system design has been the focus of considerable research and there is a great deal of evidence linking financial systems with economic development. The literature is rich in the debate surrounding the pros and cons of the two most popular financial systems—market-based systems such as those in the United States and the United Kingdom, and financial intermediary-centered systems such as those in Germany and Japan. This debate has been centered on the role of financial intermediaries and markets in the financial system. However, little attention has been paid to the mode of financial contracting. The existence and role of debt and debt-based financial instruments has been taken for granted. However, given the events of 2007 and the ensuing financial crisis, researchers will in all likelihood expand the debate to consider financial system design, including the building blocks of financial contracting.

The economic and financial principles of Islam offer an alternative perspective on financial system design. Whereas financial globalization shares the principle of risk sharing with Islamic financial principles, designing a friendly risk-sharing financial system is a challenge. The ongoing financial crisis has highlighted several areas of improvement and enhancement for developing a more efficient and stable financial system. In this chapter, we review the lessons learnt from recent progress in the conventional financial system and discuss theoretical and operational issues relevant to developing an Islamic financial system.

6.1   Lessons from the Conventional Financial System

Designing a financial system has been the subject of extensive research—both theoretical and empirical—in modern economics and finance. In addition, experience in dealing with a number of financial crises at both the domestic and international levels has provided a great deal of practical appreciation of the day-to-day workings of a financial system. We begin by presenting some lessons and observations before discussing the design of a financial system in Islam.

6.1.1 Financial system is a set of functions

A financial system is better understood when viewed as a set of functions it performs in an economy. As opposed to the traditional view of restricting the role of a financial system to mere capital mobilization, a functional view expects an expanded role from the financial system. Most poignantly, by restricting the financial system to capital mobilization, the deeper role of a financial system under uncertainty—where risk allocation becomes critical—is ignored. In addition, given information asymmetries and incentive problems, capital markets may offer more efficient contracting through marketing for corporate control.[1] Another argument favoring a functional view of a financial system is that its functions do not change significantly over time and space, while the forms and functions of institutions and intermediaries are subject to change.

Although the most fundamental role of a financial system is still financial intermediation, the following are the core functions expected from an efficient financial system:

a. **Efficient capital mobilization.** The ultimate function of a financial system is to perform efficient resource allocation through capital mobilization between savers and users of capital. This function is performed efficiently when the economic agents have access to capital through a liquid market for varying maturity structures—that is, from very short-term to very long-term needs. Access to capital has to be easy, transparent, cost-effective, and with minimal transaction costs and free of information asymmetries.

b. **Efficient risk allocation.** Under uncertainty and volatile market conditions, the function of risk sharing, risk transfer, and risk pooling becomes critical in a financial system. In the absence of such functionality, the financial system will discourage projects requiring high risk but with high value-added to the economy. The function of "insurance" is vital for any financial system, and the availability of efficient risk-sharing facilities promotes diversification and allocational efficiencies.

c. **Pooling of resources and diversification of ownership.** A financial system provides a mechanism for the pooling of funds to undertake large-scale indivisible investments that may be beyond the scope of any one individual. It also allows individual households to participate in investments that require large lump sums by pooling their funds and then subdividing shares in the investment. The pooling of funds allows for a redistribution of risk, as well as the separation of ownership and management.[2]

d. **Efficient contracting**. A financial system should promote financial contracting that minimizes incentive and agency problems arising from modern contractual arrangements among owners, managers, regulators, and other stakeholders. Both financial institutions and financial markets have distinct incentive problems due to the conflicting interests of investors, managers, owners, and regulators; and therefore a financial system should encourage financial contracting, which minimizes distortion and enhances allocation efficiency.

e. **Transparency and price discovery**. A financial system should promote efficient processing of information, such that all available information pertaining to the value or price of an asset is available at the lowest cost and is reflected in that value or price. This price discovery function of a financial system results in the allocation of capital to the most productive use and in the most efficient manner.

f. **Better governance and control**. Advances in modern finance have highlighted the importance of good governance, especially with respect to financial institutions and markets. A financial system should facilitate transparent governance and promote discipline in management through external pressures or threats, such as takeovers, so that any misallocation or misappropriation is minimized.

g. **Operational efficiency**. A financial system should provide smooth operation of financial intermediaries and financial markets by minimizing any operational risk due to the failure of processes, settlement, clearing, or electronic communication. Smooth and transparent execution of financial transaction develops a good reputation and "trust" among economic players and therefore is beneficial in attracting external resources. This is especially applicable for emerging economies that are eager to attract foreign investors.

6.1.2　Intermediation, disintermediation, and re-intermediation

Traditionally, intermediation provided by an institution such as a bank has been considered as the main source of capital mobilization, but with the passage of time and the development of capital markets, some of the functions have been shifted from formal bank-like institutions to sophisticated financial markets. At the same time, bank-based intermediation has changed from basic commercial banking to more specialized institutions in the form of investment banks, universal banks, mutual funds, and non-banking financial institutions—all having an active role in supporting financial and derivative markets. This transition has raised questions about the best form of intermediation—that is, institutions or markets, and who is best suited to perform this function more efficiently.

Research shows that during the early stages of development of an economy, a bank-like institution is a better form of intermediation; however, with the development of economies and markets, a market-based financial system becomes more efficient. It is often claimed that a trend toward a market-based financial system is also a trend toward disintermediation. However, a market-based financial system does not necessarily have to be characterized as a "disintermediated" system. Rajan (2006) argues that moving away from traditional bank-centered intermediation does not amount to "disintermediation." If more financial transactions are conducted at arm's length, it does not mean that intermediaries have disappeared. In fact, individuals have shifted a significant portion of their saving allocation from traditional deposit-taking institutions to indirect investments in financial markets through mutual funds, insurance companies, and pension funds, and indirectly in firms via (indirect) investments in venture capital funds, hedge funds, and other forms of private equity. Rajan (2006) uses the term "investment managers" to describe the managers of these financial institutions that have displaced traditional banks and have "re-intermediated" themselves between individuals and markets. Investors prefer to delegate to such a specialist in order to cope with the sheer complexity of financial instruments and the increasing volume of information. It is interesting to note the similarities between the term "investment manager" and the Islamic contract of *mudarabah* (principal/agent partnership), which is considered a cornerstone of Islamic finance.

In short, financial intermediation is a vital function of a financial system, and the emergence of more specialized players intermediating between investors and markets does not eliminate this function. With the development of markets and the increasing complexity of the financial system, intermediation by a single traditional institution is no longer efficient. It is necessary to redistribute the intermediation function among layers of specialized institutions with focused knowledge of diverse segments of the market.[3]

6.1.3   The significance of institutions

Research has confirmed the critical role that well-established institutions play in the economic and social development of all countries. Because of the distinct characteristics of financial contracts, the need for adequate institutions in financial markets is most critical among economic institutions.[4] As the financial markets grow, the significance of an appropriate legal framework and adequate enforcement of the rights and constraints of all the parties involved in the contract also grows. Beck and Levine (2003) show that financial development is higher in countries where legal systems enforce private contracts and property rights, and where creditor rights are protected. If that is not the case, typical problems of moral hazard, adverse selection, and time inconsistency due to informational asymmetries can affect the smooth enforcement of contracts, and many of these problems can be mitigated through well-designed contracts and proper "institutions."[5]

Fergusson (2006) undertook a detailed survey of the literature concerning the development of institutions and legal frameworks, and of their linkage with financial development. A condensed version of his main arguments and relevant empirical evidence is given in Table 6.1.

6.1.4 Positive and negative roles of financial engineering and innovation

Financial innovation has been the highlight and the driving force of financial markets in recent times. The key to innovation has been that market forces have been allowed to operate. However, financial innovations have also proved to be a double-edged sword, receiving much of the blame for the unprecedented financial crisis that was triggered in the sub-prime mortgage market. Financial engineering was the result of breakthroughs in financial theory, such as portfolio theory and option pricing, advancements in communication and computational technology, liberalization of markets, and increased volatility in markets. New products were introduced to offer customized solutions to corporate finance and hedging needs, and to exploit arbitrage opportunities. As a result, markets moved to greater efficiency through market integration, price discovery, lower transaction costs, enhanced liquidity, and wider access to markets.

With increased complexity in the system, new risk frontiers stimulated further the need for innovation to share and mitigate the wider spectrum of new, emerging risks. At the same time, the prevailing regulatory philosophy favored the least degree of involvement in free market forces, which led to instruments and practices that were complex, multilayered, highly integrated, dependent on quantitative rather than qualitative decision making, and based on unrealistic assumptions. The result was a more fragile system with a lower tolerance to local shocks. The financial crisis that started in 2007 raised serious questions about the role of innovations, the innovative process through financial engineering, and their contribution to the financial system. While we wait for further research on and insight into these

TABLE 6.1 The Importance of Institutions and Legal Frameworks in the Development of Financial Systems

	Main Theoretical Arguments	Empirical Research
Institutions	Better protection of creditor rights increases the breadth and depth of capital markets. Laws and their enforcement influence the extent to which insiders can expropriate outside investors who finance firms. Credibly pledging collateral reduces asymmetric information problems.	Shareholder and creditor rights indices (for 49 countries with publicly traded companies) increase opportunities for external finance (La Porta et. al., 1997a, 1998). Creditor rights and law enforcement are also positively correlated with bank development (Levine, 1998, 1999), firms' ability to raise capital (Kumar et. al., 2001; Beck et. al., 2003), efficiency of equity markets (Morck et. al., 2000), efficiency of capital re-allocation (Beck and Levine, 2002; Wurgler, 2000), corporate and bank valuations (Claessens et. al., 2000, 2003; La Porta et. al., 2000) and ability to fund faster-growing firms (Demirgüç-Kunt and Maksimovic, 1998), and firms with less collateral (Claessens and Laeven, 2003). Law enforcement and creditor protection also reduces credit cycles and currency and banking crises (Johnson et. al., 2000; Galindo et. al., 2001, 2004; Boucher, 2004).

Legal framework	Alternative view: strict protection of creditor rights (e.g. right to repossess collateral) might be inefficient and may impede continuation of efficient projects. Pro creditor rights reduce risk-taking incentives for entrepreneurs. Protection of creditors reduces their incentives to screen projects and to discourage investment by overconfident entrepreneurs.	Extending La Porta et. al's (2000) exercise by including additional macroeconomic controls, Padilla and Requejo (2000) find that, although an efficient judicial system improves the size and efficiency of the credit market, the effect of creditor protection is inconclusive. By extending the sample (15 additional developing countries), Galindo and Micco (2001) find that the positive effect of creditor protection does hold, even after controlling for macroeconomic variables.
	Legal framework and corporate governance: by shaping firms' incentives, a weak protection of creditor rights and weak law enforcement might encourage adoption of remedial rules, higher ownership concentration, and excessive reliance on tangible and liquid assets.	Countries with weak laws and enforcement tend to introduce remedial rules such as mandatory dividends and reserve requirements (La Porta et. al., 1998), display more ownership concentration (Zingales, 1994; La Porta et. al., 1998; Claessens et. al., 2000; Himmelberg et. al., 2000; Roe, 2000; Caprio et. al., 2003; Dyck and Zingales, 2004), and invest more in tangible assets (Claessens and Laeven, 2003) and liquid assets (Pinkowitz et. al., 2003).
Other institutions (trust or social capital)	Trust: increasing the perception that others will cooperate facilitates cooperation in large and impersonal markets.	Social capital and financial development are strongly connected in Italy, according to household data (Guiso et. al., 2000). Beyond Italy (in a sample of 48 countries), trust is positively correlated with the size and activity of financial intermediaries, bank efficiency, and stock and bond market development (Calderoń et. al., 2001).

Source: Fergusson (2006).

developments, we can't deny the value-added role of innovation in a financial system that is supported by a long list of success stories resulting from financial engineering. Debate will continue on how to put checks and balances into the system to promote "good" innovation, which is transparent and contributes to the stability of the system, and how to prevent innovation that is counter-productive and exposes the system to instability.

6.1.5   Drawing regulatory boundaries

Until the recent financial crisis, the United States and most of the other industrial economies subscribed to a regulatory philosophy that emphasized minimum and selective regulation and safety and soundness oversight. This philosophy was influenced indirectly by the dominant economic philosophy, which is to promote a market-based economy and to let market forces discipline and regulate markets. The need for regulation was felt where there was market failure. This approach resulted in the development of a sound regulatory framework for limited but "core" financial institutions, with less or no regulation for institutions on the "periphery."

In the US, the core consisted of institutions for which market discipline was relatively weak and those considered systemically important, such as all federally insured depositories (approximately 7,380 commercial banks, 1,270 thrifts, and 8,362 credit unions), the government-sponsored enterprises (GSEs) active in mortgage securitization and investment (Fannie Mae and Freddie Mac), and the largest broker–dealers (organized into the "big five" investment banking groups). The periphery consisted of all other financial entities, including small broker–dealers, insurance companies, finance companies, mortgage companies, funding corporations, and institutional investors ranging from pension funds and mutual funds to real estate investment trusts, asset-backed securities (ABS) pools, hedge funds, and private equity funds.[6]

With the expansion of financial markets as a result of globalization, the pace with which new financial institutions entered the market, and the kinds of financial products that were starting to emerge in the financial system, the gap in size between the core and the periphery began to widen. By mid-2000, the core had contracted to less than one-third of total financial sector assets in the US.[7] New financial institutions introduced complex legal structures with multiple layers of entities, and the financial instruments deployed introduced a high degree of leverage, complexity, and non-transparency in the financial system. All this development escaped the scrutiny of regulators and the constraints of prudential supervision because the regulators failed to keep pace with the changes in the financial system, due either to political pressures to let the markets function or to mere negligence.

The result was that the heavy reliance on market discipline and the negligence of regulators led to the onset of the financial crisis in 2007. Academic investigations have begun to understand the failure of markets and regulations that were considered to be playing complementary roles. It is certain that the new financial landscape that will emerge once the current financial crisis settles will expand the regulatory net to include a wider range of financial institutions and determine the boundaries for the complementary roles of market discipline and regulation.

6.1.6 Leverage, complexity, and fragility

The financial crisis of 2007–09 is attributed to several factors, including the failure of regulation and market discipline, flaws in corporate governance, irresponsible corporate behavior, and the breakdown of traditional risk management. Unmonitored credit expansion and abundant liquidity, supported by cheap money policy and low interest rates, led to speculative booms and asset price bubbles. Financial innovations, Ponzi finance schemes, swindles, and fraud often develop during a speculative boom when many illiquid credit instruments become monetized—for instance, through securitization—and fuel further liquidity.

As more research is undertaken to pinpoint the root causes of the crisis of 2007–09, it is clear that there are a number of systemic issues that should also be addressed. One can make some general observations about the linkages between excessive leverage in the system due to easy credit expansion and the fragility of the system. The current financial system was highly leveraged and becoming very complex, with multiple tiers of financial vehicles, which created a wide distance between the investor and the ultimate asset being financed. The result was a very delicately balanced system with a low tolerance to shocks. Inevitably, a crisis in one segment of the system immediately brought the whole system to a halt, not just domestically but also at the international level.

6.2 Gaps in the Islamic Financial System and its Practice

Despite the rapid growth in *Shari'ah*-compliant products, the current practice of Islamic finance represents only a fraction of the theoretical possibilities in a comprehensive financial system. When compared with the conventional system, the current form of Islamic finance offers very limited functionality. As mentioned in Section 6.1, examining financial systems

TABLE 6.2   Functional Assessments of Islamic Financial Markets

Function	Assessment
Capital mobilization	Limited set of instruments; concentration in short-term maturities; low depth and breadth of markets; and lack of liquidity.
Managing risk	No derivative markets or organized mechanism for risk mitigation. High geographic and sector concentration. Limited diversification opportunities.
Pooling and diverse ownership	Absence of or limited stock markets in Islamic countries, due to illiquid and poorly supervised stock markets, and limited opportunities for the pooling of ownership and the diversity of ownership. In non-Islamic countries, limited *Shari'ah*-compliant stocks available to Islamic investors.
Efficient contracting	Lack of civil and commercial law based on Islamic law in several Islamic countries where the legal system is predominantly conventional limits efficient contracting. In non-Islamic countries, it may not be possible to replicate *Shari'ah* law in its intended form, which hinders efficient contracting.
Transparency and price discovery	Illiquid, shallow, and poorly supervised capital markets inhibit the process of price discovery and limit the ability to arbitrage.
Governance and control	Not all stakeholders participate in the governance of financial institutions offering Islamic financial services. Lack of transparency in governance of *Shari'ah* boards.
Operational efficiency	High perception of operational risk due to the lack of proper accounting standards, clearing and settlement processes, and trainer personnel.

Source: Adapted for Islamic financial markets based on Ul-Haque (2002).

from a functional view provides some critical insights. Table 6.2 provides a functional assessment of Islamic financial markets as they exist today.

In the next section, we discuss some of the major gaps in the Islamic financial system.

6.2.1   The reluctance to develop risk-sharing products

One of the most serious gaps in Islamic finance is the reluctance of market players to promote risk-sharing financial products. Institutions to support risk-sharing, partnership-based, and equity-style financing and investment are the most critical to achieving the full potential of an Islamic financial system. One of the major criticisms of Islamic financial institutions is their low appetite for holding risk-sharing assets.[8] By design, Islamic financial institutions and markets should encourage partnerships and equity-sharing securities, but in practice, the proportion of such assets on the balance sheets of Islamic banks is minimal. For example, Table 6.3 shows the asset composition of selected banks from 1999 to 2002; it is evident that Islamic financial institutions' first preference is for financing instruments that are generated through sale contracts and leasing instruments. Informal observation of more recent balance sheets shows a similar picture. Islamic banks' heavy usage of the sale-based financing instrument *murabahah* has earned this practice the name "*Murabahah* syndrome."[9]

Islamic institutions' reluctance in regards to risk-sharing instruments such as *musharakah* (equity partnership) and *mudarabah* (principal/agent partnership) is problematic for achieving the true potential and benefits of

TABLE 6.3   Asset Composition of Select Islamic Banks, 1999–2002 (percent)

	1999	2000	2001	2002
Murabahah and deferred sales	80.1	83.0	86.7	84.3
Istisna	10.8	8.7	7.5	7.0
Ijarah (leasing and hire purchase)	2.5	2.4	1.9	2.9
Mudarabah (partnership)	1.6	1.6	1.2	3.1
Musharakah (equity participation)	0.9	0.8	1.3	1.2
Qard hasan	0.2	0.3	0.4	0.5
Other	0.2	0.2	0.5	3.0

Source: Islamic Banks and Financial Institutions Information System (IBIS).

globalization. Islamic financial markets are dominated by Islamic banks and there are very limited activities in capital markets. Activities in capital markets are further limited to products that emulate conventional-style fixed-income "debt-like" securities and defeat the main goal and objective of Islamic financial principles. As mentioned earlier, stock markets in several Islamic countries are still developing, and most of them operate with low efficiency and are not fully compliant with *Shari'ah*. Risk-sharing instruments, by design, require close monitoring, which requires proper infrastructure and incurs additional costs. Currently, there are no systemic-level mechanisms and institutions to provide efficient monitoring through compliance with standards, rating agencies, financial disclosures, and availability of timely information. Similarly, a stock market operating according to *Shari'ah*, which prohibits the use of leverage (use of margin accounts) and excessive speculation (including short sales), is yet to be developed in any Islamic country.

6.2.2 Limited market-based financial intermediation

Banks and financial markets play complementary roles. More transactions are now done in markets, as well as by institutions that have an arm's-length relationship with their clients. This has not, however, marginalized traditional institutions such as banks and their relationships. The changes have allowed such institutions to focus on their core business of intermediation, customization, and financial innovation, as well as risk management. Financial institutions are able to perform their core functionality more efficiently if there are supporting markets to provide liquidity, risk transfer, and insurance. As the "plain vanilla" transaction becomes more liquid and amenable to being transacted in the market, banks wishing to be competitive will embrace more illiquid transactions.[10]

Institutions specializing in *Shari'ah*-compliant products have been functioning based on the same business model for some time and without much innovation in their mode of operations. Due to the lack of supporting money, capital, and derivative markets, financial intermediations are retaining excessive exposure, especially exposure to liquidity risk, and are missing out on diversification opportunities. In order for the Islamic financial system to function properly, financial intermediaries need to specialize in mobilizing deposits, identifying investment opportunities, originating, structuring, and packaging securities, and managing risks, while allowing the complementary financial and capital markets to fill the remaining gaps and provide liquidity and risk sharing. Unless complementary financial markets are developed, financial intermediaries will continue to dominate with their limited scope and functionality.

6.2.3 Limited risk management functionality

The purpose of a traditional financial intermediary or bank is to warehouse risks that are manageable; and then, when appropriate, to offload the risks to the rest of the financial sector, replacing them with more complicated risks. After offloading "plain vanilla" risks, the financial intermediary can focus on those risks that better utilize its distinctive warehousing capabilities. This is possible only when there are mechanisms in place for transferring risks.

In the current financial landscape of Islamic financial institutions, the functionality of risk transfer is very limited. There are no organized markets for offloading risks to achieve diversification. Whereas conventional finance developed hedging mechanisms through derivative products, the Islamic financial markets have not introduced any viable mechanism for transferring risk. This has serious consequences for the financial intermediaries, who are exposed to a wide array of credit, market, and operational risks but are unable to properly hedge most of their risks. With the increasing complexity in international financial markets, financial integration, and growing uncertainty in the markets, the risk exposure of Islamic financial institutions will increase.[11]

6.2.4 Entrepreneurship and financing of the poor

As is well known, within the present dominant economic system, there are a number of serious market failures that cannot be resolved without external intervention. One such failure is the inability of the prevailing credit system to satisfy loan demands from segments of the population that cannot access formal credit channels or do not have sufficient collateral against which to borrow. These groups—commonly referred to as "non-banked" or "non-bankable"—include not only the poor but also would-be entrepreneurs with projects or ideas that have potentially high rates of return.

Islamic finance encourages entrepreneurship through risk sharing and partnership financing, and its emphasis on social justice calls for facilitating financing for the poorer segments of society. There is also a growing realization in the conventional system that a "financing gap" exists for small and medium-sized enterprises (SMEs) that could use funds productively if they had access through the formal financial system. SMEs and entrepreneurship are now recognized worldwide to be a key source of dynamism, innovation, and flexibility in advanced industrialized countries, as well as in emerging and developing economies.[12] If the SME sector does not have access to external funds for investment, the capacity to raise investment per worker, and thereby improve productivity and wages, is seriously impaired.

SMEs' difficulty in obtaining financing is compounded when the business environment lacks transparency and the legal system is weak—prevalent conditions in several Islamic countries wishing to promote Islamic finance.

According to some estimates, 72 percent of people living in Muslim-majority countries do not use formal financial services. Even when financial services are available, due to being non-compliant with *Shari'ah*, they remain unengaged. In countries where there are *Shari'ah*-compliant financial institutions, such institutions are engaged in commercial banking activities and ignore the poor sectors of the economy. Microfinance institutions, on the other hand, have been successful in conventional markets—so much so, that there are only a few cases of such institutions operating on Islamic finance principles.

It is primarily for this reason that there are very limited *Shari'ah*-compliant microfinance activities. In 2007, CGAP (Consultative Group to Assist the Poor) conducted a global survey on Islamic microfinance, collecting information on over 125 institutions operating in 14 countries. The key findings of this survey (summarized below) clearly show a dearth of Islamic microfinance services and a noticeable gap between the demand for and supply of these services:[13]

- Islamic microfinance has a total estimated global outreach of only 380,000 customers and accounts for only an estimated one-half of 1 percent of total microfinance outreach. The supply of Islamic microfinance is very concentrated in a few countries, with the top three countries (Indonesia, Bangladesh, and Afghanistan) accounting for 80 percent of global outreach. In Bangladesh, which has the largest segment of conventional microfinance, market share of *Shari'ah*-compliant microfinance is only 1 percent.
- Several studies show that more than 25 percent of potential customers in Jordan, 21 percent in Algeria, 40 percent in Yemen, and 43 percent in Syria cited religious reasons for not accessing conventional financial markets.
- Islamic microfinance accounts for a very small portion of countries' total microfinance market. For example, only 3 percent and 2 percent of the total microfinance market in Syria and Indonesia, respectively, is based on *Shari'ah*.
- The average client base of all 126 institutions surveyed was only 2,400 customers, with the largest being less than 50,000.
- There exists potential demand for *Shari'ah*-compliant microfinance products, as survey respondents in various countries show a clear preference for such financial services.[14]

In addition, the traditionally well-known Islamic vehicles of *waqf* (trust), *zakat* (alms), and *qard-ul-hassan* (no-cost loans) are not being practiced, or are not being properly utilized to promote economic development and to empower poor segments of the society in underdeveloped Islamic countries.[15] Islamic finance's promise of social justice cannot be implemented unless the prevailing "financing gap" is filled through the promotion of SMEs and microfinance.

6.3   Policy Recommendations

In the previous section, we highlighted the gaps between the current practices of Islamic finance and its paradigm version. Policy makers in countries that are serious about developing a financial system according to the principles of Islam should appreciate the challenges in developing such a system and the approach to take in overcoming those obstacles. In this section, we list some recommendations.

6.3.1   Development of institutions

There is no doubt that well-developed political, economic, and legal institutions are essential to facilitate financial contracting and are a necessary element of a robust financial system. Better institutions promoting checks and balances and the quality of governance can affect financial markets in several ways. For example, Akitoby and Stratmann (2009) show that better institutions lead to better fiscal policy, which reduces a country's default risk and, ultimately, lowers its cost of borrowing. The significance of institutions increases with market integration and globalization, where economies with established institutions attract investors and capital, as opposed to economies where institutions are weak, ineffective, and inefficient. Starting with the legal system, unless there is clarity with respect to creditors' and borrowers' rights, the protection of property rights, and rights on collateral in cases such as default, it will be difficult to build an efficient financial system. The prevailing legal systems are predominantly based on the conventional legal system, which may or may not have provisions for handling specific treatment of *Shari'ah* rules. Furthermore, legal systems in place in Islamic countries have enforcement shortcomings, which are a deterrent for any investor. Therefore, the development of supportive legal and tax codes, and of a harmonized regulatory framework based on Islamic law, is critical for the Islamic financial services industry.

Development institutions, such as rating agencies, audit agencies, trade associations, and dispute resolution organizations, also play a vital role. The function of rating agencies should not be limited to the rating of creditworthiness, but should also be extended to evaluating and giving an opinion on compliance with and the quality of *Shari'ah* practices. The scope of institutions such as the International Islamic Rating Agency (IIRA) should be expanded to rate large numbers of counterparties with whom a financial institution may engage in a *mudarabah*-like partnership. Development of private credit-rating agencies in all Muslim countries to facilitate the task of Islamic financial institutions in choosing their counterparties has been proposed.[16] Similarly, the scope of an audit should include the effectiveness of controls on new product development to ensure *Shari'ah* compliance.

6.3.2 Strengthening of the regulatory and governance framework

One may notice the omission of a detailed discussion on the regulation of Islamic financial institutions. The reason for this omission is that regulation is one area where there have been stark developments in recent years and the progress in this respect is worth appreciating. Credit goes to the collective efforts of setting up the Accounting and Auditing Organization of Islamic Financial Institutions (AAOIFI), followed by the Islamic Financial Services Board (IFSB), with the help of multilaterals such as the IMF and Islamic Development Bank (IDB). In its short life, the IFSB has made a noticeable mark on international financial circles in promoting Islamic finance and developing standards and other regulatory frameworks. If this trend continues, there is optimism about further globalization of Islamic finance. However, more work needs to be done.

Whereas the current financial crisis has highlighted vulnerabilities in financial systems, it has also recognized new challenges facing the regulation of cross-border and highly integrated financial markets. Prior to the crisis, the emphasis was on market discipline and on promoting standardization and harmonization of rules and practices. International financial intermediation was subject to the growing set of standards and codes, such as the Basel Core Principles on Banking Supervision, transparency and monetary management guidelines, IOSCO capital markets standards, corporate governance rules, anti-money laundering (AML), and counter-financing of terrorism (CFT). The objective was to enhance the efficiency of the system by delivering the best services at the lowest cost to the consumer. However, the financial crisis has exposed the need to strengthen the stability of the system, which has led to the development of a consensus that there is a need for more regulation.

The current situation offers both opportunities and challenges for the Islamic financial industry. In terms of opportunities, the stakeholders of the industry can influence policy formulation at early stages to ensure that the new regulatory environment is more "Islamic finance friendly" and addresses some of the key issues in regulating Islamic financial institutions. These issues include the treatment of investment account holders (IAHs) as stakeholders, enhancing transparency in financial disclosure, and standardization. This will require active participation in the debate and formulation of the new regulatory environment at local and international forums.

The real challenge will be the enforceability of new rules and standards. Islamic financial institutions are mostly operating in dual-system set-ups, which impose additional responsibilities on the regulators to maintain regulatory and supervisory standards for both conventional and Islamic institutions. This practice is resource intensive as well as expensive. With stricter standards, the challenge will be to ensure that Islamic financial institutions get due attention and priority in this process. At present, regulatory and supervisory standards, including compliance with Basel II, are being developed for Islamic financial institutions, though their enforceability is in question. Since the majority of Islamic financial institutions operate in developing economies, it requires extra effort to enforce the standards irrespective of how good or bad they are.

Islamic financial institutions are perceived to have higher exposure to operational risk due to the lack of proper risk systems and trained staff. In the new financial environment, there will be more reliance on risk monitoring and management. New techniques for monitoring credit and liquidity risk will be introduced, and old techniques such as value-at-risk will be refined to reflect better exposures. Islamic financial institutions should start thinking about addressing this issue by updating their risk systems. At the same time, regulatory bodies are required to devise proper training for their staff as well as for financial institutions. Regulators and supervisors should also develop a better understanding of certain practices of the financial institutions in assessing and monitoring risks.

6.3.3 Financial engineering

The financial crisis of 2007–09 has also been attributed to financial engineering, resulting from the introduction of complex and risky assets. While financial engineering will survive as both an art and a financial tool, it will become the subject of much closer scrutiny, with market and regulatory forces imposing new ethical and moral elements in its evolution and practice going forward.

For the Islamic financial industry, financial engineering is vital. Iqbal (1999), Iqbal and Mirakhor (2007), and Askari et. al. (2008) have repeatedly argued for the role of financial engineering in Islamic finance. Al-Suwailem (2006) lays down four principles for financial engineering from an Islamic perspective. First, the "principle of balance" asks for an integrated and balanced approach where all aspects of economic and social values—such as justice inclusiveness, cooperation, and competition—are considered. Second, he advocates the "principle of acceptability," that all economic dealings are generally acceptable unless otherwise stated by *Shari'ah*. This principle, linked to freedom of contract in Islam, has been the cornerstone for innovation in Islamic history. Third, the "principle of integration" states that an integrated real and financial sector are essential for sustainable growth; therefore, the foremost objective of any innovation should be to enhance integration between the two sectors. Finally, the "principle of consistency" states that the form and substance of Islamic products must be consistent with each other—that is, form should serve substance, and means should conform to ends.

The challenge of financial engineering is serious and should be met seriously. For Islamic financial institutions, a financial engineering challenge is to introduce new *Shari'ah*-compatible products that develop much-needed money and capital markets and enhance liquidity, risk management, and portfolio diversification. Generally, attempts to apply financial engineering techniques to Islamic banking will require the commitment of a great deal of resources to understanding the risk–return characteristics of each building block of the system and building new products with different risk–return profiles that meet the demands of investors, financial intermediaries, and entrepreneurs for liquidity and safety.

The practice of reverse engineering—or imitating, or attempting to replicate a conventional security—should be discouraged if and when such a practice means cutting corners and compromising the essence of the principles of Islam. The Islamic financial industry and policy makers should encourage the application of financial engineering to develop and introduce new products with their own distinct risk–return profiles. Given the current state of affairs, financial engineering should be targeted to the following areas:

- The current financial crisis has exposed all major financial institutions, as well as financial markets, to liquidity risk. Liquidity risk is higher in Islamic financial markets due to the lack of liquidity-enhancing products; therefore, liquidity management qualifies to be the first candidate for financial engineering. There is a need to develop products to establish a vibrant intra-bank market and to cater for different maturity structures.

■ The market for *sukuk* was hit from two sides in 2008—first, by objections raised by some *Shari'ah* scholars who questioned the authenticity of the structures and certain practices; and second, by the financial crisis, which was triggered by securitized products. Financial engineering should introduce *sukuk,* which are truly asset-based and at the same time are based on transparent structures. The corporate debt market is driven by a vibrant government debt market, which serves as a benchmark for other markets. In the case of Islamic financial markets, there are very limited sovereign or government *sukuk* issuances available in the market. The public sector in countries serious about Islamic finance should apply financial engineering to mobilize funds for that sector so that proper benchmarks are established.

■ Risk management will continue to be a critical area. The use of derivatives may slow down, but it will not be eliminated from the system. Products for sharing or transferring risk are very limited and, therefore, require the attention of financial engineering.

6.3.4 Transparent securitization

One of the main features of an Islamic financial system advocated by economists is that there is a direct linkage between the real and the financial sector of the economy.[17] Through securitization, conventional financial markets introduced the concept of "asset-based" securities, which have benefited the markets enormously. The art of securitization introduced much-needed liquidity in the market, allowed the enhancement of yield, provided portfolio and risk management opportunities, and—even more importantly—developed a market-based, "collateralized," low-risk security. The success of securitization can be judged by the fact that, before the advent of the subprime crisis, the spreads between Treasury yields, swaps markets, and securitized assets had narrowed considerably. The main reason for such narrow spreads was that the security was considered to be backed by a real asset.

Despite these various benefits, many blame innovative securitization itself for the financial crisis. While we cannot deny the benefits and positive contributions of securitization to the development of the financial markets, the fault lies in making securitization too complex and remote from the real asset. The Islamic financial industry can learn from this episode and develop securitization, which has similar features to conventional securitization but is not remote from the underlying asset, is transparent, and is truly "asset-linked" as opposed to "asset-based." The Islamic financial industry also needs to learn from the current practice of securitization in the form of *sukuk* and their associated problems. One of the major criticisms of some of the existing *sukuk* structures is that, contrary to theoretical and *Shari'ah* teachings, the asset is not subject to "true sale" or, often, to the prevailing market values.

Properly developed securitization has huge potential benefits for Islamic finance. For example, currently, there are no means to offload *mudarabah*-based receivables on a bank's balance sheet because these are credit sales and therefore cannot be sold as a financial loan. A securitization of such contracts can bring several benefits, such as freeing up a bank's asset side for other assets, the development of short-term liquid money markets, diversification opportunities, and transfer of risks.

6.3.5 Promotion of SME financing

The Islamic financial industry and policy makers should develop ways (i) to develop products to promote SMEs, and (ii) to facilitate SMEs' access to the formal financial sector. The Islamic contract of *mudarabah*, based on principal/agent principles, is well suited for developing such products. However, the *mudarabah* contract has not been institutionalized through proper legal infrastructure and a regulatory framework in most Muslim countries. Whereas conventional banks' conservative approach to risky assets and protective regulatory regimes prevent them from extending credit to SMEs, this should not be the case for Islamic banks that can hold *mudarabah*-based assets with no regulatory constraints. Furthermore, Islamic financial institutions are encouraged to enter into equity partnerships (*musharikah*) that can be used to promote the SME sector. There is a need to develop these instruments through the banking or non-banking sector in order to promote SME financing.

In order to facilitate the operation of the SME sector, OECD (2006) makes the following suggestions, which are equally applicable for the Islamic financial industry:

- Government measures to promote SMEs should be carefully focused, aiming at making markets work efficiently and at providing incentives for the private sector to assume an active role in SME finance.
- Public policy should improve awareness among entrepreneurs of the range of financing options available from official programs, private investors, and banks.
- The principles of risk sharing should be observed, committing official funds only in partnership with those of entrepreneurs, banks, businesses, or universities.
- The tax system should not inadvertently place SMEs at a disadvantage.
- The legal, tax, and regulatory framework should be reviewed in order to ensure that the business environment encourages the development of venture capital, including opportunities for exit.

6.3.6 Promotion of *Shari'ah*-compliant microfinance

Given the state of affairs in Muslim countries and the need for rapid economic development, Islamic finance can make its mark by helping to alleviate poverty in less-developed Muslim countries. Microfinance should be given serious consideration as a tool to promote economic development and reduce poverty. Policy makers can take several steps in this respect. First, they could develop incentives to promote microfinance by encouraging existing Islamic financial institutions to engage in microfinance. Such incentives may include tax breaks, centralized databases for monitoring credit risk, standardizing of products, and customer protection. Second, they could design a regulatory framework to monitor and supervise the performance and risk of institutions offering *Shari'ah*-compliant microfinance. Defining performance measurement tools and benchmarks can help with the monitoring and supervising of financial institutions.

Third, policy makers could offer choices to customers to match their needs. The CGAP survey showed that the *murabahah* product appears to be the most dominant (over 70 percent) and the product of choice by the institutions surveyed. This practice has led to two issues. The first issue is that *murabahah* contracts are good for commodity and asset pricing, but are not ideal for working capital purposes. The second, and more serious, issue is that the mark-up used in these transactions is often similar to the high interest rates charged by conventional microfinance institutions. This problem also creates confusion in the minds of customers who cannot understand, or cannot distinguish the difference between, mark-up and interest rates. These problems should be addressed by promoting other instruments, such as equity participation (*musharakah*), principal/agent (*mudarabah*), and leasing (*ijarah*). In this way, the provider of the service can be more effective in achieving different goals using different products.

Fourth, policy makers should develop a risk management framework— especially a credit risk framework that is not based on peer pressure and/or fear of future credit sanctions, as adopted by the conventional microfinance industry. Instead, a close working relationship could be developed with the client, leading to a better understanding of each client's circumstances.[18] Finally, Karim et. al. (2008) make a good recommendation for establishing the authenticity of products and practices through education and capacity building. Because the client base of microfinance institutions is the poor segment of society, who also happen to be less educated, there is a need to provide good education on the quality of Islamic products and their compliance with *Shari'ah* in order to promote Islamic microfinance and avoid any misuse by the providers of such services. In this respect, policy makers can work closely with local and international standard-setting bodies to develop standard products, practices, manuals, and audit mechanisms.

Credible *Shari'ah* scholars can explain the products and risks–rewards in simple language for clients.

6.3.7 Promotion of Islam's redistributive instruments

The objectives of socio-economic justice and equitable distribution of wealth are at the core of Islamic economic principles. The *Qur'an* places great emphasis on the redistribution of income and wealth, and legislates institutions for this purpose, the most important of which are the institutions of inheritance, *sadaqat* (charity), *zakah*, *waqf*, and *qard-ul-hassan*, which all have wide-ranging economic development implications and therefore are needed for the welfare of society. These instruments are vehicles for ensuring just conduct and maintaining a healthy level of wealth distribution.

Sadaqat (charity) has special significance in Islam and could be a major source of financial support in the economy if managed properly. Trust financing or endowment funds as practiced by conventional finance have their roots in the Islamic institution of *waqf*, which has long made enormous contributions to the economic development of Muslim societies. Throughout Islamic history the system of *awqaf* has provided all the essential services at no cost to the state. This means that a successful revival and implementation of the system can imply a significant cut in government expenditures and downsizing of the state sector.[19] In addition, the Islamic financial system offers unique instruments that do not have any direct counterparts in conventional finance. One such example is the institution of *qard-ul-hassan* (interest-free loans), which has been proven to be an effective means of economic development and poverty alleviation. Microfinance based on *qard-ul-hassan* has merits over conventional finance and should be promoted for economic development purposes.

There is a need to develop institutions to formalize the implementation of the redistributive instruments of Islam. Formal institutions to channel these flows in the most effective fashion should be developed. These could be dedicated institutions specializing in the distribution of funds in a manner that is most cost-effective and has the most development impact. If there are well-functioning Islamic financial intermediaries, these can become a distributive channel and provide these social welfare services as an integral part of their normal customer services. Furthermore, there is the need to develop the legal framework to encourage and protect such non-banking financial institutions so that they can operate in a friendly environment.[20]

6.3.8 Proper sequencing

In industrial countries, the development of financial markets followed a particular historical sequencing: commercial banks developed first; they were followed in turn by primary markets for government debt and paper, primary markets for equity and commercial paper, secondary markets, and finally, markets for derivatives. Motivated by the view that less-developed countries follow the development path of advanced countries, development advice has also tended to follow this historical sequencing. This approach, however, does not permit any "institutional leap-frogging." The difficulty with the stages of financial market development is that it does not emphasize the need for developing a full set of institutions necessary for market development early in the development cycle. As a result, a partial set of institutions is developed that, very often, exacerbates market incompleteness.[21]

Emphasis should be placed on developing the "functionality" of a financial system, rather than following a given sequence. Experience and knowledge of conventional finance can enable emerging markets, such as Islamic financial markets, to avoid some painful aspects of developing a financial system.

6.4   Concluding Remarks

The discussion in the preceding sections highlights the major issues the industry faces in developing a fully functional Islamic financial system. As mentioned earlier, developing a financial system requires large-scale efforts and coordination at the international level. The main issue is: Who can take on this task? It cannot be done alone, by one individual, or institution, or country; it has to be a collective effort. In this respect, the Islamic Development Bank—a regional development institution focused on Islamic finance—should take the lead and bring all the stakeholders together for this effort. The IDB should join hands with the IFSB and its member central banks to devise plans to develop and promote Islamic finance. The IDB and IFSB have prepared a 10-year master plan for the Islamic financial industry. This plan now needs to be put into action.

Endnotes

1 Ul-Haque (2002).
2 Ibid.
3 Occasionally, there are calls for traditional banks to be broken up and "narrow banking" introduced. ("Narrow banking" is where money market funds invested in liquid securities offer demand deposits, while finance companies funded through long-term liabilities make loans.) These alternative proposals do not make a great deal of sense, and yet they resurface every few years. See, for example, Simons (1948) and Bryan (2001).
4 Fergusson (2006).
5 Ibid.

6 Bhatia (2007).
7 Ibid.
8 Askari, Iqbal, and Mirakhor (2008).
9 Ali and Ahmad.
10 Rajan (2006).
11 Although it is too early to conclude that Islamic financial institutions are immune from the current financial crisis, there is a growing realization that Islamic financial institutions' excessive exposure to the illiquid real sector can bring serious financial distress to such institutions down the road.
12 OECD (2006).
13 Karim et. al. (2008).
14 In the West Bank and Gaza, more than 60 percent of low-income survey respondents showed a preference for Islamic products over conventional products, and more than 50 percent indicated they would be willing to pay a higher price for such products (Karim et. al., 2008).
15 See Askari et. al. (2008).
16 Chapra (2006).
17 Mirakhor (1989).
18 Karim et. al. (2008) suggest that an appeal to their sense of religious duty to meet their commitments can be used with the help of community elders to complement peer pressure.
19 Çizakça (1998).
20 Askari et. al. (2008).
21 Ul-Haque (2002).

CHAPTER 7

Conclusions and the Future of Islamic Finance

We have indicated throughout this book that the process of globalization is reversible, as evidenced by history. We nevertheless believe that, despite the current financial crisis and what may turn out to be a long pause in the globalization process, it will continue in the foreseeable future. The pause, induced by the worst financial turmoil since the Great Depression, may afford the global community the opportunity to adopt a financial structure, and financial regulations and supervision, that will be supportive of more orderly growth in the future. Since much of what we have to say in this concluding chapter on the convergence of conventional and Islamic finance may depend on the continuation of globalization, we will start out by briefly detailing our views on this all-important premise of this concluding chapter.

7.1 The Future of Globalization

As we have indicated, the history of globalization does not indicate a smooth progression toward a more interconnected world. There have been important reversals, the most recent being during the period of the two world wars. What the future holds in store is by no means clear. There are a number of dark clouds on the horizon.

As we have seen, the process of globalization can be generally expected to bring economic benefits to a country if its institutional structure and economic and financial policies are supportive. However, the distribution of these benefits is by no means uniform within a country. Frequently, a large segment of society not only does not benefit but may instead incur immense costs as a direct result of globalization. And in most societies, while the absolute level of individual economic prosperity is important, relative economic prosperity may be even more critical to those that are adversely affected. Globalization can affect both the absolute and relative levels of economic prosperity within a country. Thus the first caution in expecting a continuation of economic and financial globalization is growing disparities in wealth and income across countries, and especially within countries. There are clear indications that there has been a growing disparity in a number of countries—for example, within the United States. The analysis of Thomas Piketty and Emmanuel Saez[1] shows the following income share figures for the highest 1 percent of the income distribution for various years: 1913: 18 percent, 1929: 24 percent, 1975: 9 percent, and 2000: 21 percent. Namely, in 2000 the income share of the top 1 percent of the population was near its pre-Great Depression level (and from all indications it has since deteriorated further), after having fallen by nearly two-thirds to about 9–10 percent of income share in the mid-1970s; it now stands at well over 20 percent. A popular opinion piece by the economist Paul Krugman in the *New York Times* of June 14, 2002 affords a glimpse of how this story plays out in the popular media:

> *In 1981 those captains of industry were paid an average of $3.5 million, which seemed like a lot at the time. By 1988 the average had soared to $19.3 million, which seemed outrageous. But by 2000 the average annual pay of the top 10 was $154 million. It's true that wages of ordinary workers roughly doubled over the same period, though the bulk of that gain was eaten up by inflation. But earnings of top executives rose 4,300 percent.*

When a significant majority of the population sees a drop in its relative economic prosperity (and possibly no improvement in its absolute economic prosperity after accounting for inflation) and reads about the outrageous earnings and wealth of a few, someone or something has to be blamed. Frustration needs an outlet. This is the reality of life. Globalization is invariably a convenient whipping boy. Of course, countries can address rising income and wealth inequalities through taxes, but they don't seem to be willing to do so and especially if it affects those who support politicians with their pocketbook. Changes in tax structure and increases in taxation are unpopular, especially with those who stand to lose, even if not absolutely but only relatively. These concerns were especially fueled in 2007–09 with rising fuel, commodity, and food prices, which threatened the most basic needs of the less advantaged members of society.

Another cloud that threatens unfettered globalization is nationalism. Populists dread the influence of the outside world on their culture and way of life. There is no denying that globalization impinges on some aspects of national sovereignty and affects a society's unfettered cultural progression.

A rise in nationalism, as was the case in the early part of the 20th century, may again reverse globalization. Again in 2007–08, the rising price of food prompted a number of countries to embargo the export of certain food-stuffs to safeguard their "national" interests. The inflow of foreign customs, language, or religion with migrant workers has, in some countries, led to anti-immigration policies, again to keep jobs for nationals and safeguard the national interest. Populist politicians, to whip up nationalistic emotions against globalization, can use any of these factors and more.

In the post-September 11 global context, religion has become a promi-nent fault line that divides societies and countries. The playing of the Muslim call to prayers on Western television sets brings a hostile reaction. Religious fanatics—be they Christians, Jews, or Muslims—can take actions that could quickly close the door to further globalization across a large part of the world, resulting in autarchic relations—even conflict—between countries of different religions. With so many disputes around the world, a full-scale conflict could break out at any time and anywhere. Religion, which should be drawing mankind together, has been used by fanatics to put the world at war with itself and to pull it apart.

A global health pandemic could threaten the movement of people and goods. Such a public health scare could threaten the forces of globalization in a number of ways and for some time; trade, and especially tourism and the movement of labor, could come to a halt. The world is due for another pandemic, be it in the form of the H1N1 virus (formerly "swine flu"), Avian influenza, or something else.

Globalization—as a by-product of trade and the movement of people—has benefited from continually declining transportation costs over a number of decades. But higher energy costs, global warming, and other environmen-tal concerns could threaten the very foundations of globalization. In 2008, energy prices reached their peak real level in over 100 years. Global warm-ing and its connection to global economic activity has become an accepted fact of life. How the world addresses these looming challenges will have a direct impact on the course of globalization.

The Doha trade round may have died in Geneva in 2008. It is imagin-able that even a relatively small trade dispute could unravel the global gains in trade liberalization under the General Agreement on Tariffs and Trade (GATT) and the WTO. The liberalizing world trading system could easily degenerate into a handful of powerful regional trading blocs with high trade barriers between them. The financial and economic collapse in the aftermath of the sub-prime meltdown has sparked protectionist sentiments. Some US lawmakers inserted "buy American" clauses in bailout legislation, a number of countries directed their banks to limit foreign lending, and still others encouraged their corporations to repatriate foreign assets. There is a clear danger that, under deteriorating economic conditions, politicians will adopt populist rhetoric and embrace protectionist measures. How far we go down this dangerous road will depend on the severity of the economic downturn. Although we readily acknowledge that with autarchy we all lose, we may be powerless to stop the drift toward autarchy once it builds momentum.

The fragility of the international financial system has been brought into clear focus with the onset of the sub-prime meltdown in the United States and its international fallout in 2007–09. Individuals, banks, non-financial institutions, and governments around the globe hold toxic assets issued in other countries. The balance sheets of thousands of institutions around the globe have been infected. Globalization, the flow of capital, inadequate mechanisms for risk assessment and risk management, and lax regulatory and supervisory architecture have paralyzed the global financial system, resulting in frozen credit markets. Banks, investment banks, and other non-bank financial institutions that were highly leveraged are now in the process of de-leveraging and, as the process unfolds, massive losses are emerging; hundreds of institutions are now technically insolvent. As the crisis continues to spread, a number of prominent non-US politicians have blamed globalization for the migration of the US crisis to their front doors. How financial globalization will be ultimately perceived and judged is by no means clear in early 2009. Will it close the doors to all financial flows, or will it deter debt flows but encourage equity flows?

Most ominous of all, conflicts and wars could trump globalization and bring all its manifestations to a screeching halt, with prolonged conflicts and wars reversing much of the gains achieved from globalization. For instance, at the time of the Russian invasion of Georgia in 2008 it was conceivable that the conflict could lead to the withdrawal of Western capital from Russia, the imposition of economic sanctions on the Russian Federation by the United States, or to other economic restrictions that in the end would impinge on globalization. It was even possible for Russia to impose temporary restrictions on its natural gas exports to Europe, invoking further reprisals from the West. Even low-level conflicts or political differences have resulted in economic sanctions that have impeded globalization. And economic sanctions, a direct impediment and barrier to globalization, have become a favored instrument of foreign policy, especially for the United States.

While any one of the above developments could threaten the process of globalization, a confluence of a number of these could reverse all that has been achieved since World War II. Although the process of globalization is invariably a push toward convergence in most variables across countries (and we contemplate the convergence of Islamic and conventional finance), it is by no means assured that even globalization will continue. If globalization comes to a halt, then divergence—not convergence—may become the order of the day in most areas. Moreover, any one of a number of global policy changes in a de-globalizing and nationalistic world may affect the very form of financial globalization as it unfolds in the future.

There is likely to be considerable retrenchment in the aftermath of the financial meltdown of 2007–09 and the pace of globalization will in all likelihood be slower than before. Yet, on balance, we remain optimistic that globalization will continue after a longish period of retrenchment and pause, though maybe not at an even pace; and that financial globalization will also proceed, though maybe not in exactly the same form as previously. But on a positive note, we feel that financial globalization will, in the future, be more deliberate, better grounded to the real sector of the economy, and with thoughtful international regulation and supervision, precisely because of the financial turmoil of 2007–09. We are optimistic, because we believe that the world still remembers that the most recent period of de-globalization and autarchy, starting around the outbreak of World War I and accelerating during the Great Depression, was truly detrimental for all countries and should be avoided at all costs.

7.2 The Evolution of Financial Globalization

While the forces that shape economic and financial globalization are not the same, economic and financial globalization share a symbiotic relationship; they go hand-in-hand and reinforce one another. Every major economy has a significant domestic financial market. Rapidly growing emerging markets, while they may not always have a highly efficient and developed financial sector, invariably rely on international finance to support their growth. The forces that will in the future shape (in addition to the factors mentioned above that will impact globalization more generally) the landscape of international finance include a number of developments. A few of those surrounding Islamic finance have been addressed in Chapter 6: the supporting architecture and institutions, international financial agreements, the role of international institutions, the nature, specifics, and enforcement of financial supervision in countries, international financial accounting standards, international financial disclosure and reporting requirements, international standards for stock exchange listing, international standards for corporate governance, international agreements on investor protection, cross-border legal recourse for financial disputes, tax laws that affect the relative attractiveness of debt versus equity financing, corporate scandals, the extent and severity of future financial disruptions and their cross-border contagion effects, the proliferation of economic and financial sanctions, and the soundness and stability of macroeconomic policies around the globe, to name but the most prominent factors.

It is difficult to predict the evolution of any of these forces with a high degree of accuracy and certainty, but to predict the evolution of these and more would be near impossible. Yet, we can get some idea about what the future may hold in store for the convergence of Islamic and conventional finance by focusing on the critical factors that will affect their union.

The key and broader issue for convergence is whether conventional and Islamic (as practiced) finance move increasingly toward risk sharing and away from debt financing. A key factor in adopting risk-sharing instruments (as opposed to debt) is trust. As mentioned in Chapter 3, risk sharing (instruments such as equity) is dependent on the prevailing level of trust. As a result, if the level of trust is high, financial sectors are deeper and more developed. In other words, there is a high correlation between trust and development of the financial sector. Also, if the level of trust is high, investors are more likely to demand financially risky assets because they feel that this risk is limited and is unlike the infinite risk of Ponzi schemes and fraud. In high-trust countries, people invest a larger portion of their wealth in stocks, use more checks, and have access to greater amounts of credit than in low-trust societies. As already mentioned in Chapter 3, low trust is a crucial factor in explaining the low level of stock market participation. Moreover, in low-trust countries, equity participation depends on observance of the rule of law and the existence of legal institutions that protect property, creditor, and investor rights, and enforce contracts. This suggests that in low-performing economies not only is the level of trust low, but property and investor rights are poorly protected, and legal contract enforcement is weak. The policy implication for these economies is to strengthen legal institutions; improve transparency, accountability, and governance—both in the private and public sectors; and provide the public with a greater amount of information on risk sharing. So, the issue of convergence critically turns on whether the levels of trust will be enhanced in countries that practice conventional finance, as well as in the Islamic countries that aspire to Islamic finance. In the spring of 2009, trust is a scarce commodity the world over, but leaders around the world have noted its importance and will have to build trust if they are to achieve a sustained economic turnaround.

From the above, we can also conjecture that a further and continuing movement toward embracing risk-sharing instruments in countries that practice conventional finance will depend on the occurrence of the following: a wider range of risk-sharing instruments being offered to investors; the elimination of the tax advantage for debt financing; answers being sought to questions about the financial stability of debt-based financing in countries that practice conventional finance; enhancement of financial regulation and supervision to afford comfort to investors; and continued demand for risk-sharing instruments on the part of investors, be they Muslims or non-Muslims, and residents or from abroad. Whether risk-sharing instruments will grow in Islamic countries will depend on: further research on Islamic finance to develop a menu of financial instruments that are *Shari'ah* compatible and satisfy investor demand for financial products; the quality of financial supervision and regulation that affords investors financial transparency, reliable information, and security; the legal environment in Islamic countries to satisfy needs of security from expropriation and the like; the quality of institutions; the performance (return to investors) of Islamic institutions relative to conventional financial institutions; financial stability in Islamic countries; and the tax advantages offered by investing abroad (in conventional finance) versus in the home country of the investor.

We believe that the financial crisis of 2007–09 will be a watershed and the catalyst for important regulatory and supervisory changes at both the country and international level. The international financial system that emerges will be less vulnerable to systemic risk. Risk will be identified and managed better. Individuals and institutions will have more confidence in the foundation of the financial system and will be willing to share and assume more transparent risk. We believe that international economic and financial policy coordination, cooperation, and monitoring will be implemented in such a manner that financial crises will be less likely in the future.

Throughout this book we have argued that for Islamic finance to truly flourish in Muslim countries, these countries must adopt better policies and institutions to enhance economic growth and simultaneously adopt a common regulatory and supervisory system to manage their bank and non-bank financial institutions. The current financial turmoil could be the impetus for Muslim countries to embrace these much-needed reforms and policies in order to develop their financial sector and achieve higher sustained economic growth. They can no longer be satisfied with their weak institutions and vulnerability to external developments, and just hope to achieve sustained economic growth.

7.3   The Expansion of Risk Sharing

While we have witnessed dramatic changes in the field of conventional finance, in innovations, in applications, and more, over the last two decades, this change has been relatively concentrated in debt, as opposed to equity, instruments. At the same time, a series of high-profile corporate scandals in the United States—such as Enron and WorldCom, to name just two—may have inhibited investor confidence in equity-based instruments. But more recently, with the financial meltdown of sub-prime mortgages and low, even negative, real returns on debt instruments, investor demand for higher returns, and demand in favor of equity-based instruments and commodities, may have been revived.

Robert Shiller has cited empirical evidence that suggests risk sharing within countries and across borders is today an insignificant fraction of its potential (Shiller, 2003). Most investors are familiar with only a very narrow range of risk-sharing instruments—namely stocks, preferred stocks, and insurance. Shiller presents six ideas for a new risk management infrastructure: insurance (long-term livelihood and home equity insurance), financial markets (macro markets), banking (income-linked loans), taxation (inequality insurance), social welfare (intergenerational social security), and agreements with other countries (international agreements). While this list of risk-sharing proposals is ambitious, it could be enlarged to include educational loans based on lifetime earnings, divorce insurance, conflict insurance, water availability and climate insurance, inflation protection, and much more.

The point is that, under the right environment (a level playing field for equity and debt, and policies and mechanisms that enhance trust, such as good institutions, a spectrum of financial products, and so on), the demand for risk-sharing instruments could increase dramatically. The sub-prime meltdown dramatically reduced the demand for debt instruments in favor of commodities. This shift, in our opinion, is the precursor of a shift toward equity-based instruments. We believe that this will be a permanent effect and will increase the demand for more equity instruments with transparent properties. Despite the setbacks to equity-based and risk-sharing products brought about by the recent financial crisis, we believe that once the markets stabilize and are deleveraged, a trend toward equity- and risk-sharing-friendly structures will emerge. Through prudent application of financial engineering, the markets will seek and promote risk-sharing financial structures that are transparent and void of complexity. Nevertheless, this will depend on how the regulatory authorities tend to favor or disfavor debt instruments.

7.4 The Likelihood of Convergence

How likely is it that conventional and Islamic finance will converge as they both go through the globalization process? The answer would be "quite likely," if global finance relied more extensively on equity or equity-like flows, on the one hand, and a wider spectrum of risk-sharing instruments was innovated/invented, on the other. A similar process of innovation in

Islamic finance coupled with financial and institutional reforms would invigorate the growth and development of Islamic finance and enable an asymptotic convergence of the two.

As we have said earlier, in the absence of frictions, firms' financial structure would be indifferent between debt and equity. In reality, tax treatment and the availability of information (information asymmetry and the related problems of moral hazard and adverse selection) bias financial structures in favor of debt-based contracts. Legal–financial systems in advanced countries are also structured, tilting in favor of debt and debt-based transactions. However, as financial market developments progress, legal and institutional developments across the world accelerate, and information technology advances, the informational problems will diminish. Whether the tax and legal treatment of equity versus debt will become less biased is a policy question.

The global financial turmoil that started in 2007 and picked up steam in 2008 has again emphasized the fragility of a debt-based financial system. Debt financing during times of turbulence is akin to relying on "hot money," compared to equity financing, which is more permanent and assumes risk. Moreover, with the rapid innovation in debt instruments, transparency has been replaced by opacity. As a result of unknown and opaque risks and failed financial regulation of debt instruments and debt financing, debt may be losing much of its attraction to investors, at least for the foreseeable future.

The fragility of a financial system operating on the basis of a fixed, predetermined interest rate was underlined by Stiglitz (1988), who argued:

> *[The] interest rate is not like a conventional price. It is a promise to pay an amount in the future. Promises are often broken. If they were not, there would be no issue in determining creditworthiness. Raising interest rates may not increase the expected return to a loan; at higher interest rates one obtains a lower quality set of applicants (adverse selection effect) and each one's applicants undertake greater risks (the adverse incentive effect). These effects are sufficiently strong that the net return may be lowered as banks increase the interest rates charged: it does not pay to charge higher interest rates.*

Keynes believed that financial capitalism left to its own devices is inherently unstable. Saving and investment come from two different subsectors of the real economy, consumer and business, and their coordinated behavior is subject to uncertainty. That their equality is not always assured even under the best of circumstances is the core of his explanation of the inherent instability of the system. Keynes believed that the existence of a financial system dominated by *ex ante*–fixed interest-based debt contracts makes achieving sustained full employment equilibrium difficult, if not impossible. The claims created by the financial sector have no relation to the real sector. The findings of the new field of information economics strengthened the arguments of Minsky (1982) and others that a debt-based financial system with fractional reserve banking—operating with a fixed, predetermined interest rate mechanism at its core—is inherently fragile and prone to periodic instability. As banks find themselves in a financial squeeze when their returns decline unable to raise interest rates on their loans, they enter a liability-management mode by increasing interest rates on their deposits. As this vicious circle continues to pick up momentum, the liability management transforms into Ponzi financing and eventually bank runs develop. As previously emphasized, legal and institutional developments, along with good governance and the adoption of standards of best practice in transparency and accountability at the level of individuals, firms, and state, buttressed by information technology advances, will mitigate the informational problems, leading to lesser reliance on debt-based contracts.

Toward the end of the 1970s and early 1980s, the existence of financial intermediaries in general, and banks in particular, was justified due to their ability to reduce transaction and monitoring costs as well as to manage risk. However, minimal attention was paid to reasons why banks operated on the basis of fixed, predetermined interest rate-based contracts—that is, on a fixed-interest basis, which rendered the system fragile and unstable, requiring a lender of last resort to regulate it. Generally, interest rate theories explain the rate as an equilibrating mechanism between supply of and demand for finance, which is a rate that prevails in the market as a spot price and not as a price determined *ex ante* and fixed, tied to the principal and the period covered by the debt contract. Bhattacharya (1982) argued: " . . . with risk-neutral preferences, when the choice of risk level is unobservable, then any sacrifice of higher mean asset payoff constitutes an inefficient choice. The classical model of intermediaries existing to save on transactions/monitoring costs in asset choice does not explain why their liability structure should not be all equity."

With the development and growth of information economics and agency literature, another explanation was added to the list of reasons for the existence of intermediaries. They served as delegated monitoring as well as signaling agents to solve informational problems, including asymmetric information existing between principals and agents. Based on the findings of the developing field of information economics (Stiglitz and Weiss, 1981), it has been argued that adverse selection and moral hazard effects in a banking system operating on the basis of fixed-fee contracts in the presence of asymmetric information—particularly in cases where this problem is acute—means that some groups will be excluded from the credit market even when the expected rate of return for these groups may be higher than for those with access to credit. Furthermore, risk–return sharing contracts— for example, equity—are not subject to adverse selection and moral hazard effects: "[T]he expected return to an equity investor would be exactly the same as the expected return of the project itself" (Cho, 1986).

The last two decades of the 20th century witnessed a number of global bouts with financial instability and debt crises, with devastating consequences for a large segment of humanity, thus raising awareness of the vulnerability and fragility of financial systems that are based, at their core, on fixed-price debt contracts. While numerous international banks, such as UBS and Citibank, have seen their reputations tarnished by the subprime crisis, Islamic banks have been left largely unscathed. They did not, and given their premise indeed *could not*, park their assets in mortgage-backed assets. Islamic banks did not practice Ponzi finance, and have thus seen their reputation enhanced. This success has spiked interest in Islamic, equity-based finance, not only in Islamic countries but also in countries that support the conventional system, by both Muslims and non-Muslims. We have argued, and demonstrated, that there are a number of reasons why an equity-based, or Islamic, financial system is inherently more stable than the conventional debt-based system. Because of the financial crisis from the subprime debt meltdown, there is a growing interest in financial stability and stable returns, and thus in Islamic finance.

Given the state of the global financial markets in 2009, the growing interest in Islamic finance outside of Islamic countries, especially in large Western financial markets such as London, could provide the all-important boost needed to internationalize Islamic finance and promote its growth. Simultaneously, this growth can be reinforced in a number of Islamic countries that have been enjoying large current account surpluses because of higher oil and natural gas prices. A number of these countries—especially Kuwait, Qatar, Saudi Arabia, and the UAE—may also affect the growth of Islamic finance through their large and growing sovereign wealth funds demanding *Shari'ah*-compliant financial products. In turn, the growing internationalization of Islamic finance will afford equity-based finance added impetus in the West. In other words, conventional finance and Islamic finance could begin to reinforce each other.

In this book, we have addressed an overarching question regarding the future of financial globalization, and of Islamic finance: Will conventional finance, at the heart of the current financial globalization, and Islamic finance converge? There is evidence that financial globalization has not been as helpful as expected, given the potential of its benefits for growth of investment, employment, and income, as well for the reduction of income inequality and poverty. In our view, the success of financial globalization will depend on the spread and degree of risk sharing around the world. The greater the momentum, the deeper the markets, and the wider the spectrum of risk-sharing instruments, the greater will be the shared ownership and participation by larger numbers of people in finance. Faster, deeper, wider financial development has a symbiotic relationship with globalization, as the feedback process between the two strengthens both. Evidence suggests that, thus far, the degree of risk sharing achieved by globalization is insignificant.

As explained, the degree of risk sharing, and the expected welfare gains from financial integration, have to date been small, for the following reasons: (i) instruments have not been developed sufficiently to allow for greater risk sharing, and (ii) many countries still need to achieve the threshold levels of financial, legal, and institutional development required to allow for greater risk sharing. It is believed that the process of liberalization of economies, the adoption of best international standards, and the development of a good legal/institutional framework and practice is gathering momentum in many countries, as is the pace of innovation of financial instruments. We suggest that parallel progress and challenges characterize Islamic finance, although with a significant time lag.

While Islamic finance has experienced phenomenal success in the last two to three decades, it still has a long way to go to achieve its objective of maximum risk sharing. We have argued that the institutional structures within which Islamic finance is to operate are those that promote good state and corporate governance, trust, protection of rights, and contract enforcement. It was suggested that, in the case of Islamic finance, the progress achieved to date is a negligible fraction of the potential. The reasons are identical to those offered in financial globalization. It is suggested that financial, legal, and institutional developments, and the greater pace of instrumentalization of the basic modes of transactions permitted, would accelerate the progress of Islamic finance. As it would appear that Islamic finance and financial globalization share a *common objective* of achieving maximum risk sharing, it is not too unrealistic to expect convergence as we continue down this path.

We have also argued that legal and institutional developments, as well as further advances in information technology, will reduce informational problems and lead to growing trust, which is essential for risk sharing. The result will be the dominance of equity in financial structures and relationships. We have presented historical evidence of a globalization period in the Middle Ages, when partnerships and equity participation were the dominant mode of finance. The breakdown of trust as a result of repeated wars and catastrophes, as well as financial innovations, particularly securitization of government debt in the late Middle Ages, created the right milieu for the dominance of debt and debt finance which has lasted to the present day. We believe that conflicts and wars are the factors that most seriously threaten the future of globalization and financial globalization. How the world handles these threats may be the single most important factor determining the course of financial globalization and the possible convergence of Islamic and conventional finance.

For Islamic finance to sustain long-term growth, Muslim countries must liberalize their economies, embrace efficient institutions, and adopt consistent macroeconomic policies. They need to grow on a sustained, more rapid basis, and address the all-important issues of social and economic justice. Their sustained economic growth would be the most important impetus for a thriving Islamic financial sector; in turn, their thriving Islamic financial sector may be the best inducement for non-Islamic countries to embrace Islamic finance and equity-based assets more generally. In a globalizing world, the developments of Islamic finance and conventional finance can be expected to reinforce one another. We believe that Islamic countries are beginning to show signs that they are on the path to faster economic growth and financial market development; and they are turning increasingly to Islamic finance and risk-sharing instruments. Affluent Muslim communities in the West are doing the same.

Ironically, we believe that the financial crisis of 2007–09 could turn out to be the major catalyst for promoting the growth and globalization of Islamic finance. The crisis has shown the inherent flaws of fractional reserve banking, debt leveraging, and the creation of money out of thin air. The impact of the financial crisis on the real sector had already been severe by the early months of 2009 and there was no end in sight. This crisis may be a major force for change in conventional finance toward greater reliance on equity at the expense of debt.

Finally, as we have seen, recent data on the flow of capital across borders appear to suggest that global finance may be experiencing an early stage of the return to dominance of equity and risk sharing through the growth of Islamic financial techniques, as well as greater innovation of equity-based instruments within conventional finance. And therein may be the initial seeds of convergence between Islamic and conventional finance.

Endnote

1 www.cbpp.org/7-10-06inc.htm.

References

Abed, G.T. and Davoodi, H.R., 2003, *Challenges of Growth and Globalization in the Middle East and North Africa* (Washington, DC: International Monetary Fund).

Abed, G.T. and Gupta, S., 2002, *Governance, Corruption and Economic Performance* (Washington, DC: International Monetary Fund).

Abu-Lughod, J., 1994, "Discontinuities and Persistence," in A.G. Frank (ed.), *The World System, Five Hundred Years or Five Thousand?* (London and New York: Routledge).

Abu-Lughod, J., 1989, *Before European Hegemony. The World System: AD 1250–1350* (New York: Oxford University Press).

Acemoglu, D. and Guerrieri, V., 2006, "Capital Deepening and Non-Balanced Economic Growth," *NBER Working Paper* No. 12475 (Cambridge, MA: National Bureau of Economic Research).

Acemoglu, D. and Johnson, S., 2003, "Unbundling Institutions," *NBER Working Paper* No. 9934 (Cambridge, MA: National Bureau of Economic Research).

Acemoglu, D. and Johnson S., 2002, *Institutions, Corporate Governance, and Crises* (Oxford University Press).

Acemoglu, D., Johnson, S., and Robinson, J., 2004, "The Institution as the Fundamental Can Be of Long-Run Growth," *NBER Working Paper* No. 10481 (Cambridge, MA: National Bureau of Economic Research).

Adarkar, B.P., 1932, "Mr. Keynes and the Canonists," Saving and Usury: A Symposium, *The Economic Journal*, March, pp. 128–31.

Adelson, H.L., 1960, "Early Medieval Trade Routes," *The American Historical Review*, vol. 65, no. 2, pp. 271–87.

Adelson, M., 2007, "The Role of Credit Rating Agencies in the Structured Finance Market," Testimony before the Subcommittee on Capital Markets, Insurance and Government-Sponsored Enterprises of the House Committee on Financial Services Regarding the Role of Credit Agencies in the Structured Finance Market, Washington, DC, September 27.

Adrian, T. and Shin, H.S., 2008, "Liquidity and Leverage," Federal Reserve Bank of New York, *Staff Reports*, No. 328.

Ahmed, H. and Tariquallah, K., 2007, "Risk Management in Islamic Banking," in M.K. Hassan and M.K. Lewis (eds.), *Handbook of Islamic Banking* (Cheltenham, UK: Edward Elgar), pp. 144–60.

Aizenman, J., 2002, "Financial Opening: Evidence and Policy Options," *NBER Working Paper* No. 8900 (Cambridge, MA: National Bureau of Economic Research).

Aizenman, J. and Jinjarak, Y., 2006, "Globalization and Developing Countries—A Shrinking Tax Base?" *NBER Working Paper* No. 11933 (Cambridge, MA: National Bureau of Economic Research).

Aizenman, J., Pinto, J.B., and Radziwill, A., 2004, "Sources for Financing Domestic Capital—Is Foreign Saving a Viable Option for Developing Countries?" *NBER Working Paper* No. 10624 (Cambridge, MA: National Bureau of Economic Research).

Akitoby, B. and Stratmann, T., 2009, "The Value of Institutions for Financial Markets: Evidence from Emerging Markets," *IMF Working Paper* No. 09/27, February.

Albuquerque, R., 2003, "The Composition of International Capital Flows: Risk Sharing Through Foreign Direct Investment," *Journal of International Economics*, vol. 1, no. 2, pp. 353–83.

Alesina, A. and La Ferrara, E., 2002, "Who Trusts Others?" *Journal of Public Economics*, vol. 85, pp. 207–34.

Alfaro, L., 2005, "Why Doesn't Capital Flow from Rich to Poor Countries? An Empirical Investigation," *NBER Working Paper* No. 11901 (Cambridge, MA: National Bureau of Economic Research).

Alfaro, L., Chanda, A., Kalemli-Ozcan, S., and Sayek, S., 2005, "How Does Foreign Direct Investment Promote Economic Growth? Exploring the Effects of Financial Markets on Linkages," *NBER Working Paper* No. 12522 (Cambridge, MA: National Bureau of Economic Research).

Al-Hassani, B. and Mirakhor A., 2003, *Essays on Iqtisad* (New York: Global Scholarly Publications).

Al-Isfahani, Al-Raqib, 1992, "Mufradat Alfaz Al Quran," *Dar Al-Qalam* (Damascus).

Al-Mustafaoui, Sh. Hassan, 1995, *Al-Tahquiq Fi Kalamat Al-Quran Al-Karim* (Tehran: Ministry of Islamic Culture and Guidance).

Al-Suwailem, Sami, 2006, "Hedging in Islamic Finance," *Occasional Paper* No. 10 (Jeddah: IRTI).

Ali, M.I., 2005, "In the Mirror of History Were the Earlier Generations Smarter or Are We?" *Finance in Islam.* http://www.financeinislam.com/article/8/1/300

Ali, S.S. and Ahmad, A., 2006, "An Overview," in S.S. Ali and A. Ahmad (eds), *Islamic Banking and Finance: Fundamentals and Contemporary Issues* (Jeddah: IRTI).

Allais, M., 1987, "The Credit Mechanism and its Implications," in G.R. Feiwell (ed.), *Arrow and the Foundations of the Theory of Economic Policy* (London: Macmillan).

Amin, S., 1994, "The Ancient World-Systems versus the Modern Capitalist World-System," *The World System, Five Hundred Years or Five Thousand?* (London and New York: Routledge), pp. 247–76.

Ammer, J., Holland, S.B., Smith, D.C., and Warnock, F.E., 2006, "Look at Me Now: What Attracts U.S. Shareholders?" *NBER Working Paper* No. 12500 (Cambridge, MA: National Bureau of Economic Research).

Anderson, J.N.D. and Coulson, N.J., 1958, "The Moslem Ruler and Contractual Obligations," *New York University Law Review*, vol. 33, no. 7, November.

Antunes, A.R. and Tiago V.C., 2003, "Corruption, Credit Market Imperfections, and Economic Development," *Working Paper* No. 17-03 (Banco de Portugal, Economic Research Department).

Archer, S. and Karim, R.A., 2007, *Islamic Finance: The Regulatory Challenge* (Singapore: John Wiley & Sons Asia).

Arfoe, L., 1987, "Cedar Forest to Silver Mountain: Social Change and the Development of Long-Distance Trade in Early Near Eastern Societies," in M. Rowlands, M. Larsen, and K. Kristiansen (eds.), *Centre and Periphery in the Ancient World* (Cambridge, MA: Cambridge University Press), pp. 25–35.

Arrow, J.A., 1974, *The Limits of Organization* (New York: W.W. Norton & Company).

Arrow, K.J. and Debreu, G., 1954, "The Existence of an Equilibrium for a Competitive Economy," *Econometrica*, vol. XXII, pp. 265–90.

As-Sadr, M. Baqir, *Our Philosophy*, translated by Sham S.C. Inati (London: Muhammadi Trust, 1987).

Ashraf, N., Iris, B., and Nikita, P., 2005, "Decomposing Trust and Trustworthiness," *Working Paper* (Department of Economics, Harvard University).

Ashtor, E., 1983, *Levant Trade in the Later Middle Ages* (Princeton, NJ: Princeton University Press), pp. 3–64.

Ashtor, E., 1976, *A Social and Economic History of the Near East in the Middle Ages* (London: Collins).

Ashtor, E., 1975, "The Volume of Levantine Trade in the Later Middle Ages," *Journal of European Economic History*, vol. 4, pp. 573–612.

Askari, H., Cummings, J.T., and Glover, M., 1982, *Taxation and Tax Policies in the Middle East* (London: Butterworth Publishers).

Askari, H., Iqbal, Z., and Mirakhor, A., 2009, *New Issues in Islamic Finance and Economics: Progress and Challenges* (Singapore: John Wiley and Sons Asia).

Atje, R. and Jovanovic, B., 1993, "Stock Markets and Development," *European Economic Review*, vol. 37, pp. 632–40.

Aurelio, M.M., 2006, "Going Global: The Changing Pattern of U.S. Investment Abroad," *Federal Reserve Bank of Kansas Economic Review*, Third Quarter.

Aydemir, A. and Borjas, G.B., 2007, "Cross-Country Variation in the Impact of International Migration: Canada, Mexico and the United States," *Journal of the European Economic Association*, June, pp. 663–708.

Ayub, M., 2007, *Understanding Islamic Finance* (Singapore: John Wiley & Sons Asia).

Ayyagari, M., et. al., 2006, "What Determines Protection of Property Rights? An Analysis of Direct and Indirect Effects," *Robert H. Smith School Research Paper* No. RHS 06-032.

Ayyagari, M. and Kosova, R., 2006, "Does FDI Facilitate Domestic Entrepreneurship? Evidence from the Czech Republic," *Working Paper Series*, Department of International Business and School of Business and Public Management (SBPM), George Washington University, September 14.

Aziz, A.A., 2007, "The Evolution of Islamic Hedging Solutions," *Islamic Finance News* (Kuala Lumpur and Singapore: RedMoney).

Bailey, W., Mao, C.X., and Sirodom, K., 2007, "Investment Restrictions and the Cross-Border Flow of Information: Some Empirical Evidence," *Journal of International Money and Finance*, vol. 26.

Balassa, B., 1978, "Exports and Economic Growth: Further Evidence," *Journal of Development Economics*, vol. 5, pp. 181–89.

Baldwin, K., 2002, "Risk Management in Islamic Banks," in S. Archer and Rifaat Ahmed Abdel Karim (eds.), *Islamic Finance* (London: Euromoney).

Balgati, B., Demitriades, P., and Law, S.H., 2007, "Financial Openness and Institution: Evidence from Panel Data," Paper presented at the Conference on New Perspectives on Financial Globalization, sponsored by the Research Department (Washington, DC: International Monetary Fund).

Baltensperger, E., 1978, "Credit Rationing: Issues and Questions," *Journal of Money, Credit and Banking*, vol. 10, no. 2, May, pp. 170–83.

Batra, G., Kaufmann, D., and Stone, A.H.W., 2003, *Investment Climate around the World* (Washington, DC: The World Bank).

BBC, 2003, "Profile: Iran's Dissident Ayatollah," British Broadcasting Corporation, January 30.

Beck, T., Demirgüç-Kunt, A., and Levine, R., 2007, "Finance, Inequality and the Poor," *Journal of Economic Growth*.

Beck, T. and Levine, R., 2004, "Legal Institutions and Financial Development," in C. Menard and M. Shirley (eds.), *Handbook of New Institutional Economics* (Dordrech, The Netherlands: Kluwer).

Beck, T. and Levine, R., 2003, "Legal Institutions and Financial Development," *NBER Working Paper* No. 10126 (Cambridge, MA: National Bureau of Economic Research).

Bekaert, G., Harvey, C.R., and Lumsdaine, R.L., 2002, "The Dynamics of Emerging Market Equity Flows," *Journal of International Money and Finance*, vol. 21, no. 3, pp. 295–350.

Bekaert, G., Harvey, C., and Lundblad, C., 2005, "Does Financial Liberalization Spur Growth?" *Journal of Financial Economics*, vol. 77, no. 1, pp. 3–56.

Bekaert, G., Harvey, C.R., and Lundblad, C.T., 2001, "Emerging Equity Markets and Economic Development," *Journal of Development Economics*, vol. 66, pp. 465–504.

Bekaert, G., Harvey, C.R., and Lundblad, C.T., 2000, "Emerging Equity Markets and Economic Development," *NBER Working Paper* No. 7763 (Cambridge, MA: National Bureau of Economic Research).

Bekaert, G. and Lundblad, C., 2006, "Growth Volatility and Financial Liberalization," *Journal of International Money and Finance*, vol. 25, pp. 370–403.

Bekaert, G. and Urias, M.S., 1996, "Diversification, Integration and Emerging Market Closed-End Funds," *Journal of Finance*, vol. 51, no. 3, pp. 835–69.

Berg, J., John D., and McCabe, K., 1995, "Trust, Reciprocity, and Social History," *Games and Economic Behavior*, vol. 10, pp. 122–42.

Bernanke, B., 2008, "Stabilizing the Financial Markets and the Economy," Speech at the Economic Club of New York (October 15), available at the website of Board of Governors of the Federal Reserve System.

Bernanke, B., 2007, "Remarks," Federal Reserve Bank of Atlanta's 2007 Financial Markets Conference, Sea Island, Georgia, May 15.

Beugelsdijk, S., de Groot, H., and van Schaik, A., 2004, "Trust and Economic Growth: A Robustness Analysis," *Oxford Economic Papers*, vol. 56, pp. 118–34.

Bhambra, H., 2007, "Supervisory Implications of Islamic Finance in the Current Regulatory Environment," in S. Archer and R.A. Karim, *Islamic Finance: The Regulatory Challenge* (Singapore: John Wiley & Sons Asia).

Bhatia, A.V., 2007, "New Landscape, New Challenges: Structural Change and Regulation in the U.S. Financial Sector," *IMF Working Papers*, August, pp. 1–24, available at SSRN: http://ssrn.com/abstract=1007943.

Bhattacharya, S., 1982, "Aspects of Monetary and Banking Theory and Moral Hazard," *Journal of Finance*, vol. 37, no. 2, pp. 371–84.

Black, B., 2000, "The Core Institutions that Support Strong Securities Markets," *The Business Lawyer*, vol. 55.

Blassa, B., 1978, "Exports and Economic Growth: Further Evidence," *Journal of Development Economics*, June, pp. 181–89.

Bookstaber, R., 2007, *A Demon of Our Own Design* (Hoboken, NJ: John Wiley and Sons, Inc.).

Borensztein, E., de Gregorio, J., and Lee, J-W., 1998, "How Does Foreign Direct Investment Affect Economic Growth?" *Journal of International Economics*, vol. 45, no. 1, pp. 115–35.

Bossone, B., 2002, "Should Banks Be 'Narrowed'?" *Public Policy Brief* No. 69 (Annandale-on-Hudson, NY: The Levy Economics Institute).

Broner, F.A. and Ventura, J., 2006, "Globalization and Risk Sharing," *NBER Working Paper* No. 12482 (Cambridge, MA: National Bureau of Economic Research).

Bryan, L., 2001, *Breaking up the Bank: Rethinking an Industry under Siege* (Homewood, IL: Dow Jones-Irwin).

Bushman, R.M. and Piotroski, J.D., 2005, "Financial Reporting Incentives for Conservative Accounting: The Influence of Legal and Political Institutions," *Journal of Accounting and Economics*.

Byrne, E.H., 1930, *Genoese Shipping in the Twelfth and Thirteenth Centuries* (doc. dated 1250) (Cambridge, MA), pp. 85–88.

Byrne, E.H., 1920, "Genoese Trade with Syria in the Twelfth Century," *American Historical Review*, vol. 25, pp. 191–219.

Calderon, C., Chong, A., and Galindo, A., 2002, "Development and Efficiency of the Financial Sector and Links with Trust: Cross-Country Evidence," *Economic Development and Cultural Change* (University of Chicago), pp. 189–204.

Cannan, E., 1932, "Saving On and Saving Up: The Ambiguity of 'Saving'," Saving and Usury: A Symposium, *The Economic Journal*, March, pp. 123–28.

Cardoso, F. and da Cunha, V.G., 2005, "Household Wealth in Portugal," *Working Paper* No. 4-05 (Banco de Portugal, Economic Research Department).

Carrington, W.J. and Detragiache, E., 1998, "How Big Is the Brain Drain?" *IMF Working Paper* WP/98/102.

Chang, H-J., 2007, *Bad Samaritans: The Myth of Free Trade and the Secret History of Capitalism* (New York: Random House).

Chapra, M.U., 2007, "Challenges Facing the Islamic Financial Industry," in M.K. Hassan and M.K. Lewis (eds.), *Handbook of Islamic Banking* (Cheltenham, UK: Edward Elgar), pp. 325–60.

Chapra, M.U., 2006, "Financial Stability: The Role of Paradigm and Support Institutions," in T. Khan and D. Muljawan (eds.), *Islamic Financial Architecture: Risk Management and Financial Stability* (Jeddah: IRTI).

Chapra, M.U., 2000, *The Future of Economics: An Islamic Perspective* (Leicester, UK: The Islamic Foundation).

Chapra, M.U., 1998, *Islam and the Economic Challenge* (Leicester, UK: The Islamic Foundation).

Chapra, M.U., 1996, "What Is Islamic Economics?" *Islamic Development Bank Winner's Lecture Series* No. 9 (Jeddah), pp. 25–26.

Chapra, M.U., 1985, *Towards a Just Monetary System* (Leicester, UK: The Islamic Foundation).

Chapra, M.U., 1979, *Objectives of the Islamic Economic Order* (Leicester, UK: The Islamic Foundation).

Chapra, M.U., 1975, *The Economic System of Islam* (London: Islamic Council of Europe).

Chari, A. and Henry, B., 2006, "Firm-Specific Information and the Efficiency of Investment," *NBER Working Paper* No. 12186 (Cambridge, MA: National Bureau of Economic Research).

Chinn, M.D. and Ito, H., 2002, "Capital Account Liberalization, Institutions and Financial Development: Cross Country Evidence," *NBER Working Paper* No. 8967 (Cambridge, MA: National Bureau of Economic Research).

Cho, Y.J., 1986, "Inefficiencies from Financial Liberalization in the Absence of Well-Functioning Equity Markets," *Journal of Money, Credit, and Banking*, vol. 17, no. 2, pp. 191–200.

Choudhry, N.N. and Mirakhor, A., 1997, "Indirect Instruments of Monetary Control in an Islamic Financial System," *Islamic Economic Studies*, vol. 4, no. 2.

Çizakça, M., 1998, "*Awqaf* in History and Its Implications for Modern Islamic Economies," *Islamic Economic Studies*, vol. 6, no. 1.

Claessens, S., 1995, "The Emergence of Equity Investment in Developing Countries—Overview," *The World Bank Economic Review*, vol. 9, pp. 1–17 (Washington DC: The World Bank).

Claessens, S. and Feijen, E., 2006, "Financial Sector Development and the Millennium Development," *World Bank Working Paper* No. 89 (Washington, DC: The World Bank).

Claessens, S. and Perotti, E., 2006, "The Links between Finance and Inequality: Channels and Evidence," Background paper for the *World Development Report 2006* (Washington, DC: The World Bank).

Clarke, G.R.G., 2004, "How the Quality of Institutions Affects Technological Deepening in Developing Countries," *World Bank Policy Research Working Paper* No. 2603 (Washington, DC: The World Bank).

Clementi, G.L. and MacDonald, G., 2004, "Investor Protection, Optimal Incentives, and Economic Growth," *Journal of Economics*, August, pp. 1131–75.

Cole, H., 1988, "Financial Structure and International Trade," *International Economic Review*, vol. 29.

Coleman, J.S., 1990, *Foundations of Social Theory* (The Belknap Press of Harvard University Press).

Coleman, J.S., 1988, "Social Capital in the Creation of Human Capital," *The American Journal of Sociology*, vol. 94, Supplement, pp. 95–120 (University of Chicago).

Cooper, G., 2008, *The Origin of Financial Crises* (New York: Vintage Books).

Coval, J.D., 1999, "Home Bias at Home: Local Equity Preference in Domestic Portfolios," *Journal of Finance*, vol. 54, no. 6.

Crafts, N., 2003, *Globalization and Economic Growth: A Historical Perspective* (London: London School of Economics).

Cummings, J.T., Askari, H., and Mustafa, A., 1980, "Islam and Modern Economic Change," in J.L. Esposito (ed.), *Islam and Development* (Syracuse University Press).

Dasgupta, P. and Serageldin, I., 1999, *Social Capital: A Multifaceted Perspective* (Washington, DC: The World Bank).

Davis, J.R., 1969, "Henry Simons, the Radical: Some Documentary Evidence," *History of Political Economy*, vol. 1, no. 2, pp. 388–94.

Day, J., 2002, *The Levant Trade in the Middle Ages, the Economic History of Byzantium: From the Seventh through the Fifteenth Century* (Dumbarton Oaks Research Library and Collection).

Dehesa, M., et. al., 2007, "Relative Price Stability, Creditor Rights, and Financial Deepening," *IMF Working Paper* (Washington, DC: International Monetary Fund).

Demirgüç-Kunt, A., Beck, T., and Levine R., 2006, "Small and Medium Enterprises, Growth, and Poverty: Cross-Country Evidence," *World Bank Policy Research Working Paper* No. 3178 (Washington, DC: The World Bank).

Dennis, L., 1932, "Usury," Usury and the Canonists: Continued, *The Economic Journal*, June, pp. 312–18.

De Somogyi, J., 1965, "Trade in Classical Arabic Literature," *The Muslim World*, pp. 131–34.

Deutsche Bank, "Pioneering Innovative *Shari'ah* Compliant Solution," *Deutsche Bank Academic Paper*.

Docquier, F. and Rapoport, H., 2004, "Skilled Migration: The Perspective of Developing Countries," *World Bank Policy Research Working Paper* No. 3381.

Doidge, C., Karolyi, A.G., and Stulz, R.M., 2004, "Why are Foreign Firms Listed in the U.S. Worth More?" *Journal of Financial Economics*, pp. 205–38.

Dollar, D., 1992, "Outward-Oriented Developing Economies Really Do Grow More Rapidly: Evidence from 95 LDC's, 1976–1985," *Economic Development and Cultural Change*, pp. 523–44.

Dollar, D. and Kraay, A., 2002, "Growth Is Good for the Poor," *Journal of Economic Growth*, vol. 7, no. 3, September, pp. 195–225.

Edison, H.J. and Warnock, F.E., 2006, "Cross-Border Listings, Capital Controls, and Equity Flows to Emerging Markets," *NBER Working Paper* No. 12589 (Cambridge, MA: National Bureau of Economic Research).

Edwards, S., 1993, "Openness, Trade Liberalization, and Growth in Developing Countries," *Journal of Economic Literature*, pp. 1358–93.

Ehrenkreuz, A., 1959, "Studies in the Monetary History of the Near East in the Middle Ages," *JESHO*, vol. 2, pp. 128–61; 1963, vol. 6, pp. 243–77.

El-Erian, M.A., 2007, "Dealing with Global Fluidity," *A Compilation of Articles from Finance and Development* (Washington, DC: International Monetary Fund).

Epstein, G., 2002, "Financialization, Rentier Interests, and Central Bank Policy," www.umass.edu/peri/finagenda.html#alphalist.

Erbas, N. and Mirakhor, A., 2007, "The Equity Premium Puzzle, Ambiguity Aversion, and Institutional Quality," *IMF Working Paper* (Washington, DC: International Monetary Fund).

Ernst & Young, 2007, "Ernst & Young Islamic Funds and Investment Report," The World Islamic Funds and Capital Markets Conference, Dubai, UAE.

Estevadeordal, A. and Taylor, A.M., 2002, "Testing Trade Theory in Ohlin's Time," *NBER Working Paper* No. W8842, March. Available at SSRN: http://ssrn.com/abstract=305065.

Evans, M. and Hnatkovska, V., 2005, "International Capital Flows Returns and World Financial Integration," *NBER Working Paper* No. 11701 (Cambridge, MA: National Bureau of Economic Research).

Exenberger, A., 2004, "The Cradle of Globalization: Venice's and Portugal's Contribution to a World Becoming Global," *Working Papers in Economics* No. 2004/02 (Austria: University of Innsbruck).

Fama, E., 1970, "Efficient Capital Markets: A Review of Theory and Empirical Work," *Journal of Finance*, vol. 25, no. 2, May, pp. 383–417.

Faria, A. and Mauro, P., 2004, "Institutions and the External Capital Structure of Countries," *IMF Working Paper* No. WP/04/236 (Washington, DC: International Monetary Fund).

Faria, A., Mauro, P., Minnoni, M., and Zaklan, A., 2006, "External Financing of Emerging Market Countries: Evidence from Two Waves of Financial Globalization," *IMF Working Paper* No. WP/06/205 (Washington, DC: International Monetary Fund).

Fazzari, S.M., 1999, "Minsky and the Mainstream: Has Recent Research Rediscovered Financial Keynesianism?" *Working Paper* No. 278 (Annandale-on-Hudson, NY: The Levy Economics Institute).

Fearson, W.E., Foerster, S.R., and Keim, D.B., 1993, "General Tests of Latent Variable Models and Mean-Variance Spanning," *Journal of Finance*, vol. 48, no. 1, pp. 131–55.

Federal Reserve Board, 2002, "Remarks by Chairman Alan Greenspan," April. Available on Federal Reserve Board website.

Ferguson, N., 2008, *The Ascent of Money* (New York: The Penguin Press).

Fergusson, L., 2006, "Institutions for Financial Development: What Are They and Where Do They Come from?" *Journal of Economic Surveys*, vol. 20, no. 1, pp. 27–69.

Ferri, P. and H.P. Minsky, 1991, "Market Processes and Thwarting Systems," *Working Paper* No. 74 (Annandale-on-Hudson, NY: The Levy Economics Institute).

Fiennes, T., 2007, "Supervisory Implications of Islamic Banking: A Supervisor's Perspective," in S. Archer and R.A. Karim, *Islamic Finance: The Regulatory Challenge* (Singapore: John Wiley & Sons Asia).

Finance and Development, 2007, "Globalization: The Story Behind the Numbers," A Compilation of Articles from *Finance and Development* (Washington, DC: International Monetary Fund).

Financial Times, 2007, Reports "Islamic Finance," May 24.

Findlay, R. and Lundahl, M., 2002, "The First Globalization Episode: The Creation of the Mongol Empire, or the Economics of Chinggis Khan," http://yaleglobal. yale.edu/about/pdfs/mongol.pdf.

Fischel, W., 1937, *Jews in the Economic and Political Life of Mediaeval Islam* (London).

Fischel, W., 1933, "The Origin of Banking in Medieval Islam," *Journal of the Royal Asiatic Society*, pp. 339–52 and 568–603. Also published in *Islamic Culture*, vol. XIV (Cairo: Bureau of Compilation, Translation and Publication).

Flood, R.P. and Garber, P.M., 1980, "Gold Monetization and Gold Discipline," *NBER Working Papers* No. 0544 (Cambridge, MA: National Bureau of Economic Research).

Frank, A.G., 1990, "The Thirteenth Century World System: A Review Essay," *Journal of World History*, vol. 1, no. 2, pp. 249–56.

Frankel, J.A. and Rose, A.K, 1996, "Currency Crashes in Emerging Markets: Empirical Indicators," *CEPR Discussion Papers* No. 1349.

French, K.R. and Poterba, J.M., 1991, "Investor Diversification and International Equity Markets," *American Economic Review*, vol. 81, no. 2, pp. 222–26.

Friedman, M., 1967, "The Monetary Theory and Policy of Henry Simons," *Journal of Law and Economics*, vol. X, pp. 1–13.

Fry, M., 1995, *Money, Interest, and Banking in Economic Development* (The Johns Hopkins University Press).

Fukuyama, F., 1996, *Trust, the Social Virtues and the Creation of Prosperity* (Free Press Paperbacks).

Garcia, V.F., Cibis, V.F., and Maino, R., 2002, "Remedy for Banking Crises: What Chicago and Islam Have in Common," World Bank and IMF Staffs, unpublished.

Garretsen, H., Lensink, R., and Sterken, E., 2003, "Growth, Financial Development, Societal Norms and Legal Institutions," *International Financial Markets Institutions and Money*, June.

Gelos, R.G. and Wei, S-J., 2002, "Transparency and International Investor Behavior," *NBER Working Paper* No. 9260 (Cambridge, MA: National Bureau of Economic Research).

Gills, B.K. and Frank, G.A., 1994a, "The Cumulation of Accumulation," in B.K. Gills and G.A. Frank (eds.), *The World System, Five Hundred Years or Five Thousand?* (London and New York: Routledge), pp. 81–114.

Gills, B.K. and Frank, G.A., 1994b, "World System Cycles, Crises, and Hegemonic Shifts, 1700 BC to 1700 AD," in B.K. Gills and G.A. Frank (eds.), *The World System, Five Hundred Years or Five Thousand?* (London and New York: Routledge), pp. 143–99.

Glaeser, E.L., 2000, "Measuring Trust," *The Quarterly Journal of Economics*, August, pp. 811–46.

Glaeser, E.L., Laibson, D., Scheinkman, J.A., and Soutter, C.L., 1999, "What is Social Capital? The Determinants of Trust and Trustworthiness," *NBER Working Paper* No. 7216 (Cambridge, MA: National Bureau of Economic Research).

Goitein, S.D., 1967, *A Mediterranean Society, The Jewish Communities of the Arab World as Portrayed in the Documents of the Cairo Geniza*, Vol. I (Berkeley and Los Angeles: Economic Foundations).

Goitein, S.D., 1964, "Commercial and Family Partnerships in the Countries of Medieval Islam," *Islamic Studies*, vol. 3, pp. 318–19.

Goitein, S.D., 1962, *Jewish Education in Muslim Countries, Based on Records of the Cairo Geniza* (Hebrew) (Jerusalem).

Goitein, S.D., 1961, "The Main Industries of the Mediterranean Area as Reflected in the Records of the Cairo Geniza," *JESHO*, vol. 4, pp. 168–97.

Goitein, S.D., 1955, "The Cairo Geniza as a Source for the History of Muslim Civilization," *Studia Islamica*, pp. 168–97.

Goitein, S.D., 1954, "From the Mediterranean to India," *Speculum*, vol. 29, pp. 181–97.

Goitein, S.D. and Shemesh, B., 1957, *A Muslim Law in Israel* (Hebrew) (Jerusalem).

Goldberg, P.K. and Pavcnik, N., 2007, "Distributional Effects of Globalization in Developing Countries," *NBER Working Paper* No. 12885 (Cambridge, MA: National Bureau of Economic Research).

Goodhart, C., 2004, *Financial Development and Economic Growth: Explaining the Links* (New York: Palgrave Macmillan and British Association for the Advancement of Science Books).

Gordon H. Hancon, 2008. "International Migration," World Bank Seminar, October 3.

Gorton, G., 2008, "The Panic of 2007," *NBER Working Paper* No. 14398 (Cambridge, MA: National Bureau of Economic Research).

Grais, W. and Pellegrini, M., 2006, "Corporate Governance and Shariah Compliance in Institutions Offering Islamic Financial Services," *World Bank Policy Research Working Paper* No. 4054, November.

Gray, R. and Archad, I., 2007, "Regulating Islamic Capital Markets," in M.K. Hassan and M.K. Lewis (eds.), *Handbook of Islamic Banking* (Cheltenham, UK: Edward Elgar), pp. 282–92.

Greenlaw, D., Hatius, J., Kashyap, A.K., and Shin, H.S., 2008, "Leveraged Losses: Lessons from the Mortgage Market Meltdown," Paper presented to the US Monetary Policy Forum.

Greenspan, A., 2004, "Risk and Uncertainty in Monetary Policy," *American Economic Review, Papers and Proceedings*, vol. 94, pp. 33–40.

Greenspan, A., 2002, "Economic Volatility," Paper presented at a symposium sponsored by the Federal Reserve Bank of Kansas City, Jackson Hole, Wyoming, August 30.

Greenwald, B.C. and Stiglitz, J.E., 1990, "Asymmetric Information and the New Theory of the Firm: Financial Constraints and Risk Behavior," *The American Economic Review*, May.

Gross, D., 2007, *POP: Why Bubbles Are Great for the Economy* (New York: Collins).

Guiso, L., et. al., 2005, "Trusting the Stock Market," *NBER Working Paper* No. 11648 (Cambridge, MA: National Bureau of Economic Research).

Guiso, L., Sapienza, P., and Zingales, L., 2004, "The Role of Social Capital in Financial Development," *The American Economic Review*, vol. 94, no. 3.

Habachy, S., 1962, "Property, Right, and Contract in Muslim Law," *Columbia Law Review I*, vol. 62, no. 3.

Halaissos, M. and Bertaut, C., 1995, "Why Do So Few Hold Stocks?" *The Economic Journal*, vol. 105, no. 432, pp. 1110–29.

Hanson, Gordon H., 2008, "International Migration," World Bank Seminar, October 3.

Harrison, A., 2006, "Globalization and Poverty," *NBER Working Paper* No. 12347 (Cambridge, MA: National Bureau of Economic Research).

Hassan, M.K. and Lewis, M.K. (eds.), 2007, *Handbook of Islamic Banking* (Cheltenham, UK: Edward Elgar).

Häusler, G., 2007, "The Globalization of Finance," *A Compilation of Articles from Finance and Development* (Washington, DC: International Monetary Fund).

Helliwell, J.F. and Putnam, R., 1995, "Economic Growth and Social Capital in Italy," *Eastern Economic Journal*, vol. 21, no. 3, Summer, pp. 295–307.

Henisz, W.J., 2000, "The Institutional Environment for Economic Growth," *Economics and Politics*, vol. 12, pp. 1–31.

Henry, P.B., 2000a, "Do Stock Market Liberalizations Cause Investment Booms?" *Journal of Financial Economics*, vol. 58, no. 1/2, pp. 301–34.

Henry, P.B., 2000b, "Stock Market Liberalization, Economic Reform, and Emerging Market Equity Prices," *Journal of Finance*, vol. 55, no. 2, pp. 529–64.

Hirshleifer, J., 1971, "The Private and Social Value of Information and the Reward to Inventive Activity," *The American Economic Review*, vol. 61, no. 4, pp. 561–74.

Homer, S., 1963, *A History of Interest Rates*, 2nd ed. (New Brunswick, NJ: Rutgers University Press).

Hong, H., Kubik, J.D., and Stein, J.C., 2004, "Social Interaction and Stock-Market Participation," *Journal of Finance*, vol. 54, no. 1, February, pp. 137–63.

Honohan, P., 2006, "Financial Sector Policy and the Poor: Selected Findings and Issues," *World Bank Working Paper* No. 43 (Washington, DC: The World Bank).

Hubbard, G., 1998, "Capital Market Imperfections and Investment," *Journal of Economic Literature*, vol. 36, pp. 193–225.

Huberman, G., 2001, "Familiarity Breeds Investment," *The Review of Financial Studies*, vol. 14, no. 3, pp. 659–80.

Huberman, G. and Kandel, S., 1987, "Mean-Variance Spanning," *Journal of Finance*, vol. 42, no. 4, pp. 873–88.

Huberman, G., Kandel, S., and Stambaugh, R.F., 1987, "Mimicking Portfolios and Exact Arbitrage Pricing," *Journal of Finance*, vol. 42, no. 1, pp. 1–9.

Ibn Mandhoor, 1984, "Lisan Al-Arab," *Nashr Adab* (Qum, Iran).

IFIS, 2008, "Japan to Raise First Sovereign Islamic Bond in Malaysia Next Month," Bernama Newswire, January 16.

Imad, A.M., 2005, "In the Mirror of History: Were the Earlier Generations Smarter or Are We?" *Finance in Islam*.

Imamuddin, S.M., 1960, "Bayt Al-Mal and Banks in the Medieval Muslim World," *Islamic Culture*, January.

IMF, 2007a, *Global Financial Stability Report* (Washington, DC), April.

IMF, 2007b, *World Economic Outlook* (Washington, DC), April.

Iqbal, M. (ed.), 1986, *Distributive Justice and Need Fulfillment in an Islamic Economy* (Islamabad: International Institute of Islamic Economics, International Islamic University).

Iqbal, Z., 1999, "Financial Engineering in Islamic Finance," *Thunderbird International Business Review*, vol. 41, no. 4/5, July–October, pp. 541–60.

Iqbal, Z. and Mirakhor, A., 2007, *An Introduction to Islamic Finance: Theory and Practice* (Singapore: John Wiley and Sons).

Iqbal, Z. and Mirakhor, A., 2004, "A Stakeholders Model of Corporate Governance of the Firm in the Islamic Economic System," *Islamic Economic Studies*, vol. 11, no. 2, March.

Iqbal, Z. and Mirakhor, A., 2002, "Development of Islamic Financial Institutions and Challenges Ahead," in S. Archer and R.A. Karim (eds.), *Islamic Finance: Growth and Innovation* (London: Euromoney Books).

Iqbal, Z. and Mirakhor, A., 1999, "Progress and Challenges of Islamic Banking," *Thunderbird International Business Review*, vol. 41, no. 4/5, pp. 381–405.

Iqbal, Z. and Mirakhor, A., 1987, "Islamic Banking," *IMF Occasional Paper* No. 49.

IRTI and IFSB, 2006, Islamic Financial Services Industry Development: Ten-Year Framework and Strategies (Jeddah: Islamic Research and Training Institution (IRTI) and Islamic Development Bank).

ISI Analytics, 2007, *Islamic Financial Services Industry* (London: ISI Emerging Markets).

ISI Emerging Market Database (London: Euromoney).

Jobst, A., Kunzel, P., Mills P., and Amadou, S., 2008, "Islamic Bond Issuance—What Sovereign Debt Managers Need to Know," *IMF Policy Discussion Paper* No. PPD/08/3.

Johnson, S., McMillan, J., and Woodruff, C., 2002, "Property Rights and Finance," *The American Economic Review*, vol. 92, no. 5, pp. 335–56.

Ju, J. and Wei, Sh-J., 2006, "A Solution to Two Paradoxes of International Capital Flows," *IMF Occasional Paper* No. 178 (Washington, DC: International Monetary Fund).

Kalecki, M., 1971, "The Determinants of Profits," *Selected Essays on the Dynamics of the Capitalist Economy* (Cambridge University Press), pp. 78–92.

Kaminsky, G. and Schmuckler, S., 2002, "Short-Run Pain, Long-Run Gain: The Effects of Financial Liberalization," unpublished Working Paper (Washington, DC: International Monetary Fund).

Kareken, J.H., 1985, "Ensuring Financial Stability," in *Search for Financial Stability: The Past Fifty Years* (Federal Reserve Bank of San Francisco).

Karim, N., Tarazi, M., and Reille, X, 2008, *Islamic Microfinance: An Emerging Market Niche*, No. 49, August 2008 (CGAP).

Karolyi, A.G., 2004, "The Role of American Depositary Receipts in the Development of Emerging Equity Markets," *The Review of Economics and Statistics*, vol. 86, no. 3, August, pp. 670–90.

Kaufman, D., Kraay, A., and Mastruzzi, M., 2005, *Governance Matters: Governance Indicators for 1996–2004* (Washington, DC: The World Bank).

Keynes, J.M., 1936, *The General Theory of Employment, Interest and Money* (New York: Harbinger, 1965).

Keynes, J.M., 1933, "A Monetary Theory of Production," reprinted in D.E. Moggridge (ed.), *The Collected Writings of John Maynard Keynes*, vol. 13 (London: Macmillan, 1973), pp. 408–11.

Keynes, J.M., 1932, "Saving and Usury," Saving and Usury: A Symposium, *The Economic Journal*, March, pp. 135–37.

Khan, M. and Mirakhor, A., 1989, "The Financial System and Monetary Policy in an Islamic Economy," *Journal of King Abdulaziz University: Islamic Economics*, Vol. 1.

Khan, M. and Mirakhor, A., 1987, "Islamic Interest-Free Banking: A Theoretical Analysis," in M. Khan and A. Mirakhor (eds.), *Theoretical Studies in Islamic Banking and Finance* (Houston, TX: IRIS Books).

Khan, M. and Mirakhor, A., 1986, "Islamic Interest-Free Banking," *IMF Staff Papers*, Vol. 33.

Kho, B-Ch., Stulz, R.M., and Warnock, F.E., 2006, "Financial Globalization, Governance, and the Evolution of the Home Bias," *NBER Working Paper* No. 12389 (Cambridge, MA: National Bureau of Economic Research).

Klein, M.W., 2005, "Capital Account Liberalization, Institutional Quality and Economic Growth: Theory and Evidence," unpublished *NEBR Working Paper* (Cambridge, MA: National Bureau of Economic Research).

Knack, S. and Keefer, P., 1997, "Does Social Capital Have an Economic Payoff? A Cross-Country Investigation," *The Quarterly Journal of Economics*, November, pp. 1251–88.

Kobayakawa, S. and Hisachi, N., 1999, "A Theoretical Analysis of Narrow Banking Proposals," *IMES Discussion Paper Series* 99-E-19 (Bank of Japan).

Kohn, D.L., 2008, "Economic Outlook," Speech at the Georgetown University Wall Street Alliance, New York, October 15 (available at the website of Board of Governors of the Federal Reserve System).

Kohn, D.L., 2006, "Monetary Policy and Asset Prices," European Central Bank Colloquium on Monetary Policy: A Journey from Theory to Practice, Frankfurt, Germany, March 16 (available on the Federal Reserve Board website).

Konstas, P., 2006, "Reforming Deposit Insurance," *Public Policy Brief* No. 83 (Annandale-on-Hudson, NY: The Levy Economics Institute).

Kose, A., Prasad, E., Rogoff, K., and Wei, Sh-J., 2006, "Financial Globalization: A Reappraisal," *IMF Working Paper* No. WP/06/189 (Washington, DC: International Monetary Fund).

Kose, A., Prasad, E., and Terrones, M., 2007, "How Does Financial Globalization Affect Risk Sharing? Patterns and Channels" (Washington, DC: International Monetary Fund).

Kose, A., Prasad, E., and Terrones, M., 2005, "The Macroeconomic Implications of Financial Globalization: A Reappraisal and Synthesis," *IMF Working Paper* No. WP/01/180 (Washington, DC: International Monetary Fund).

Kose, A., Prasad, E., and Terrones, M., 2003, "Financial Integration and Macro-economic Volatility," *IMF Working Paper* No. WP/03/50 (Washington, DC: International Monetary Fund).

Kourides, P.N., 1970, "The Influence of Islamic Law on the Contemporary Middle Eastern Legal System: The Foundation and Binding Force of Contracts," *Columbia Journal of Transnational Law*, vol. 9, no. 2, pp. 384–435.

Kregel, J., 1997, "Margin of Safety and Weight of Argument in Generating Financial Fragility," *Journal of Economic Issues*, vol. 31, no. 2, pp. 543–48.

Krichene, N. and Mirakhor, A., 2008, "Resilience and Stability of the Islamic Financial System—An Overview," Public lecture, IFSB, November.

Krueger, A.O., 1980, "Trade Policy as an Input to Development," *American Economic Review*, May, pp. 288–92.

Labib, S.Y., 1969, "Capitalism in Medieval Islam," *Journal of Economic History*, vol. 29, no. 1, pp. 79–96.

Laiou, A.E., 2002a, "The Byzantine Economy in the Mediterranean Trade System: Thirteenth–Fifteenth Centuries," in A.E. Laiou, *Gender, Society and Economic Life in Byzantium* (Hampshire, 1992), pp. 177–223.

Laiou, A.E., 2002b, "The Levant Trade in the Middle Ages, The Economic History of Byzantium: From the Seventh through the Fifteenth Century," *Dumbarton Oaks Research Library and Collection*, No. 39.

Lane, E.W., 2003, *An Arabic–English Lexicon* (Lahore: Suhail Academy).

Lane, F.C., 1944, "Family Partnerships and Joint Ventures in the Venetian Republic," *Journal of Economic History*, vol. 4, no. 2, pp. 178–96.

Lane, F.C., 1937, "Venetian Bankers, 1496–1533: A Study in the Early Stages of Deposit Banking," *Journal of Political Economy*, vol. 45, pp. 187–206.

Levchenko, A. and Mauro, P., 2006, "Do Some Forms of Financial Flows Help Protect from Sudden Stops?" *IMF Occasional Paper* No. 202 (Washington, DC: International Monetary Fund).

Levine, R. and Zervos, S., 1998, "Stock Market, Banks and Economic Growth," *American Economic Review*, vol. 88, pp. 537–58.

Levine, R. and Zervos, S., 1997, "Financial Development and Economic Growth," *Journal of Economic Literature*, vol. 35, pp. 688–726.

Lewis, K.K., 1996, "Consumption, Stock Returns, and the Gains from International Risk-Sharing," *NBER Working Paper* No. 5410 (Cambridge, MA: National Bureau of Economic Research).

Lieber, A.E., 1968, "Eastern Business Practice and Medieval European Commerce," *Economic History Review*, 2nd Series, vol. 21, pp. 230–43.

Lim, M.M-H., 2008, "Old Wine in a New Bottle: Subprime Mortgage Crisis—Causes and Consequences," *Working Paper* No. 532 (Annandale-on-Hudson, NY: The Levy Economics Institute) (available on the LEI website).

Lindert, P.H. and Williamson, J.G., 2001, "Does Globalization Make the World More Unequal?" *NEBR Working Paper* No. 8228 (Cambridge, MA: National Bureau of Economic Research).

Lopez, R.S., 1976, *The Commercial Revolution of the Middle Ages, 950–1350* (Cambridge University Press).

Lopez, R.S., 1955, "East and West in the Early Middle Ages: Economic Relations," *Relazioni del X Congresso Internazionale di Scienze Storiche* (6 vols., Florence) III, pp. 129–37.

Lopez, R.S., 1952, "The Trade of Medieval Europe: The South," *The Cambridge Economic History of Europe*, vol. 2 (Cambridge University Press), pp. 257–354.

Lopez, R.S., 1951, "The Dollar of the Middle Ages," *Journal of Economic History*, pp. 209–34.

Lopez, R.S. and Raymond, I.W., 1955, *Medieval Trade in the Mediterranean World*, Records of Western Civilization Series (Columbia University Press).

Lopez-de-Silanes, F., La Porta, R.F., Shleifer, A., and Vishny, R.W., 1997, "Trust in Large Organizations," *The American Economic Review*, vol. 87, no. 2, *Papers and Proceedings of the Hundred and Fourth Annual Meeting of the American Economic Association*, pp. 333–38.

Lorenz, E., 1999, "Trust, Contract and Economic Cooperation," *Cambridge Journal of Economics*, vol. 23, pp. 301–15.

Lucas Jr., R., 2000, "Some Macroeconomics for the 21st Century," *Journal of Economic Perspectives*, vol. 14, no. 1, pp. 159–78.

Lucas Jr., R., 1990, "Why Doesn't Capital Flow from Rich to Poor Countries?" *American Economic Review Papers and Proceedings*, vol. 80, May, 1990 pp. 92–96.

Lucas Jr., R., 1988, "On the Mechanics of Economic Development," *Journal of Monetary Economics*, vol. 22, pp. 3–42.

Martin, M., 2007, "The Globalisation of Islamic Banking," *Middle East Economic Digest*, vol. 51, no. 36, pp. 33–36.

Mauro and Ostry, *IMF Survey*, September 2007.

Mehra, R., 2006, "The Equity Premium in India," *NBER Working Paper* No. 12434 (Cambridge, MA: National Bureau of Economic Research).

Mehra, R., 2003, "The Equity Premium: Why is it a Puzzle?" *Financial Analysts Journal*, pp. 54–69.

Mehra, R. and Prescott, E.C., 1985, "The Equity Premium: A Puzzle," *Journal of Monetary Economics*, vol. 15, pp. 145–61.

Metzler, L.A., 1951, "Wealth, Saving, and the Rate of Interest," *Journal of Political Economy*, vol. 59, pp. 93–116.

Michie, R.C., 2007, *The Global Securities Market: A History* (Oxford University Press).

Miller, M.H., 1988, "The Modigliani–Miller Propositions After Thirty Years," *Journal of Economic Perspectives*, vol. 2, no. 4, pp. 99–120.

Miller, M. and Modigliani, F., 1963, "Corporate Income Taxes and the Cost of Capital: A Correction," *American Economic Review*, vol. 53, no. 3, pp. 433–43.

Minsky, H.P., 2008, *Stabilizing an Unstable Economy* (New York: McGraw Hill).

Minsky, H.P., 1994, "Financial Instability and the Decline of Banking: Public Policy Implications," Paper presented at the Conference on the Declining Role of Banking, Federal Reserve Bank of Chicago.

Minsky, H.P., 1993, "Finance and Stability: The Limits of Capitalism," *Working Paper* No. 93 (Annandale-on-Hudson, NY: The Levy Economics Institute).

Minsky, H.P., 1992a, "The Financial Instability Hypothesis," *Working Paper* No. 74 (Annandale-on-Hudson, NY: The Levy Economics Institute).

Minsky, H.P., 1992b, "The Capital Development of the Economy and the Structure of Financial Institutions," *Working Paper* No. 72 (Annandale-on-Hudson, NY: The Levy Economics Institute).

Minsky, H.P., 1986, "Global Consequences of Financial Deregulation," *Working Paper* No. 96 (Washington University, Department of Economics).

Minsky, H.P., 1984, "Central Banking and Money Market Changes: A Reprise," *Working Paper* No. 72 (Washington University, Department of Economics).

Minsky, H.P., 1982, *Inflation, Recession and Economic Policy* (London: Wheatsheaf Books).

Mirakhor, A., 2005a, "Globalization and Islamic Finance," Paper presented at the Sixth International Conference on Islamic Economics and Finance, Jakarta, Indonesia, November.

Mirakhor, A., 2005b, "A Note on Islamic Economics," invited lecturer at the Islamic Development Bank for Research in Islamic Economics, April.

Mirakhor, A. 2003a, "General Characteristics of an Islamic Economic System," in B. Al-Hassani and A. Mirakhor (eds.), *Essays on Iqtisad* (Maryland: Nur Publications, 1989; republished New York: Global Scholarly Publications).

Mirakhor, A., 2003b, "Muslim Contribution to Economics," Paper presented at the Annual Meeting of the South-Western Economic Association, March 1983 and reproduced from *Essays on Iqtisad* (Maryland: Nur Publications, 1989; republished New York: Global Scholarly Publications).

Mirakhor, A., 2003c, "Islamic Economic System," in B. Al-Hassani and A. Mirakhor (eds.), *Essays on Iqtisad* (Maryland: Nur Publications, 1989; republished New York: Global Scholarly Publications).

Mirakhor, A., 2003d, "Theory of an Islamic Financial System," in B. Al-Hassani and A. Mirakhor (eds.), *Essays on Iqtisad* (Maryland: Nur Publications, 1989; republished New York: Global Scholarly Publications).

Mirakhor, A., 2002, "Hopes for the Future of Islamic Finance," *New Horizon*, no. 121, July–August, pp. 5–8.

Mirakhor, A., 1997, "Outline of an Islamic Economic System," Zahid Husain Memorial Lecture Series, No. 11, March 22, State Bank of Pakistan.

Mirakhor, A., 1990, "Equilibrium in a Non-Interest Open Economy," IMF, published in *Journal of King Abdulaziz University: Islamic Economics* (1993), vol. 5, pp. 3–23.

Mirakhor, A., 1989, "Islamic Economic System," in B. Al-Hassani and A. Mirakhor (eds.), *Essays on Iqtisad* (Maryland: Nur Publications).

Mirakhor, A., 1985, "Theory of an Islamic Financial System," published in B. Al-Hassani and A. Mirakhor, *Essays on Iqtisad* (New York: Global Scholarly Publications, 2003).

Mirakhor, A., 1983, "Muslim Contribution to Economics," Paper first presented at the Midwest Economic Association Meeting, April 7–9; reprinted in B. Al-Hassani and A. Mirakhor, *Essays on Iqtisad* (Maryland: Nur Publications; republished New York: Global Scholarly Publications, 2003).

Mirakhor, A. and Iqbal, Z., 2007, "Profit-and-Loss Sharing Contracts in Islamic Finance," in M.K. Hassan and M.K. Lewis (eds.), *Handbook of Islamic Banking* (Cheltenham, UK: Edward Elgar), pp. 49–63.

Mirakhor, A. and Iqbal, Z., 1988, "Stabilization and Growth in an Open Islamic Economy," *IMF Working Paper* No. 22.

Mirakhor, A. and Krichene, N., 2009, "Recent Crisis: Lessons from Islamic Finance," Unpublished manuscript, January.

Mishkin, F.S., 2005, "Is Financial Globalization Beneficial?" *NBER Working Paper* No. 11891 (Cambridge, MA: National Bureau of Economic Research).

Modigliani, F. and Miller, M.H., 1958, "The Cost of Capital, Corporate Finance, and the Theory of Investment," *American Economic Review*, vol. 48, no. 3, pp. 261–97.

Mody, A. and Murshid, A.P., 2005, "Growing up with Capital Flows," *Journal of International Economics*, vol. 65, pp. 249–66.

Munro, J., 2003, "The Late-Medieval Origins of the Modern Financial Revolution: Overcoming Impediments from Church and State," *Working Paper* No. 2. Online version: www.chass.utoronto.ca/ecipa/wpa.html (University of Toronto, Department of Economics and Institute for Policy Analysis).

Oakley, D., 2007, "Capital Takes a Leading Role," *FT Report: Islamic Finance* (London: Financial Times).

Obstfeld, M., 2009, "International Finance and Growth in Developing Countries: What Have We Learned?" *NBER Working Paper* No. 14691 (Cambridge, MA: National Bureau of Economic Research).

Obstfeld, M., 1994, "Risk-Taking, Global Diversification, and Growth," *The American Economic Review*, vol. 84, no. 5, December, pp. 1310–29.

Obstfeld, M., 1992, "International Risk Sharing and Capital Mobility—Another Look," *Journal of International Money and Finance*, vol. 11, pp. 115–21.

Obstfeld, M. and Taylor, A., 2003, *Global Capital Markets: Integration, Crisis and Growth* (Cambridge: Cambridge University Press).

Obstfeld, M., et. al., 2003, "Globalization and Capital Markets," in M.D. Bordo, A.M. Taylor, and J.G. Williamson (eds.), *Globalization in Historical Perspective* (Chicago: NEBR, University of Chicago Press).

OECD, 2006, *The SME Financing Gap: Theory and Evidence, Vol. I: Organisation for Economic Co-operation and Development* (OECD Publications).

O'Hara, K., 2004, *Trust from Socrates to Spin* (Duxford, UK: Icon Books).

Ozden, C. and Schiff, M. (eds.), 2006, *International Migration, Remittances and the Brain Drain* (The World Bank and Palgrave Macmillan).

Palley, T.J., 2007, "Financialization: What It Is and Why It Matters," *Working Paper* No. 525 (Annandale-on-Hudson, NY: The Levy Economics Institute).

Papadimitriou, D.B. and Wray, L.R., 1999, "Minsky's Analysis of Financial Capitalism," *Working Paper* No. 275 (Annandale-on-Hudson, NY: The Levy Economics Institute).

Papadimitriou, D.B. and Wray, L.R., 1998, "Narrow Banks in Today's Financial World: U.S. and International Perspective," in G. Bager and M. Szabo-Pelsoczi (eds.), *Global Monetary and Economic Convergence* (Aldershot, UK: Ashgate Publishing).

Payandeh, A., 1984, *Nahjulfasahah: Collected Short Sayings of the Messenger* (Tehran: Golestanian).

Perotti, E.C. and van Oijen, P., 2001, "Privatization, Political Risk and Stock Market Development in Emerging Economies," *Journal of International Money and Finance*, vol. 20, pp. 43–69.

Perotti, E.C. and van Oijen, P., 1995, "Credible Privatization," *American Economic Review*, vol. 85, pp. 847–59.

Phillips, R.J., 1995, "Narrow Banking Reconsidered," *Public Policy Brief* No. 18 (Annandale-on-Hudson, NY: The Levy Economics Institute).

Phillips, R.J., 1992a, "Credit Markets and Narrow Banking," *Working Paper* No. 77 (Annandale-on-Hudson, NY: The Levy Economics Institute).

Phillips, R.J., 1992b, "Chicago Plan and New Deal Banking Reform," *Working Paper* No. 76 (Annandale-on-Hudson, NY: The Levy Economics Institute).

Phillips, R.J., 1989, "The Minsky-Simons-Vebleu Connection: Comment," *Journal of Economic Issues*, vol. XXIII, pp. 889–91.

Phillips, R.J., 1988, "Vebleu and Simons on Credit and Monetary Reform," *Southern Economic Journal*, vol. 55, no. 1, pp. 171–81.

Pierce, J.L., 1991, *The Future of Banking. A Twentieth Century Fund Report* (New York: Yale University Press).

Pinkowitz, L., Stulz, R.M., and Williamson, R., 2004, "Do Firms in Countries with Poor Protection of Investor Rights Hold More Cash?" unpublished *NEBR Working Paper* (Cambridge, MA: National Bureau of Economic Research).

Posen, A.S., 2001, *A Strategy to Prevent Future Crises: Safety Shrink the Banking Sector* (Peter G. Peterson Institute for International Economics).

Postan, M., 1957, "Partnership in English Medieval Commerce," *Studi in Onore Di A. Sapori*, vol. 1 (Milan), pp. 521–49.

Postan, M., 1928, "Credit in Medieval Trade," *The Economic History Review*, vol. 1, no. 2, pp. 234–61.

Power, D. and Epstein, G., 2003, "Rentier Income and Financial Crises," *Working Paper* No. 57 (Amherst, MA: Political Economy Research Institute, University of Massachusetts).

Prasad, E., Rogoff, K., Wei, S., and Kose, M.A., 2004, "Effects of Financial Globalization on Developing Countries: Some Empirical Evidence," *IMF Occasional Paper* No. 220 (Washington, DC: International Monetary Fund).

Rajan, R.G., 2006, "Has Finance Made the World Riskier?" *European Financial Management*, vol. 12, no. 4, pp. 499–533.

Rajan, R.G., 2005, "Has Financial Development Made the World Riskier?" *NBER Working Paper* No. 11728 (Cambridge, MA: National Bureau of Economic Research).

Rajan, R.G. and Zingales, L., 2003, "The Great Reversals: The Politics of Financial Development in the Twentieth Century," *Journal of Financial Economics*, vol. 69, pp. 5–50.

Ranciere, R., Tornell, A., and Westermann, F., 2006, "Decomposing the Effects of Financial Liberalization: Crises vs. Growth," *NBER Working Paper* No. 12806 (Cambridge, MA: National Bureau of Economic Research).

RatingsDirect, 2009, "Rated Gulf Islamic Financial Institutions and Takaful Companies Have Shown Resilience to Global Market Dislocation, But They Are Not Risk Immune," Standard & Poor's, www.standardandpoors.com/ratingsdirect, February 20.

Ravallion, M., 2005, "Inequality is Bad for the Poor," *World Bank Policy Research Working Paper* No. 3677 (Washington, DC: The World Bank).

Ravallion, M., 2004a, "Looking beyond Averages in the Trade and Poverty Debate," *World Bank Policy Research Paper* No. 3461 (Washington, DC: The World Bank).

Ravallion, M., 2004b, "Competing Concepts of Inequality in the Globalization Debate," *World Bank Policy Research Paper* No. 3243 (Washington, DC: The World Bank).

Ravallion, M. and Chen, S., 2001, "How Did the World's Poorest Fare in the 1990's?" *Review of Income and Wealth Series*, vol. 47, no. 3, pp. 283–300.

RedMoney, 2009, "Islamic Finance in the UK: A Review of 2008," *Islamic Finance News* (Malaysia).

RedMoney, 2007, *The 2007 Guide to Opportunities and Trends in Islamic Finance* (Kuala Lumpur: RedMoney).

Robbins, L., 1952, *The Theory of Economic Policy in English Classical Economics* (London: Allen & Unwin).

Rodriguez, F. and Rodrik, D., 2000, "Trade Policy and Economic Growth: A Skeptic's Guide to the Cross-Sectional Evidence," *NBER Macroeconomics Annual*, vol. 15, pp. 261–325.

Rodrik, D., 2004, "Getting Institutions Right," *Unpublished Working Paper* (Cambridge, MA: Harvard University).

Roemer, P.M., 1987, "Crazy Explanations for the Productivity Slowdown," in S. Fischer (ed.), *NBER Macroeconomic Annual* (Cambridge, MA: MIT Press).

Roemer, P.M., 1986, "Increasing Returns and Long-Run Growth," *Journal of Political Economy*, no. 94, pp. 1002–37.

Ross, S.A., 1978, "Mutual Fund Separation in Financial Theory—the Separating Distributions," *Journal of Economic Theory*, vol. 47, pp. 254–86.

Ross, S.A., 1976, "The Arbitrage Theory of Capital Asset Pricing," *Journal of Economic Theory*, vol. 13, pp. 341–60.

Sachedina, A.A., 2001, *The Islamic Roots of Democratic Pluralism* (New York: Oxford University Press).

Sachedina, A.A., 1988, *The Just Ruler in Sh'ite Islam* (New York: Oxford University Press).

Sachs, J. and Warner, A., 1995, "Economic Reform and the Process of Global Integration," *Brookings Papers on Economic Activity*, vol. 1, pp. 1325–43.

Sachs, J., Warner, A., Aslund, A., and Fischer, S., 1995, "Economic Reform and the Process of Global Integration," *Brooking Papers on Economic Activity*, pp. 1–118.

Saleh, N.A., 1992, *Unlawful Gain and Legitimate Profit in Islamic Law: Riba, Gharar, and Islamic Banking*, 2nd ed. (London: Graham & Trotman).

Sandwell, B.K., 1932, "Mr. Keynes and the Canonists," Saving and Usury: A Symposium, *The Economic Journal*, March, pp. 131–35.

Sauer, J.B., 2002, "Metaphysics and Economy—The Problem of Interest. A Comparison of the Practice and Ethics of Interest in Islamic and Christian Cultures," *International Journal of Social Economics*, vol. 29, no. 1/2, pp. 97–118.

Schmidt, D., 2007, "Globalization at Work," *A Compilation of Articles from Finance and Development* (Washington, DC: International Monetary Fund).

Schmukler, S., 2004, "Financial Globalization: Gains and Pain for Developing Countries," *Economic Review*, Second Quarter, pp. 39–66 (Federal Reserve Bank of Atlanta).

Scott, K.E., 1998, "Mutual Funds as an Alternative Banking System," *Journal of Institutional and Theoretical Economics*, vol. 154, pp. 86–96.

Sebastiani, M. (ed.), *Kalecki's Relevance Today* (London: Macmillan).

Shane, R.M., 1984, "Capital Theory and the Dynamics of Growth," *American Economic Review*, vol. 64.

Shiller, R.J., 2003, *The New Financial Order: Risk in the 21st Century* (Princeton University Press).

Shirazi, I.M., 2001, *War, Peace, and Non-Violence: An Islamic Perspective* (Fountain Books).

Shleifer, A. and Wolfenson, D., 2002, "Investor Protection and Equity Markets," *Journal of Financial Economics*, vol. 66, pp. 3–27.

Siddiqi, M.N., 2006, "Shariah, Economics and the Progress of Islamic Finance: The Role of Shariah Experts," Seventh Harvard Forum on Islamic Finance, Cambridge, Massachusetts, April 21.

Siddiqi, M.N., 2001, *Economics, An Islamic Approach* (Islamabad: Institute of Policy Studies; Leicester, UK: The Islamic Foundation).

Siddiqi, M.N., 1985, *Partnership and Profit-Sharing in Islamic Law* (Leicester, UK: The Islamic Foundation).

Siddiqi, M.N., 1981, *Muslim Economic Thinking* (Leicester, UK: The Islamic Foundation).

Siegel, J., 2005, "Can Foreign Firms Bond Themselves Effectively by Renting U.S. Securities Laws?" *Journal of Financial Economics*, vol. 75, pp. 319–59.

Simons, H., 1948, *Economic Policy for a Free Society* (Chicago: University of Chicago Press).

Simons, H., 1936, "Rules versus Authorities in Monetary Policy," *Journal of Political Economy*, vol. 44, no. 1, pp. 1–30.

Simons, H., 1934, "A Positive Program for Laissez Faire: Some Proposals for a Liberal Economic Policy," *Public Policy Pamphlet* No. 15 (University of Chicago).

Skidelski, R., 2008, "The Remedist," *The New York Times Magazine*, December 12.

Smarzynska, B.K. and Wei, Sh-J., 2000, "Corruption and the Composition of Foreign Direct Investment: Firm-Level Evidence," *NBER Working Paper* No. 7969 (Cambridge, MA: National Bureau of Economic Research).

Somerville, H., 1932, "Usury and Standstill," Usury and the Canonists: Continued, *The Economic Journal*, June, pp. 318–23.

Somerville, H., 1931, "Interest and Usury in a New Light," *The Economic Journal*, vol. XLI, no. 164, pp. 646–49.

Soros, G., 2008, "The Crisis and What to Do About It," *The New York Review of Books*, December 4, pp. 1–6.

Soros, G., 1987, *The Alchemy of Finance* (New York: Simon & Schuster).

Spikes, S., 2008, "Qatar Islamic Unit Wins UK Banking Licence," *Financial Times*, February 5.

Spong, K., 1996, "Narrow Banks: An Alternative Approach to Banking Reform," in D. Papadimitriou (ed.), *Stability in the Financial System* (New York: St. Martin's Press).

Spong, K., 1993, "Narrow Banks: An Alternative Approach to Banking Reform," *Working Paper* No. 90 (Division of Bank Supervision and Structure, Federal Reserve Bank of Kansas City, Kansas City, Missouri).

Spong, K., 1991, "A Narrow Banking Proposal" (Federal Reserve Bank of Kansas City).

Spulber, D.F., 1996, "Market Microstructure and Intermediation," *Journal of Economic Perspectives*, vol. 10, no. 3, pp. 135–52.

Spuler, B., 1970, "Trade in the Eastern Islamic Countries in the Early Centuries," in D. Richards (ed.), *Islam and the Trade in Asia*, pp. 11–20.

Stiglitz, J., 2006, *Making Globalization Work* (New York: W.W. Norton).

Stiglitz, J., 2003, *Globalization and its Discontents* (New York: W.W. Norton).

Stiglitz, J., 1988, "Money, Credit and Business Fluctuations," *Economic Record*, vol. 64, no. 187, pp. 307–22.

Stiglitz, J.E., 1987, "The Causes and Consequences of the Dependence of Quality on Price," *Journal of Economic Literature*, vol. XXV, March.

Stiglitz, J.E. and Weiss, A., 1992, "Asymmetric Information in Credit Markets and Its Implications for Macro-economics," *Oxford Economic Papers*, vol. 44, no. 4, pp. 694–724.

Stiglitz, J.E. and Weiss, A., 1981, "Credit Rationing in Markets with Imperfect Information," *American Economic Review*, vol. 71, no. 3, pp. 333–421.

Stulz, R., 2006, "Financial Globalization, Corporate Governance, and Eastern Europe," *NBER Working Paper* No. 11912 (Cambridge, MA: National Bureau of Economic Research).

Stulz, R., 2005, "The Limits of Financial Globalization," *Journal of Finance*, vol. 60, no. 4, August.

Stulz, R., 1999a, "International Portfolio Flows and Security Markets," in M. Feldstein (ed.), *International Capital Flows* (Chicago: Chicago University Press).

Stulz, R., 1999b, "Globalization, Corporate Finance, and the Cost of Capital," *Journal of Applied Corporate Finance*, vol. 12, no. 3, pp. 8–25.

Tesar, L.L., 1995a, "Evaluating the Gains from International Risk-Sharing," *Carnegie-Rochester Conference Series on Public Policy*, vol. 42, June, pp. 95–143.

Tesar, L.L., 1995b, "Home Bias and High Turnover," *Journal of International Money and Finance*, vol. 14, August, pp. 467–92.

The Banker, 2007, Special Supplement: Top 500 Financial Islamic Institutions, November 1.

The Message of the Qur'an (Translation of the *Qur'an* by Muhammad Asad), 1980 (Gibralter: Dar al Andalus Limited).

Tornell, A., Westermann, F., and Martinez, L., 2004, "The Positive Link Between Financial Liberalization, Growth, and Crises," *NBER Working Paper* No. 10293 (Cambridge, MA: National Bureau of Economic Research).

Tuma, E.H., 1965, "Early Arab Economic Policies," *Journal of the Central Institute of Islamic Research* (Karachi), vol. 4, no. 1, pp. 1–24.

Turgeon, L., 1996, *Bastard Keynesianism* (Westport, CT: Praeger).

Udovitch, A.L., 1970a, "Commercial Techniques in Early Medieval Islamic Trade," in D. Richards (ed.), *Islam and the Trade of Asia*, pp. 37–62.

Udovitch, A.L., 1970b, *Partnership and Profit in Medieval Islam* (Princeton University Press).

Udovitch, A.L., 1967a, "Credit as a Means of Investment in Medieval Islamic Trade," *Journal of the American Oriental Society*, vol. 87, no. 3, July–September, pp. 260–64.

Udovitch, A.L., 1967b, "Labor Partnership in Medieval Islamic Law," *Journal of Economic and Social History of the Orient*, vol. 10, pp. 64–80.

Udovitch, A.L., 1962, "At the Origins of the Western Commenda: Islam, Israel, Byzantium?", pp. 198–207.

Ul-Haque, N. and Mirakhor, A., 1999, "The Design of Instruments for Government Finance in an Islamic Economy," *Islamic Economic Studies*, vol. 6, no. 2.

Ul Haq, I., 1995, *Economic Doctrines of Islam* (Virginia: The International Institute of Islamic Thought).

Van Greuning, H. and Iqbal, Z., 2007, *Analyzing Risk for Islamic Banks* (Washington, DC: The World Bank).

Van Wincoop, E., 1999, "How Big are Potential Welfare Gains from International Risk Sharing?" *Journal of International Economics*, vol. 47, February, pp. 109–235.

Van Wincoop, E., 1994, "Welfare Gains from International Risk Sharing," *Journal of Monetary Economics*, vol. 34, October, pp. 175–200.

Wallace, N., 1996, "Narrow Banking Meets the Diamond-Dybvig Model," *Federal Reserve Bank of Minneapolis Quarterly Review*, vol. 20, no. 1, winter 1996, pp. 3–13.

Watkins, K., 2007, "Making Globalization Work for the Poor: Point, Counterpoint," *A Compilation of Articles from Finance and Development* (Washington DC: International Monetary Fund).

Wei, Sh-J., 2005, "Connecting Two Views on Financial Globalization: Can We Make Further Progress?" Paper prepared for the 18th Annual TRIO Conference, organized by Shin-ichi Fukuda, Takeo Hoshi, Takatoshi Ito, and Andrew Rose, University of Tokyo, Japan.

Wei, Sh-J., 2002, "The Life-and-Death Implications of Globalization," Paper presented at the National Bureau of Economic Research Inter-American Seminar in Economics, Monterrey, Mexico, November, *IMF Working Paper* (Washington, DC: International Monetary Fund).

Wei, Sh-J., 2001, "Domestic Crony Capitalism and International Fickle Capital: Is There a Connection?" *International Finance*, vol. 4, Spring, pp. 15–46.

Wei, Sh-J., 2000a, "How Taxing is Corruption on International Investors?" *Review of Economics and Statistics*, vol. 82, February, pp. 1–11.

Wei, Sh-J., 2000b, "Local Corruption and Global Capital Flows," *Brookings Papers on Economic Activity: 2* (Washington, DC: Brookings Institution), pp. 303–54.

Wei, Sh-J., 2000c, "Natural Openness and Good Government," *NBER Working Paper* No. 7765 (Cambridge, MA: National Bureau of Economic Research).

Wei, Sh-J., 1997, "Why is Corruption Much More Taxing than Tax? Arbitrariness Kills," *NBER Working Paper* No. 6255 (Cambridge, MA: National Bureau of Economic Research).

Wei, Sh-J. and Wu, Y., 2002, "Negative Alchemy? Corruption, Composition of Capital Flows, and Currency Crises," in S. Edwards and J. Frankel (eds.), *Preventing Currency Crises in Emerging Markets* (Chicago: University of Chicago Press), pp. 461–501.

Whalen, C.J., 2008, "Understanding the Credit Crunch as a Minsky Moment," *Challenge*, vol. 5, no. 1, pp. 91–109.

Whalen, C.J., 2001, "Integrating Schumpeter and Keynes: Hyman Minsky's Theory of Capitalist Development," *Journal of Economic Issues*, vol. XXXV, no. 4.

Whalen, C.J., 1999, "Hyman Minsky's Theory of Capitalist Development," *Working Paper* No. 277 (Annandale-on-Hudson, NY: The Levy Economics Institute).

Whalen, C.J., 1991, "Stabilizing the Unstable Economy: More on the Minsky-Simons Connection," *Journal of Economic Issues*, vol. XXV, no. 3, pp. 739–63.

Whalen, C.J., 1989, "The Minsky-Simons-Veblen Connection: Reply," *Journal of Economic Issues*, vol. XXIII, pp. 891–95.

Whalen, C.J., 1988, "The Minsky-Simons Connection: A Neglected Thread in the History of Economic Thought," *Journal of Economic Issues*, vol. XXII, no. 2, pp. 533–44.

Wilson, R., 2007, "Islamic Finance in Europe," *RSCAS Policy Papers* No. 2007/02 (Florence: Robert Schijman Centre for Advanced Studies, European University Institute).

Wray, R.L., 2008a, "Financial Markets Meltdown: What Can We Learn from Minsky?"

Wray, R.L., 2008b, "Lesson from the Subprime Meltdown," *Challenge*, vol. 51, no. 2, pp. 40–68.

Wray, R.L., 2006, "Can Basel II Enhance Financial Stability? A Pessimistic View," *Public Policy Brief* No. 84 (Annandale-on-Hudson, NY: The Levy Economics Institute).

Wray, R.L., 1992, "Alternative Theories of the Rate of Interest," *Cambridge Journal of Economics*, vol. 16, pp. 69–89.

Yartey, C.A., 2006, "The Stock Market and the Financing of Corporate Growth in Africa: The Case of Ghana," *IMF Occasional Paper* No. 201 (Washington, DC: International Monetary Fund).

Zak, P., 2003, "The Neurobiology of Trust," *Corante Tech News*.

Zak, P. and Knack, S., 2001, "Trust and Growth," *The Economic Journal*, vol. 111, April, pp. 295–321.

Zaman, S.M.H., 1999, *Economic Guidelines in the Quran* (Islamabad: The Islamic Institute of Islamic Thought).

Index